To Bert Sparrow —

But for you, my
friend, I'd be a retired
ribbon clerk — or with
the homeless, today —

With best wishes
and warm regards —

Sincerely —

Bill Quinn

Buffalo Bill
Remembers

BUFFALO BILL
REMEMBERS

Truth and Courage

LT. GEN.

WILLIAM W.

"BUFFALO BILL"

QUINN

Library of Congress Catalog Card Number: 91-05063

ISBN: 0-923568-23-9

Typesetting by
The Boufford Typographers
3886 Sheldrake Avenue ⌑ Okemos, Michigan 48864

PUBLISHED BY

Wilderness Adventure Books
320 Garden Lane
P.O. Box 968
Fowlerville, Michigan 48836

Manufactured in the United States of America

To Sally, Donna, and Bill, Jr.,
who, upon hearing these stories,
forced me into "writing them up."

CONTENTS

Contents

Contents

Contents

FOREWORD

There isn't a man or woman who has ever served in the Armed Forces of our nation, and then retired from his service, who hasn't periodically sat down with his family, old buddies, or with friends, and recalled a memorable instance in a war, or an anecdote in connection with their military service.

General Quinn is an unusually talented man, an outstanding graduate of West Point, who served his country exceedingly well in the fields of command and intelligence in both World War II and Korea. In the latter conflict, he distinguished himself as an Infantry regimental commander, compiling an enviable combat record. Besides his other decorations, he wears two medals for heroism and a Purple Heart.

He and I have spent many hours talking about things that happened to both of us, and because of his fine memory, and the wonderful stories he accumulated, many of us have implored him to record these experiences, so the rest of us could enjoy them.

That's what this book is all about. You might call it a portable bull session, where the General has put down the things he remembers from two wars, and his recollections of memorable events during his lifetime.

This isn't a book that has any particular continuity to

it. It's a book that one can open at any chapter and find something extremely interesting and sometimes very funny.

It has been my great pleasure to keep up with this book as it was being written, and I can assure any reader, be he an ex-service person, or just an interested civilian, that the reading of this book will give that person a much better view of a life of service in the Armed Forces of our country.

Barry Goldwater

January 1, 1991

AUTHOR'S NOTE

This effort is not an autobiography, as there is no attempt to portray my life in a beginning to (nearly) the end sequence.

It is a potpourri of events, personalities, articles, etc., either experienced by me, or known by me to be true. It has no rhyme, but it does have reason.

Through the years I have related some of these experiences to my children and close friends, and because of the historical significance of some of them, I have found myself being continually bombarded with, "Daddy, why don't you write that up?"

So I have.

In an attempt to avoid redundancy, I ran into difficulty, as I wanted each chapter to stand by itself. Consequently, the reader may open the book at any chapter and read on, in the main, without reference to other chapters.

I'm sure I've erred in names, places, and dates, as a lot of territory has been covered. So forgive those mistakes, as they were honest ones. You will soon appreciate the fact that I am a story teller and not an historian.

I sincerely hope that you find something of interest herein.

Bill Quinn

November 1, 1990

PREFACE

To my regimental junior officer replacements in Korea in 1951:

> "No combat commander can be successful unless he is provided with accurate information. An inexperienced officer tends to exaggerate the enemy strength and capabilities. In your reporting to your immediate supervisor, you must report the TRUTH as you honestly know it and not as you fearfully suspect."

> "COURAGE is the foundation upon which leadership is built. In your platoon or company, from time to time, you must join your leading elements in a fire fight. Your troops must know that you will place yourself at the same degree of risk as do they. With you, their leader, in their company, they will fight even harder."

"Buffalo Bill" Quinn
C.O. 17th Inf. (Buffaloes)

PROLOGUE:
BARRY GOLDWATER,
L.B.J. AND ME

The Goldwaters and the Quinns met at a party hosted by Joe and Helen Borda some time in 1959. Goldwater was in the Senate, and we became friends that night and continued to see each other socially for the next two or three years. As a matter of fact, with Joe and his wife and the J. Hunter Drums, we formed a small club that used to meet annually—four couples in all—at the Greenbriar in West Virginia. So, through the years Bette and I became more intimate with Peggy and Barry.

They began to invite us to participate in an annual "safari" to the Grand Canyon. For years, Barry had been conducting this pilgrimage with a number of his friends, mostly from Phoenix. A lot of them were former Air Force associates. The club was called the Grand Canyon Hiking, Loving and Singing Club, for lack of a better name. Our friendship progressed that way though the years, a very slow but solid type of relationship. At that time I was in Washington on duty at the Pentagon as the Army's Public Relations Officer.

On the first of March, 1964, I was given command of the Seventh Army in Germany, and Betty and I proceeded to Stuttgart. This, of course, reduced to zero any contact with the Goldwaters. However, once we got established in the summer of 1964, during which time Barry was campaigning for the Presidency, I dropped him a note which read, "Whenever you feel that you can break away from whatever you are doing, you and Peggy are cordially invited to come to Germany and visit Bette and me."

I don't even recall whether I got an answer or not, but that is not material. What is important is that in the early fall, just before the election of '64, during the height of the campaign, Barry was at a fundraiser or some kind of function, and a female member of the press asked him what he and Peggy were going to do after the election, "win, lose, or draw." Barry said he thought they might accept an invitation from Bill and Bette Quinn to visit them in Germany. He thought that he and Peggy might as well go somewhere and rest after the election was over. And that was the end of the conversation.

The next day this item was in this lady's column in one of the Washington papers. A benign article, it just simply stated that after the election Barry and Peggy Goldwater would in all probability visit the Quinns in Germany and that General Quinn commanded the Seventh Army, etc. Lyndon Johnson's people picked this up and somehow got together with Daniel Schorr of CBS.

Daniel Schoor, who was in Germany at the time, wrote a very vicious article about Barry and me. Just what his connection was with the Johnson forces, I don't know, but in any event, this dispatch to CBS (and he cites it in his own book) stated in effect that the Goldwaters were coming to Germany on a special visit after the election to visit with the right wing Nazi Party types in Germany and that he and General Quinn were going to Berchtesgarten on a special trip to visit Adolph Hitler's mountain retreat, the purpose of the exercise being to pay tribute to Hitler.

When this hit the news in the States, Barry was in San Francisco and became so upset and incensed that he barred CBS from further coverage of his campaign and refused to have them come into his room or anywhere else associated with his campaign where he was in control. He told the CBS hierarchy that unless Daniel Schorr was fired, the bar would prevail, because Schorr was a liar. CBS reluctantly did remove Schorr from Germany and "technically" separated him from CBS.

In any event, it caused a hell of a lot of embarrassment to me as well as to the Senator, because I began to get queries from all over, including Stephen Ailes, the Secretary of the Army, as to what my politics were in regard to Adolf Hitler. In other words, was I getting involved in right wing politics in Germany, and was I visiting or consorting with Nazi Party officials? This was blow number one, from which I never recovered. The Secretary of the Army apparently believed a lie.

The second blow was about a month or so before the election. President Johnson had invited Barry to the White House publicly to receive an intelligence briefing. The President was going to show what a big heart he had and how fair he was, giving Goldwater a complete briefing on the international situation and the intelligence associated with it. I heard later that Barry had said there was no way he was going to the White House, because it was just a sham, and he knew damn well what would happen; Johnson would give him a couple of drinks of bourbon, they would b.s., and the next day, of course, the

Democratic propaganda machine would indicate that Goldwater had received all the information and that L.B.J. was a great guy, a fair play man, etc.

So Barry regretted the invitation to go to the White House for a briefing.

The next day, however, the Johnson machine did have something to say, and it wasn't what they had planned. What they put out to Douglas Kiker of the *New York Herald Tribune* was as follows:

> Goldwater did not have to go to the White House to get briefed by the President on intelligence matters because he was being fed by the so-called "back channel" (a confidential method of dispatching messages) from Lt. General William W. Quinn, now commanding general of the Seventh Army. Quinn had been feeding Goldwater on a daily basis with the intelligence-connected aspects of his political campaign.

Of course, this was a politically motivated lie. It was not designed to damage me, but it did. The design was to indicate that Goldwater was not playing the game fairly and that he did not have to go and see the President because he was getting intelligence illegally from a former friend through messages to the Pentagon. Once again, the queries rolled in from the Secretary of the Army and the Chief of Staff, General Harold K. Johnson (a classmate at West Point), asking me to explain my conduct.

I replied with an information copy to Mr. McNamara, Secretary of Defense, that the article was untrue, hence libelous, and I requested the Judge Advocate General of the Army to assist me in pressing a libel suit against Douglas Kiker and the *New York Herald Tribune*.

I received a very prompt reply from Secretaries Ailes and Johnson, saying they had great faith in me, I was a good boy, etc. In order to make sure I didn't muddy the political waters during the campaign by any legal action on my part, they advised me that the Army Judge Advocate General had reviewed my case and determined that I had received insufficient injury to warrant a suit.

Subsequently, I was told by civilian lawyers that I did, in fact, have a good case, but it was too late. In connection with writing this section I asked under the provisions of the Freedom of Information Act for copies of these cables and messages, but was denied them.

At this time, however, my Army career was dead in the water, and I decided to retire prematurely. Before doing so, I proceeded to Washington to see Johnny Johnson and to volunteer for a command in Vietnam.

Johnny said, "Bill, you're too damn old. The 'Whiz Kids' up in Defense think 'Westy' (Westmoreland) is over the hill."

So we agreed that I could check out—retire. At my retirement ceremony in Stuttgart, Germany, I received messages from Barry Goldwater, General Eisenhower, General Lemnitzer, a tribute by a German Corps commander, and a decoration by the President of the Federal Republic of Germany.[1]

---

[1]The following is an exerpt from Ward Just's *Military Men*, page 125: "Another candidate (for Chief of Staff U.S. Army) was the Commander of the Seventh Army in Europe, Lt. Gen. William Quinn, but Quinn had been ruined by the lunatic newspaper furor over his invitation to an old friend, Presidential candidate Barry Goldwater, to his summer retreat in the mountains of Bavaria. If Quinn had had a villa in S'ngano or a ski hutch in Gstaad there would have been no trouble, but what he had was a hunting lodge in Brechtesgaden, and when the newspapers got through with him (Quinn was charged—wrongly—with leaking classified documents to Goldwater, among other matters), his career was in shambles."

PART I

WHERE IT ALL STARTED

1

IT ALL STARTED HERE

I almost didn't go to West Point.

One night at dinner, after a session with my professor in high school, I asked my father if he would help get me an appointment to West Point, whereupon he said, "West Point! Whatever gave you that idea? You're not going to West Point!"

"Why can't I?"

"Because the family has decided that they need a lawyer. Bud's the president of the bank (Uncle Lorie), we've got the newspaper, and Burt's the mayor. What you're going to do is this, you're going to Johns Hopkins University to get your B.A. degree, and then you're going to the University of Virginia for law."

"Who said so?"

"The family decided that that's what you're going to do; and I told you, we need a lawyer in the family."

"Dad, I'm not going to do any of those things," I replied, "I'm going to West Point." We had a big row, and I left the dinner table. My mother was very upset, as I was their only child.[1]

Well, the next day I went to my cousin Lorie, Jr. Lorie, Jr. was an entrepreneur in the news business and at one time controlled practically all the weekly newspapers on the Eastern Shore of Maryland. When I told him what had happened, he asked, "Do you really want to go to West Point?"

"Yes," I replied, "I asked Dad to help me get an appointment, but he refused."

"Well," he said, "I'll help you, son."

I loved my cousin Lorie, Jr., more than I did my father. He was childless and loved me very much. He was the one that I usually got the baseball mitt from, or a pair of soccer shoes. My father didn't seem to be interested. So my cousin Lorie paid for my tuition to Columbian Preparatory School (Chadman's) in Washington, which would prepare me for the entrance examination for West Point. He also gave me a small allowance.

In Chapter Five of this book there is a dissertation and a story that relates to Professor Gardner—a session in which I was motivated to go to West Point. That chapter will explain precisely why I asked my father to help me.

In any event, I proceeded to Chadman's; Mr. Chadman was a one-armed man with a goatee, very distinguished looking. I soon realized that my high school education was rather weak, primarily because I was not a very good student.

In high school I was very athletic. I played first base on the high school baseball team. In my senior year I was all-Maryland fullback on the soccer team and captain of the high school basketball team. I also entered in relays

[1]See Appendix A for a thumbnail sketch of my childhood years in Crisfield, Maryland.

and high jumping in track meets and was a strong swimmer, having won several meets at states fairs and other novice events. The athletics that I played in high school held me in good stead in later years. I was a "jock" and thought about sports every waking moment and consequently didn't study very hard.

So, when I got to Chadman's I found that the mathematics and English requirements for passing the West Point exam were very demanding. I had difficulty keeping up with the class to the extent that I was forced to drop out at Christmas time, as I realized I was costing my cousin money unnecessarily. I was determined not to go home, but to keep trying for West Point somehow.

I answered an ad and secured a job in Washington with Collier's magazine corporation. *Collier's* at that time was a popular magazine, as were *Life, Redbook, Good Housekeeping* and others of that nature. I sold magazines from door-to-door. I had family friends in Washington who put me up for a short time, and then I rented a very small room in a not-too-promising neighborhood in the Southeast, for which I paid a dollar and a half a week.

I kept this job for several months and then applied for, and got, a job at the Government Printing Office, working in the Superintendent of Documents Division. Here I worked in a series of bins which had various government publications; small booklets and handbooks on everything from agriculture to animals—you name it. Orders would come in from Congress or from citizens, requesting certain publications. It was my job to fill the orders; that is, to go from bin to bin and pick out the publications, and if they weren't there, to make a note for the inventory and also indicate on a buck slip that they were not available, which alerted somebody to answer the letters. I was paid sixty dollars a month for that job.

During that period I ran into someone who told me about Homer Millard's Prep School. Millard was located at 1918 N Street NW, in Washington, and he prepped primarily for West Point. Millard was a West Pointer and a taskmaster when it came to teaching. Although his school started in September and went through February, when the mental examinations for West Point were held, I went to see him around November first and asked him if he would take me in his school. He said, "You are two months behind. However, you did go to Chad's." Then he added, "I'll take you in, you can come and move in with me. We are going through the books now from the beginning, for the second time."

Millard's system was to go through the math and English books, upon which the examination for West Point was based, three times. He made his class go through all of the texts in two months, i.e., September — October and November — December, and then on the first of January for the third time. To make sure that there was nothing overlooked, every problem in each book had to be solved and understood.

So, "Beany" Millard took me in. I told him that I didn't have a dime and that my father would not give me any money. So he said, "Well, try your uncle or cousin."

I had failed to get into West Point the first year, and I was embarrassed to ask them for any more help. However, my cousin Lorie, Jr. gave me a little money and his brother, Wallace, said he would loan me a couple hundred dollars.

Then Beany said, "I'll tell you what I'll do, for what they can't come up with. I'll stake you, because you're going to West Point. Let me have what your cousins gave you, and you can pay me the difference when you graduate."

Well, this was incredible, but true. So, I moved in with Millard and he said, "Not only are you going to move into this house, you are going to move into my room. I'm going to coach you and see that you get caught up with the others."

So I roomed with the head man of the prep school. There was a desk in the room, and he ordered me to sit down and study and study, as this was the first of November, and I had missed the first practice test in September and October.

I studied so much that one night I lost my vision. I went completely blind. He was lying on his bed reading a magazine. I yelled, "Beany, I'm blind!"

He jumped up and said, "Lie down here." He got a cold towel and put it over my eyes and said, "Just keep it on for about five or ten minutes." I did so with my eyes closed. In about five minutes, he took the towel off and said, "Open your eyes." I did. I could see. I was all right. He said, "Knock it off for tonight."

The next morning he took me down to an optometrist who examined my eyes, and told me nothing was wrong. After we explained the circumstances to the doctor, he said, "Your eyes, for some reason, rejected the continuous light due to its intensity, et cetera. You should take several breaks during your studying; don't spend too many hours at one time in the same position in the same degree of light."

I stayed at Millard's until the end of his course in early March. On Saturday, two days before I was to take the entrance and physical examinations at Walter Reed Hospital in Washington, I went to Annapolis with some friends to see the Army—Navy basketball game. I left Washington in a snow storm, and on my way to the Washington—Baltimore—Annapolis Railroad I got my feet wet. I walked from the WB&A Station to Dalghren Hall, met my friends, and we went to the basketball game.

During all this time my feet were wet. Wet all that day. We went to the dance as the guests of some midshipmen we knew, and after the dance I walked back to the railway station, my feet still wet. When I got home, my feet were shriveled up and almost frozen. Sunday morning I woke up with a severe cold.

Monday morning I had a fever of 102° and had pneumonia but didn't know it. In any event, I had to go to Walter Reed Hospital to take these examinations. I went to Walter Reed and I took one examination in mathematics with this temperature. I returned to Millard's and went to bed, taking whatever was available to cut down the fever. The next morning I got up, again with a high fever, went back to Walter Reed to take the second part of the examination. When I finished the second and third parts of the examination, I passed out. Of course, as a civilian, I had no rights in the hospital. It was just a convenient place to take the examination, since the physical examination was to be conducted there, also.

I was taken back to Millard's and put in bed in somewhat of a coma. Beany knew that I had friends in Maryland, the Gormans. Mrs. Grace Gorman lived on an estate in Howard County not far from Washington. She was the widow of former State Senator Gorman, and they were a very distinguished family in Maryland. I had dated her niece and was almost like one of the family. Aunt Grace told Beany to bring me out there, and they would get a doctor from Johns Hopkins to come and take a look at me.

In any event, I was taken there, still feverish and out of it. A local doctor was called who said I was very sick and that I had pneumonia with probable complications.

A specialist from Johns Hopkins came from Baltimore and diagnosed my problem as empyema and said that an operation would be necessary. I was therefore moved to Johns Hopkins Hospital for the surgery, which amounted to an opening in the right cavity of the chest under my right arm and an insertion of a tube to drain out the pus, or inflammation, which had formed in one of the lobes. Had that not taken place, I would have died from the infection.

I was at Johns Hopkins for over two months with this tube in my side. During this period I received a notice almost every ten days from West Point or the Department of the Army notifying me that I had passed the entrance examination. This notification also included a summons to take the physical examination. It was now early June 1927, and I was supposed to enter West Point on the first of July. When I got out of Johns Hopkins, I looked like the hunchback of Notre Dame, as my right shoulder had completely collapsed and was at least two or three inches lower than my left shoulder, and I was somewhat stooped over as well, by virtue of nursing this wound in my right side all that time.

I went to Walter Reed Hospital for my physical exam about the middle of June, just two weeks before I was supposed to enter West Point. The doctors gave me one look, and without looking at my teeth, eyes, or heart or anything, just said, "There's no reason for you to take this examination, because you're obviously incapacitated for anything. Your right side is collapsed, and consequently, Walter Reed would not authorize you to enter West Point. Even if you did enter, you would not be able to withstand the physical requirements of your plebe year. You can forget the Military Academy, because there's no way you can ever pass the physical entrance examination due to the incapacitating results of empyema."

Of course, I was heartbroken and very sick and depressed about this prediction. So I went home to Crisfield a cripple. What further depressed me was the attitude of my father, who seemed to derive a great deal of satisfaction that I had failed to get to West Point. Almost gleefully he cracked, "Now I guess you're ready and willing to listen to the family and do what you were told to do. This fall you will enter Johns Hopkins University." Here we were in mid-June, and it looked like I would not go to West Point, that year or ever.

A few days after I had returned home after failing the physical examination, I went to see Dr. Fuller. Dr. Steven Fuller was a dentist and a major of infantry in the Maryland National Guard. Company L of the 29th Division was based in Crisfield. I told him that come hell or high water I had to go to West Point. Dr. Fuller listened to my story and said, "Well, Bill, maybe we can work something out. I'll talk to Dr. Norris." Dr. R.R. Norris, a neighbor of ours and a brother of Aunt Grace Gorman, was a medical officer in the regiment of which Company L was a part. He and Dr. Fuller got their heads together and came up with the following plan.

As it happened, Company L had no place to practice marksmanship off-season. They were able to practice only when they went to Camp Ritchie, Maryland, for two weeks each year. For some time it had been hoped and planned that Company L could have a small rifle range somewhere in the environs of Crisfield so that during the year, say on Saturdays or holidays, it would be possible for members to go to a range and practice marksmanship. A rifle range, in those days, had a deep ditch at the target end. The targets were raised up so that the bottom of the target was at the level of the ground, and after one fired at the target, it was lowered back down in the ditch to be marked and scored.

Dr. Fuller and Dr. Norris saw an opportunity to kill two birds with one stone, that is, build a two-or-three target range and build up Billy Quinn so he could enter West Point. They laid out the range. They staked out where the firing line was to be and where the pits, or the ditch, was to be dug. They gave me a shovel and a sketch and told me to dig the ditch six feet deep and about twenty feet long. They also told me what to do with the spoil, that is, to build up the butts in front of the target so that the pits would not have to be so deep.

So beginning around the first of July 1927, I started digging a ditch. I worked roughly seven hours a day, with a shovel and a wheelbarrow and some other tools. I was paid twenty-five cents an hour. By the end of August, I finished the range pit; however, being right-handed, I had also built up my right side to where it was almost as strong, and possibly stronger, than my left shoulder and left arm. The two months of daily and strenuous exercise had put me in excellent shape.

At about this time, about mid-August, "Toady" Riggs, the football coach at St. Johns College in Annapolis, Maryland, came to Crisfield on a scouting trip. Now, remember, Crisfield High was such a small school that they did not play football, only soccer. However, Toady Riggs had the idea that an athlete was an athlete and if you could play one sport, well, you could play them all. In his book, football experience was not the only criterion in recruiting.

He looked me up. We had a chat, after which he said, "I'd like you to come to St. Johns. I can get you a football scholarship, and I can arrange for you to work in the dining hall. That'll take care of your food; I can also arrange for you to work in the gym, and that'll take care of your room."

I said, "Well, Mr. Riggs, let me think about it. I don't really have any plans now, except that, and you have to know this, I plan to go to West Point."

"Then this might be a good thing for you to do. If you're not going to West Point this year, you should do something constructive, both in athletics and academics. You ought to come to St. Johns. I can promise that you will play football for me."

Well, my father was still working on me. One night at dinner, about the third week in August, my father and I had a real rhubarb. My father said, "Listen, you're just as stupid as hell. You've got everything laid out for you for the future, but you insist on this damn West Point idea. You know you're not going, you can't get an appointment, and you know I'm not going to help you a damn bit."

Actually, I don't remember what I said, but I was so mad and hurt that I got up and said, "Well, I realize that, because I resent being herded like a sheep. I'm not welcome here any more, so I'll just take off."

Well, my mother fell apart. Sobbing, she cried, "Oh, William, please don't do anything rash."

As I had only one dollar in my pocket, I said, "Mother, let me have five dollars so I can get to St. Johns." The next morning I left home. I was not a Tom Sawyer type with a stick-held bandana slung over my shoulder, but damn near. I had a small suitcase with a few clothes in it, and off I went to St. Johns or somewhere—hopefully, to West Point.

I hitchhiked my way to Annapolis and St. Johns and reported to Toady Riggs in his office in the gymnasium. He said, "I'm glad to see you. I think you're going to do well here. Did you ever play any lacrosse?"

"No."

"Well, you'll play lacrosse as well as football. Now go on up to McDowell Hall and register."

"I don't quite understand what you mean, 'register.' "

He said, "you've got to sign in, to become a student here; they have to know who you are and get statistics on you." Then he added, "It'll only cost you ten dollars."

"Well, Toady," I said, "I don't have ten dollars."

"You don't?"

"No, I've only got six."

"Well," he said, "that does make it a little tough, doesn't it?"

"Yeah, I guess I can't register."

"Oh, yes you can." He reached in his pocket and pulled out a five-dollar bill and gave it to me, and I went up and registered.

I must point out that I went to St. Johns for a year and a half, and *that* money was the total amount that I ever paid the college, that is, five dollars of mine and five of Toady's. The reason I didn't have to pay anything was because I became a main cog in the wheels that were running the college, in a way.[2]

---

[2]I waited on the tables in the college dining room, working in the gym, being a school librarian two nights a week, and organizing a window washing and rug beating group in Annapolis. We washed the windows of the police station, courthouse and several banks, and provided a babysitting service, primarily for naval academy officers. Finally, I delivered all special delivery, insured, and registered items which arrived at the college.

2

FROM ST. JOHN'S
TO WEST POINT

Around Christmas of 1928 I received a principal appointment to West Point from Senator Goleman Dupont of Delaware. I had passed the mental examination for entrance several years earlier, but it was necessary for me to take the physical. This physical was to take place some time in late March or April, so it was necessary for me to go to Walter Reed Hospital. In the meantime, there was no need for me to stay in St. John's.

A Kappa Alpha fraternity brother of mine named "Red" Zimmerman had graduated some years before and was an officer at the Bethlehem Steel Company at Sparrow's Point, Maryland. One weekend he said, "Bill, I understand that you, Foxy Hunter, and Tommy Andrews are headed for West Point. If you're not going to hang around at St. John's until you enter, why don't you come with me, and I'll get you a job at Sparrow's Point in the pipe mill? You could make six or eight bucks a day."

I decided I would do just that. Red lived with his sister and mother, and they had a room for me in Baltimore. So

I moved in with them and went to work with Red every day from Baltimore to Sparrow's Point.

In this steel mill I had a job as an assistant pipe inspector. Now, the pipe inspector in this case had a crushing machine by which he could test the weld of a pipe. Before I discuss the machine, I'll tell the uninitiated that pipes are made basically from a flat strip of metal which, in the *butt weld*, is the exact dimension of the circumference. The end of this flat iron strip, while red hot, is pulled through a loop which forces it to close so that the two edges butt each other. The other kind of a weld is where the same idea prevails, except the circumference of the finished pipe is smaller than the metal strip because one side of the metal plate will overlap, and it's called a *lap weld*.

I was in the butt weld factory, and my job involved the so-called *crop ends*—when a piece of pipe is drawn through and is butt-welded, the pipe is then laid on a rack to cool; as soon as it's cooled, the foreman cuts the pipe into specified lengths. Now, when a pipe—we'll say a 20-foot pipe—comes out, it's actually 22 to 23 feet long, because each end is not necessarily a good weld. The ends which are cut off to make the pipe exactly 20 feet long are called the crop ends.

My job was to take a crop end, put it into a press, and crush the pipe so that I could see, after it had been mashed, whether or not the two butt ends of the pipe had crystallized. In other words, if it hadn't crystallized, the pipe was not very good and would probably have to be recycled. Sometimes the ends do not crystallize because the furnace is too cold or too hot. In any event, for the pipe to be good, there has to be crystallization. So much for that.

Once, I was on a night shift which I got every two or

three weeks. This particular week I had been putting in some bad reports on some of the welds. Now, the welders were mostly Polish, from the Polish district in Baltimore. They were a pretty tough bunch of people; at least, my particular group was. I had been sending in reports indicating that the welding was not being done properly. This caused the foreman to get pretty uptight with me, but of course, I wasn't under him—I worked for the inspector. One night, one of these great big characters rolled into my office (I had a little office and from time-to-time would go out to my crusher and take some samples). He came in and told me that I was causing a lot of trouble by giving them bad reports and they didn't like it at all. He explained that what I should do was to understand their problems and not give them bad reports.

I said, "I'm just doing what I'm told to do, and I can show you that you have a bad weld here in a soft batch."

He answered, "I don't care about that. I'm warning you."

Well, I kept on. Then one night I heard a man yell "RUN!" I ran, and my God, an overhead crane had dropped an empty steel bucket right where I had been standing.

Consequently, I went to Red and said, "Red, you know I want to go to West Point. I just think probably you'd better get somebody else to do this damn job. I'm not gonna lie, but I know if I stay here those guys will kill me! Red, they tried." And I told him what happened.

"Well," he said, "Okay, Bill. You've got enough money anyway, to have a little fun before you go to the Point."

I said, "As a matter of fact, Foxy Hunter called me. He's going to leave St. John's and wants me to join him on a ship on the James River Fleet." These were freighters from World War I which had been parked and lashed together in the Hudson and York Rivers and several other places, including the Sacramento River in California.

I left Sparrow's Point, and Foxy and I worked on this boat, chipping, painting, and working the machinery until a week or so before entering West Point—which we did on July 1, 1929.

In connection with the entrance physical examination, I had a close call in passing, not because of my empyema, but because I was partially deaf.

While I was at Sparrow's Point, the tremendous noise of the pipes rattling on racks was almost deafening, and the decibels were extremely high. I didn't realize it, but the few months I worked there I suffered a loss of hearing and didn't really know it. This did not surface until I took my physical examination immediately prior to entering West Point.

We were at Walter Reed Hospital in Washington, and I had passed everything until I came to the hearing tests. In this test we were ushered into a room in which there were several doctors—the eye, ear, nose, and throat clinic. In the ear exam, several potential cadets were being tested at the same time in a partitioned cubicle. My doctor began to whisper numbers to me, such as 66, 45, 22, and 31, and I didn't hear a damned one of them. So he marked me "failed." He said, "You've failed. You didn't hear anything I said."

"You mean I didn't pass?"

"That's right."

WHAM!

I was told to move towards another desk. I just don't know how it got mixed up, but anyway, there was a man in front of me named Burt Sparrow who had my hearing deficiency on his form, while I had been given a clean bill of health. When he got up to the table the officer there said, "Son, I'm sorry, but you've failed the exam."

Sparrow said, "I couldn't have!"

When I heard this, knowing I had failed, I grabbed him and said, "Could I talk to you for a minute?"

"Certainly."

"Listen, they've made a mistake. Can you hear okay?"

"I can hear perfectly."

"Would you mind going back and taking a retest?"

"Not at all, I'd be glad to."

So he did, and came out with a corrected score, no problem. I passed the physical, but if it hadn't been for Burt Sparrow, I would probably be jerking sodas or pumping gas as a filling station attendant today.

3

WEST POINT FOOTBALL

Plebe Year at West Point is a difficult year physically. Certainly, during the so-called "Beast Barracks," the first two months after one's entry into West Point, it's all physical. One runs everywhere at all times, even climbing stairs. During this period also, one has to participate in all of the sports that are available at the Academy, with the possible exception of ice hockey and golf, if one doesn't know how to play either.

In that connection, when I arrived at West Point in July, 1929, one of the first people to greet me or to "recognize" me, as it's called, was a first classman by the name of Packard, who was the forthcoming captain of the Army soccer team. He had learned somehow that I had been selected as All-Maryland fullback in my senior year in high school. That was the only sport in which I felt I really had any qualifications. I had been captain of my high school basketball team, and I'd also played first base on the high school baseball team, but was not good enough in those sports for the Army team.

In any event, we Plebes went out and played soccer, and then later switched to football. We had several first classmen who were the regulars on the first string Army team who stayed behind to coach and work with the Plebes. One of these was "Red" Cagle, who was all-American, a famous football player and a fine person. Red was the passer and the quarterback or tailback for West Point. Another "Beast Barracks" coach was Johnny Merrill, who was from Texas, a fine coach and another nice guy.

When we went out to exercise in football, Red Cagle began to throw the football to Plebes who were going down under passes, and he threw one to me which looked impossible to catch, but I reached up with one hand, caught it, pulled it down, and kept on running. This caught his attention; he had me stand in line again. He threw a couple more passes, and I caught them. He then took me aside and, one-on-one, began to throw passes; I was catching them all. He soon said, "You're going out for football, I'm sure."

"No, I hadn't planned to. Mr. Packard asked me to . . ."

Cagle interrupted, "The hell with Mr. Packard, the hell with soccer. You're going out for football. You're going to be on the Plebe Team as an end."

And that's precisely what happened. I didn't go out for soccer. I went out for the Plebe football team, and I made left end. On the other end was Dick King. We had a great freshman team. In the backfield we had Ken Fields, tailback and quarterback; Tom Kilday, fullback; Bill Firenzel and Eddie Herb as halfbacks; Bus Evans at center; Abe Lincoln and Johnny Armstrong as tackles; and Milt Somerfelt and Sam Mundell as guards. We beat the hell out of every freshman team we played, and on two occasions beat the varsity in practice scrimmages, much to the chagrin of "Biff" Jones, the Army head coach.

But our plebe coach, Gar Davidson (who later became head coach), loved it. It was during one of those games that I got really clobbered. I was in the Post Hospital for a week, conscious but out of my mind. Late one afternoon after practice, the whole coaching team came to see me, including "Babe" Bryan, the assistant football coach. Babe had put on a lot of weight and was very heavy. I said to him, "I know you, you're Babe Bryan, and look at you, you're going to have a baby." Well, I thought the coaching staff would break up.

In any event, we had a great freshman team, and Dick King and I held down the two ends. As a matter of fact, some sports writer on the *New York Times*, in writing about us, remarked in his article about the Army Plebe's "royal pair of ends, King and Quinn." It was a great year.

On the two occasions when we went out and scrimmaged with the Army first team and beat them, I caught two passes and scored two touchdowns. That so infuriated some of the first team players that they began to beat us up in the line.

We had such a good team that when Army was invited to go to the West Coast to play Stanford in a post-Christmas game in 1929, the army coaching staff took our plebe team along with them to practice and scrimmage with the first team all across the country. Our train would stop every afternoon at some town having a football field, dressing room and showers. I recall one stop in Hutchinson, Kansas. We went to the local high school and worked out there, then got back on the train. Then, of course, we worked out in Palo Alto in the Stanford stadium.

Although Army led Stanford at the half, we lost the

game, primarily because of the heat, which was around
85−90°. We were accustomed to near-zero weather at
West Point. As a matter of fact, one of our tackles,
"Buster" Perry, lost 17 pounds in that football game. After the game, however, we went to the Saint Francis Hotel in San Francisco for a big dance and dinner as the
guests of Herb Fleishacker, who played fullback for
"Pop" Warner at Stanford. We plebes had a good time on
the West Coast, even though the varsity lost the game.

In connection with the temperature that day, I remember a player named Smith, who sat on the bench in
uniform but never got into the game, lost five pounds.

So much for football.

• • •

After that season, during the winter, I decided to go
out for swimming and diving. I had won several swimming
prizes while I was in high school at several camp meetings,
fairs, etc. Usually the race was out to a buoy and back, no
particular distance, just a matter of speed. The prize was
usually a $10 gold piece.

I was interested in diving and could dive quite well for
a person with no training. When I tried out at West Point,
the swimming coach signed me up for both swimming and
diving. As I was practicing in the pool one day about a
week after I signed up, a football coach came in. It was either Babe Bryan or Ralph Sassy who caught me swimming and ordered me out of the pool. He said, "Quinn, as
long as you're at West Point, don't you go in that pool any
more, unless you're on summer vacation. Understand?" I
didn't. Later on, I asked him why, and he explained.
"Swimming muscles, that is, muscles developed by swimming, are not those we need for football. For that we

need an entirely different kind of muscle."

That ended my swimming and diving career, except that I won a high diving contest at Delafield Pond the next summer. I don't think the coach knew about that. If he did, he never mentioned it.

During my second, third, and last years at the Academy, I roomed with Tom Kilday of San Antonio, Texas, and Steven "Shamrock" Mack from Illinois. All three of us were football players. Shamrock was a back, and Tom, who had gone to St. Edwards in Texas, was first string fullback.

During this period and for all four years, as a matter of fact, we had to take riding, as the Army was mounted at that time, and tanks were few and far between. The cavalry, naturally, was horse borne. It so happened that Kilday, in spite of being from Texas, didn't like horses very much, and as a result found it difficult to get a good seat on any horse. One day in the fall of 1932 (we had a pretty good team that year; we beat Navy twenty to zero) we went out for an afternoon riding class. This was at the beginning of the football season, and Tom, either because of a jump or a shied horse, was thrown from the saddle. He landed in a pile of fresh manure. He picked himself up and continued to ride. Later, when he returned with us to our room in the barracks and took off his leather leggings, a whole pile of manure that had been jammed in them during his fall fell out on the floor. Tom said, "This is it. I'm getting the hell out of here. I didn't come to West Point to be thrown around in horse shit. I'm packing up."

With that, he did. He went down to the basement trunk room and brought up a suitcase and a foot locker. I said, "Tom, wait a minute, let's not—you know—don't rush . . ."

Shamrock said, "Tom, you don't know what you're

doing."

"The hell I don't! I'm getting out. I'm just not going to take this crap anymore."

I immediately went to the orderly room and called Major Ralph Sassie, then the head football coach. I said, "Coach, you'd better get over here to our room in the barracks right away."

"Why?" He asked.

"Tom Kilday is packing up. He's going to leave. He's going to resign."

"Why, Bill?"

"Coach, just get over here, and hurry, because—I'll just give you one reason why, and it has to do with horse manure."

"I'll be right there." Within five minutes, Coach Sassie came in and said, "Tom, what in the world is the matter?"

Tom told him. "I just am not a good horseman," he said. "I hate horses, I'm not going in the cavalry. This is not the first time I've been thrown, but it's the last."

The coach said, "Tom, just stay right there, and don't do anything. What if I can get you excused from riding?"

"If I don't have to go to that damn riding hall again, I'll be happy."

The coach replied, "It's done." And it was done.

Tom got a medical excuse based on some kind of allergy, and I don't believe he ever got on another horse—certainly not at West Point.

Tom Kilday was a great fullback player and a great guy.

4

EMBARRASSING MOMENTS AT WEST POINT

In everyone's life there is an occasion or two which causes one a great deal of embarrassment, to him/herself or to another party. I had my share of red-faced incidents while attending West Point.

During the winter months, there was a dance every other Saturday night. I had a date for this particular dance, which was held in Cullum Hall, a beautiful, museum-like building at West Point, with the ballroom on the second floor.

After the dance, my date and I were proceeding down the steps on our way to her hotel. In front of us was another couple. The girl was exactly in front of me and was wearing a very long dress, so long that as she went down the steps, the dress trailed like a train. I had turned to talk to my partner and in so doing, stepped on the bottom of the dress, and the young lady walked out of it. There she stood in her briefs with her dress on the floor. It was a moment of infinite embarrassment to both of us. Then she grabbed the dress, threw it around her waist, and took off for the ladies' room. I never found out who she was. That was an error, as I could have apologized and invited her to another dance. She did have a good-looking behind.

• • •

The second incident occurred at Christmastime in my third year at West Point. I was invited to a debutante ball in Baltimore during the holidays. The ball was held in the Old Leonart Hotel. I had known some midshipmen in Washington earlier, and it was through them that I got this invitation. They were there, and introduced me to some of the girls they knew. At one point, I sat down at a table with a midshipman, his girl, and another girl. After a little conversation, the latter asked, "How did you get to West Point?"

"Oh, it was a fast manuever. I kind of conned the Duponts into sending me to West Point."

"What do you mean?"

"Well, it's a long story, but here's a quicky version. A friend of mine in Wilmington named Phillip Carpenter was a close friend of Governor Robinson of Delaware. Phil was also Chairman of the State Republican Party. It was through Phil and Governor Robinson, who influenced Senator Coleman Dupont to give me a principal appointment, that I got into West Point. I'm not really from Delaware at all; I'm from Crisfield, Maryland. However, the Duponts didn't know that. They were really taken."

Then I added, "You know, I'd like to know you; I'm sorry I didn't catch your name when we were introduced."

She said, "My name is Ethel."
"And your last name?"
"Dupont."

• • •

During the summer of 1932 at the beginning of our
First Class, or senior year, at West Point, my class (1933)
was ordered to Fort Bragg, North Carolina, for field and
anti-aircraft artillery training.

On arrival at the post, Ken Fields, the First Captain of
the Corps of Cadets, was instructed by the Commandant
of Cadets to make a courtesy call on the Commanding
General, then Major General Magnus McCloskey.

Bill Frentzel and I were "conned" into going with
Fields to make the call. So, that Sunday afternoon we
dressed in our highly starched whites and proceeded to
the General's quarters. As we started up the walkway to
the quarters, General and Mrs. McCloskey were coming
out of their front door headed for some function on the
post. When they saw us coming, they immediately turned
around and re-entered the house.

When we rang the doorbell an orderly opened it immediately and bid us to enter. Mrs. McCloskey was
standing by. Ken introduced himself, Frentzel and me. As
I stepped forward to greet her, I slipped on a small scatter
rug in the foyer and fell flat on my back. I can still see the
face of Mrs. McCloskey leaning over me and asking me if
I was hurt. No, I wasn't, just very embarrassed, that's all.

We were guided to a screened porch and asked to
have seats. I chose a swing and sat on the right side. On
the arm of the swing was an ash tray loaded with cigarette
butts, which I had not noticed. At this point, the General
made an entrance, and as I rose to greet him, my elbow

hit the ash tray and sent it and its contents all over the floor. The orderly was called and soon had the mess cleaned up, but I was now bleeding.

I thought as the conversation became animated my transgressions would be dismissed. However, after being asked if we would care for a soft drink, we were served Coca-Colas by the orderly. I reached out of the swing and took the glass, which slipped out of my hand and fell on a Persian rug in front of the swing. Coke seemed to envelop the whole porch. By now I was dying, and if I had been playing some kind of a game, I would have asked the coach to take me out. As they say, some days. . . .

5

FLASHBACK TO CRISFIELD HIGH

"William, that's the most ridiculous declaration of all. In the first place, boy, you don't have sense enough to get into West Point, and if by some miracle you SHOULD make it, you couldn't possibly muster enough brains to stay there."

• • •

Such was the statement made to me by Professor Gardner one day in May 1925—and in front of everybody.

Professor Gardner was the principal of our high school in Crisfield, Maryland. He had been principal as long as anyone could remember. At that time he was an elderly man, stout, wore an old fashioned handlebar mustache, and was considered by the townspeople as somewhat of a philosopher. He had a wonderful twinkle in his eye and a sense of humor that I never appreciated until several years after I had departed his paternal influence.

In addition to his administrative duties Professor

27

Gardner taught trigonometry to the senior class. On one lazy spring afternoon, he didn't show up for our class as scheduled. There were about ten of us taking trig and when he failed to appear, we sneaked out into the school yard to play catch or just loaf in the sun. Fifteen or twenty minutes later we heard him bellow from the school door, "Come in here you rapscallions, before I thrash every one of you."

After we resumed our seats, he proceeded to lecture us on the *Twenty Elements of Character,* one of his favorite themes which we had heard a hundred times.

"And so—you couldn't wait for me!" He went on, "That shows you have proven your lack of two of the primary elements of character—persistence and patience. You'll never amount to anything. As a matter of fact, I venture to say that none of you have even thought about your future. I think I'll prove it by a little test. Now, let's see . . . Foster, what do you plan to do?"

"I plan to be a mining engineer, sir," Foster replied.

"You'll never make it in this world," scoffed the professor. "You have no patience, boy. How about you, Susan?"

"I want to be a doctor, Professor," she answered.

"A doctor! You won't make it either, girl," he said. "After this exhibition this afternoon, I hold out no hope for you, or for that matter, anyone here."

I knew he was going to get to me next. Although I had heard my family discussing a future in law for me, I had never considered it seriously, because the only lawyers I knew were old, pompous and unpopular. Under the circumstances I brushed that course of action aside.

But I had to think of something—and fast—because here it came.

"And you, William?"

Suddenly I had it! Only the evening before I had seen an impressive movie called *West Point,* starring William Boyd. Here was an answer—here was something to do— and just as good as being an engineer or a doctor. I cleared my throat and answered,

"I'm going to West Point."

First he smiled. Then he put his hands across his ample stomach to keep it from bobbing up and down as he chuckled. *Then he made that statement.*

And everybody laughed.

That afternoon, in my mind's eye, is still as clear as a bell. That remark seared my insides and burned deep at the roots of my pride. As I left the school that afternoon, avoiding my classmates, I said to myself, "I'll show him. I'll *really* get that old goat."

That evening at dinner I asked my father how one went about getting into West Point. He told me that congressmen and senators made appointments—but why did I ask? I told him I was going.

"Have you lost your mind?" he snapped. "Whatever gave you that idea? Don't you know your Uncle Lorie has just fixed it up for you to enter Johns Hopkins this fall? After you get out of there, you're going to University of Virginia law school. We don't have a lawyer in the family —but you're going to be one. It's all settled, so get that West Point notion out of your head."

But it wasn't settled. My father and I had one more session in August which resulted in my mother crying and my leaving home the next morning—for West Point— sometime and somehow.

Once I was in, I wondered whether or not I should write Professor Gardner and tell him a thing or two. I decided against it, because he also said I wouldn't last. It was better to wait until I was sure I'd get through.

A year and a half went by and I was sure I could complete West Point—I was also on my way home for my first Christmas leave. The first morning after I arrived, I dressed up in my full dress uniform with its forty-four large brass buttons and proceeded to Prof Gardner's downtown office, where he conducted a small marine insurance business.

Almost six years had passed since I had seen him—almost six years since he had said *it*. I entered his dimly lit office and saw him sitting behind an old fashioned roll-top desk, littered high with books, papers and bric-a-brac. Here it was!

I walked smartly up to his desk, cracked my heels together and at the same instant saluted in my snappiest military manner. He glanced up over his specs, looked me up and down slowly and finally said, "Why, it's William."

"Yes sir." I replied, as if the two words were one.

"Well, William, what's that get-up you've got on?" he asked with a puzzled look on his aging face.

"Sir, this is the uniform of a cadet of the United States Military Academy at West Point," I replied crisply.

"You don't say. Well, well, well. 'Must say it's a mighty fancy costume, William," he said, stroking his big mustache.

"This isn't a costume, Professor Gardner," I rebutted quickly, itching to get to the issue, "It's a uniform, and if you will recall, sir, it's one which you said I'd never wear."

Boy was this sweet! I was really lowering the boom—he was going to eat those words.

"I don't understand you, William," he responded slowly, with a surprised look of new interest.

"Well, sir, I'll refresh your memory," I continued, getting slightly excited. "You told me one day just before I graduated from high school, nearly six years ago, that I didn't have enough sense to get into West Point. Well, I did, and here I am to prove it."

For a minute or so he said nothing. He seemed to be searching his memory. Slowly he began to smile, particularly with his eyes.

"William, I said that?" he finally answered, half question, half denial.

"You did, sir."

"Well, William, you must have a good memory. That's commendable, my boy, because memory is one of the twenty basic elements of character. Did I ever discuss them with you when you were in school?"

Did he ever . . . ? But wait, this old boy was changing the subject. He wasn't going to get away with it.

"What about it, Professor? You remember saying it, don't you?"

"William, for the life of me I don't. I just don't know why such a thing would come to mind as I've always thought of you as a fine intelligent boy. I remember, however, that during your last year in high school, you didn't pay much attention to your studies. You were captain of this sport or president of that society—just racing around. I also recall that once during that period I said to myself, 'I'm going to have to challenge that boy, he's not looking over the horizon.' Maybe that's what prompted my remark, William, if you insist I made it."

He continued gravely, "In any event, son, I've followed your career with great interest. I remember the day you entered West Point. I remember your Uncle Lorie telling me the news in front of the bank. I told him then I had always known you would succeed in whatever you endeavored to do."

It was all over. I suddenly realized that I had been victimized. He really hadn't meant what he said—he just

wanted to shake me into consciousness of the future—
make me "look over the horizon." He would never really
know how successful he had been. His parting remarks
were these: "Now go ahead, William, and finish up, and
when you do graduate from West Point, be a good officer
and do your duty well."

After the graduation exercise in which General
MacArthur presented our diplomas, I walked slowly back
to my barracks room. I unfolded on my desk the parch-
ment which I noticed had been duly signed, by the Commandant of Cadets, the Dean of the Academic Department and the Superintendent. As I studied the document
my mind slipped back to that day in high school—and
Professor Gardner. During this reverie my eyes again
moved down to the bottom of the diploma, and although
I don't understand it to this day, I plainly saw for a second, something new below the other signatures, which
read:

BY DIRECTION OF:

F.E. GARDNER
PRINCIPAL, C.H.S.

PART II

FORT MCKINLEY, MAINE

6

SERGEANT WARWICK

When I graduated from the Military Academy, I was ordered to Fort McKinley, Maine, which is in Casco Bay on Great Diamond Island. It had formerly been a coast artillery fortress, and with Fort Prebble and Fort Williams, constituted the coastal defense of Portland Harbor and environs. The guns had been replaced or removed, but the bulwarks, or rather, the fortifications, were still there. Since practically all of the senior company officers were on Civilian Conservation Corps (CCC) duty in running camps in Maine, New Hampshire, and Vermont, there was a void from the standpoint of command of various companies. Right out of West Point I was given command of a company of infantry. This was unusual, in that normally it would take one maybe ten or eleven years to get command of a company.

When I was given command of Company L of the 5th Infantry, I didn't sleep that night. How was I going to tell Sergeant Warwick, who was the first sergeant of the company, how to conduct the affairs of the company? I thought and thought and thought. Here was Sergeant Warwick with 28 years' service, and I walked in to take over the command of his company without one day of service. I didn't know how to handle this. Many of my classmates from West Point had also been given companies, and I didn't know what the other officers were going to do. We talked about it at mess, but I never disclosed my plans.

The second morning I was on the post I went to the company and entered my small office off the Orderly Room in which the First Sergeant and Company Clerk had desks. I asked Sergeant Warwick to come in my office. He came in and saluted. I said, "Sit down, Sergeant." He was a little embarrassed, because we were very formal in those days, and that was a rare type of protocol. A soldier who was reporting in to the commander usually stood in front of the desk and was told what was going on and what to do. Very rarely were there any long conversations.

Sgt. Warwick said, "Yessir," and sat down. Though he was embarrassed, it didn't matter to me, because I was very nervous about what I had to say.

I started, "Sergeant Warwick, I have just graduated from the Military Academy and I am now in command of Company L. Here are the facts. The first fact I think should be discussed is that I don't know my ass from third base about running a company. An additional fact is that you know it and I know it. So here's what the future will hold: I'm going to take your advice and your recommendations as to discipline, of rewards and punishments, of planning, of training, things to do, when to do it, how to do it, the mess, the food, the morale, etc. Now, the final fact is that I don't know what I am doing today, but Sergeant Warwick, I *will* know someday, and it won't be too far off. So I will just let that rest with you."

Sgt. Warwick got up from the chair, stood in front of the desk, saluted, and said, "Lieutenant, I appreciate what you just said. I understand completely, and we're going to have the best company in the regiment."

And I think we did. As a matter of fact, I know we did.

7

CALL TO ARMS

Casco Bay is very beautiful, and of course at one time was an impregnable harbor guarded by some of the largest coastal artillery guns we had in our inventory. The Fort was highly organized and operational during the Spanish-American War, but with the event of air power, the Coast Artillery faded out of the picture.

The Fifth Infantry Regiment, which had been in occupation in Germany in the twenties, was moved from Germany to the United States. There apparently was no infantry establishment capable of accepting a regiment of Infantry, so it was stationed at three forts: Fort Williams, Fort Prebble, and Fort McKinley. Williams and Prebble were on the mainland at Cape Elizabeth, a suburb of Portland. These were the coast artillery fortresses that had guarded the Portland Harbor and environs. The guns were still there, but no ammunition or projectiles, and only a handful of coast artillerymen were left to maintain the weapons.

There were seven companies of the regiment, from two battalions of the Fifth Infantry at Fort McKinley, on one end of Great Diamond Island in Casco Bay and hence only accessible by a small Army launch. I'm sure

36

readers who have sailed the Casco Bay will know Great Diamond and Little Diamond islands. Now that the locale is identified, we'll proceed with the story.

General Fox Connor was at that time the Army Corps Commander with headquarters in Boston. He lived up to his name in being very foxy and a real martinet. It so happened at that point in time the Civilian Conservation Corps camps had drained all the regular Army units of company commanders and majors. Hence, we lieutenants, just out of West Point, were given command of companies. This was a great break for us.

We were due for an annual inspection by General Connor in the fall of 1933. He was a rough tough type of individual and very caustic. The first place Fox Connor hit on his annual inspection was a small Army post named Fort Banks, in New Jersey.

All alone except for his chauffeur, he drove into Fort Banks one day and proceeded immediately to the guard house. Now, in those days the guard house was manned by an Officer of the Day, who had other duties to perform and therefore was not there all the time. But the sergeant of the guard was always there. The guard consisted of those two people and several enlisted men who stood guard at the stables, commissary, post exchange, the gate, etc., primarily during the night. Also always on duty at the guard house was a bugler.

When General Connor drove up to the guard house, the sergeant of the guard came out to see who it was. When he recognized the general, he saluted and stood at attention. Fox Connor jumped out of his sedan, returned the salute, and asked, "Sergeant, you have a bugler on duty?"

"Yes, sir," the sergeant said.

"Well, send him out here."

The sergeant yelled, *"Bugler!"* The bugler double-timed out.

"Report to the general."

The bugler saluted and said, "Bugler on duty reporting, sir."

Fox Connor asked, "Do you know fire call?"

"Yes, sir."

"Well, blow it."

The bugler went to a megaphone, which is normally located at the guard house as an amplifier so the sound can be heard all over the post, and blew fire call. Nothing happened. Although there was a fire-fighting detachment, half duty and half volunteer on the post, it never reacted. Probably Fort Banks had not had a fire in years.

General Conner said, "That's all, thank you, bugler." He then proceeded to the headquarters at Fort Banks, went into the post commander's office and literally tore him apart. He raged, "The place could burn down. Not one soul reacted to fire call." The post commander was absolutely mortified and apologetic. *No one ever knew what happened to him.*

In any event, the news of this incident went through the Corps area like a forest fire.

Next, General Connor visited a small battalion post outside of Providence, Rhode Island, before it was alerted. He did the same thing he had done at Fort Banks, exactly, with the same results. Nothing or nobody moved on the fire call.

We were braced for his visit. Sure enough, he came to Fort McKinley. As usual, he went to the guard house. The sergeant of the guard reported to him. General Connor said, "Do you have a bugler on duty?"

The Sergeant replied, "Yes, sir."

"Have him report."

The bugler reported.

The General asked, "Do you know 'Call to Arms'?" ("Call to Arms" signals the troops to report in formation with individual weapons, grenades, and ammunition; machine guns and mortars are assembled with ammunition and spare parts; all units are ready to fight.)

The bugler blew "Call to Arms." *I was ready.* I had had the foresight and initiative to fill two pails of water. When we heard the bugle, I yelled at the barracks, "Let's go!" You've never seen such action. We had practiced hauling out ladders and getting our hose unreeled to near perfect. We were ready to put out any fire. But it wasn't a fire call.

But Quinn and Company L were ready. Quinn formed his troops with speed and great aplomb, standing tall in front of them with his two pails of water. And the fire engines came roaring out of their houses headed for the post headquarters.

Major McGuire, the post commander, retired not long thereafter.

8

C.C.C. And Pat Fox

During the period 1933—36 when I was stationed at Fort McKinley, Maine, in the Fifth Infantry, we were in the middle of the Civilian Conservation Corps (CCC) program. This program caused a heavy drain on the Regular Army captains and majors who were dispatched to organize and command these camps. Although the CCC was not military, the government decided that the Army should be the agency to run the camps and operate them on a para-military basis, i.e., from the standpoint of organization and discipline.

There followed a great deal of competition for excellence among the various camps all over. Our regiment was responsible for monitoring and servicing the CCC camps in Maine, New Hampshire, and Vermont.

General Fox Conner, the Corps area commander in Boston, conceived the idea of enhancing the quality of the camps by formally establishing a Best Camp Award in his corps area. He instructed the commanding officer of the Fifth Infantry to dispatch a "board" to conduct, not an investigation, but a kind of team to inspect all of the CCC camps in Maine, New Hampshire, and Vermont and to report to him its findings and recommendations as to the best camp in the three states.

When the board was selected, it was comprised of two people. One was Major Alonzo P. "Pat" Fox, member and President of the Board (and also the father of Mrs. Alexander Haig). The second was Second Lieutenant William W. Quinn, member and Recorder of the Board. In February, 1935, off we went with a driver and an old sedan on its last legs and with an unreliable heater. That winter, Maine had a snowfall of over 14 feet, but with chains we muscled through the countryside somehow.

The first night we went to a camp in Lewiston, Maine. When we got there, we bought an evening newspaper. The editor must have had a sense of humor, as the lead story announced a *heat wave*. The article went on to explain that the temperature had dramatically risen from 30° below zero to 8° below.

That night it was very cold. We were in an old barracks in a squad room furnished with two Army cots, two chairs, and a pot-bellied wood-burning stove. Later when I crawled into bed I had trouble going to sleep, as I had about forty pounds of blankets over me. They were so heavy I could hardly breathe. After dinner, we huddled around the stove and began talking about one thing and another about the regiment. All that time I was thinking of the two quarts of Laird's Apple Jack in my suitcase under my bunk. I didn't know Major Fox very well, and I wasn't about to take a drink or even mention drinking in his presence. Since I wanted to make sure I made first lieutenant, I didn't want to bump heads with a teetotaller. I reasoned that sometime I'd sneak a drink when he wasn't watching.

Suddenly Fox said, "Bill, you know I've been in the Army a long time, yet I never seem to learn. Believe it or not, I've started out in this Arctic wilderness without a damn drop of whiskey.

Well, I busted both knees hitting the floor to get under my bunk and pull out my suitcase. I hauled out a bottle of Apple Jack. I also had two small jiggers, just in case. In literally seconds, I had poured two jiggers of Apple Jack, and we began to sip that nectar. Major Fox exclaimed, "This is great. Now, I'll tell you what we'll do, as soon as I can get somewhere where I can buy Apple Jack, I'll stock up myself."

In any event, we sat there and talked and sipped those jiggers of Apple Jack and then went to bed and slept like hell.

It followed that every night during that whole trip, wherever we were, we went through this same routine of getting out the two jiggers, of which I was custodian. Maybe it would take us a half an hour or more to drink the two shots, during which time we had great conversations. As a result of that trip, and not necessarily because of the Apple Jack, I have held General Fox in the greatest of esteem and admiration—one of the finest men I ever knew.

This trip had some very interesting aspects to it. I recall inspecting the camp on Moosehead Lake in Maine. Now, Moosehead Lake is magnificent in the summertime. The terrain is varied. There are places where you can launch boats and other places where there are palisades. The camp we were in was on one of the palisades, and it was a sheer drop of several hundred feet down to the lake.

Because the lake was so deserted at that time of year, the "chick sales" for the camp, or at least for the officers, was built out over the lake. There was no toilet to be flushed; the droppings went down hundreds of feet into the lake. I went out to this structure one morning early after breakfast for my morning call. I sat down. The wind was literally shaking the shack. It was trembling like a leaf. But I had to go. However, I was afraid to do what I had to do, because the wind was so powerful on the updraft that it was all I could do to hold myself down on the seat. I chickened out, left the place, and went over to the enlisted men's latrine, which was more comfortable, and certainly less threatening.

At Ellsworth, Maine, I had another such confrontation with the cold and the call of nature. I awoke at daybreak one morning, jumped out of my cot, and ran for the outside john. I was in trouble because I had a touch of diarrhea. I rushed to the outhouse only to find the door frozen shut, with the exception of about a foot at the top, or maybe 18 inches. With superhuman effort, I scaled that door and dropped inside just in time.

After I had finished my duties, I couldn't get out. The effort that I used to get in had usurped all my strength, or at least, it didn't seem as urgent to get out as to get in. I tried and tried and tried, to no avail. I had no tools to chisel the ice down below, and I just stood there and yelled for help. Finally, somebody heard me and got an axe to chop me out.

The bottom lines of these experiences were: (1) The North Country is a hard country; (2) Pat Fox and I became great friends; and (3) if I am at a party where someone mentions Apple Jack, my left knee begins to swell.

9

UNDERHILL CENTER, VERMONT

The regiment to which Company L belonged was organized in three battalions. Each battalion had three infantry companies and a machine gun company. In those days, the machine gun company was transported by mules pulling caissons carrying the machine guns and ammunition. Because the company was mule-transported, the officers of the company were mounted on horses.

Machine gun companies, like D, H, and M Companies, went off annually to Underhill Center, Vermont, for intensive machine gun target practice, training, manuevers, etc. I was assigned to Company D at the time, and my boss was Captain Dorr Hazelhurst. He was a great guy. Since all we had for officers in this machine gun company were a captain and a lieutenant, naturally I did all the work.

This particular year, we took off from Fort Williams, Fort McKinley, and Fort Prebble. As I said, Fort Williams and Fort Prebble were on the mainland outside of Portland, and Fort McKinley was on an island. We were all mounted, with the men riding the caissons pulled by the mules, and the officers mounted on horses.

No sooner had we arrived and begun pitching camp than I got a call to report to the camp commander, a major. He said, "Quinn, you're the post exchange officer."

Well, that was news to me. I didn't know anything about post exchanges. "Yes, sir," I said, "where do you want me to set up?"

"There's a shed over here, a lean-to against the headquarters building. You can go downtown and get some chewing tobacco, snuff, beer, cigarettes, candy, etc. You don't have to build a large inventory."

I went to Captain Hazelhurst's tent and told him they had made me the PX officer.

In the three companies of infantry and support services there were maybe two to three hundred men involved. I went to the nearest town, Underhill. I soon found a wholesale house and bought candy, soft drinks, tobacco, cigarettes, etc. I also learned there was a liquor distributor in the area, so I went to him and ordered about ten cases of Canadian beer.

Unfortunately, it was payday. The troops had been paid that afternoon. I had some containers and ice and was working like hell to get this PX open by evening. With the help of a couple of men from my company who were carpenters, I finally set up in this shed. They constructed shelving and put a lock on the door. I opened up at six o'clock. The first ten soldiers in line each bought a case of beer and wiped me out. As a result of the subsequent complaints, the major called me in and said, "What is this about your running out of beer?"

"Yes, sir, I just bought ten cases, and I thought that would be enough. But it wasn't."

"Don't let that happen again."

"Yes sir."

The next day I went downtown and bought a carload of beer, a tractor-trailer full of a brew called "Mulehead." New problem: How was I going to handle a carload of beer?

The headquarters was an old deserted farmhouse on the reservation. It was an Army training area at that time. The house had been used as headquarters for units training at the center. There was one empty first-floor room not being used by the staff, so I asked the major if I could store the beer there. He told me to go ahead.

So with some of my men from Company D and the distributor, we began to unload the beer. When we had almost emptied the tractor-trailer, the floor of the room gave way, and all of the beer dropped to the ground. Fortunately, not a bottle was broken, for the simple reason that it didn't crash, it just settled slowly. In any event, the beer was on the ground, as well as the floor under it. I caught hell again from the major for buying too much beer and for putting too much weight on the room and partially destroying the headquarters. So I went back in the dog house, but damn it, I never ran out of beer again during the encampment!

While we were there, I got somebody to sub for me in the PX one weekend. Captain Hazelhurst and I decided we'd go to Quebec, as long as we were that close to Canada. Neither of us had been to Canada before, and we'd heard so much about the Chateau de Frontenac that we decided we would live it up for a day or two. We packed no suitcases, just a musette bag with our toilet articles, a change of underwear, and a bottle of bourbon. I had a Ford at the time, so we took off for Quebec.

When we arrived in Quebec City, we immediately went to the Hotel Frontenac. Since we had no suitcases and looked kind of disheveled, the reservation clerk said, "I'm sorry, gentlemen, but you'll have to pay in advance for this one night."

So we paid in advance and went upstairs to our room. I must say, Captain Hazelhurst loved his bourbon, and on the way to Quebec he had taken a nip or two every now and then. When we got settled in our room, we broke out the bourbon again. At about six-thirty, we decided we would go downtown. We asked at the desk about a good restaurant and were given the name of a highly recommended one. We got in my car, found the restaurant, parked, and went in. By this time, the Captain was feeling absolutely no pain. I wasn't hurting anywhere either.

We sat down and the waiter brought a menu. Dorr said, "You know, I think I'm gonna order some soup."

We looked at the menu, and the first soup named was *soupe du jour*. Dorr said to the waiter, "What flavor is *soupe du jour?*"

"Well, Monsieur," the waiter replied, "I am not sure. It is *soupe du jour.*"

Hazelhurst said, "I understand what it says here; it says *soupe du jour.*" (Of course, he didn't know what that meant.) He said in a loud voice, "I'm just asking what-the-hell flavor it is!"

By now we had the attention of everybody in the restaurant. The waiter shook his head and left to get the maitre d', who came over to our table and said, *"Maintenant,* what is your problem?"

"Your waiter won't tell me what kind of soup you've got. I want that *soupe du jour,* and he won't tell me what flavor it is."

"Monsieur, 'soupe du jour' means 'soup of the day.' It can be anything the chef decides to make. It is not a tomato soup or something like that."

Dorr answered, "Hell, it's got a flavor, hasn't it?"

Apparently, the maitre d' didn't know what it was; so he went back to check with the chef, and it turned out to be cream of asparagus. Things then quieted down, even though we continued to be the objects of great interest.

In any event, we got out of there without an altercation and went back to the hotel to bed. The next day we got up and drove back to Underhill. One day and one night—that was our grand tour of Canada.

As we closed up the camp at the end of our training, I had some beer left over. I had to load it in a truck and ride with it so nobody would steal it. However, I got the beer back to Fort Prebble and sold it to the post exchange.

Later on I was billed $2.67 for my share of the repairs to the floor of the headquarters building.

Lesson learned: Don't let your inventories break the house down.

PART III

THE PHILIPPINES

10

MIGRAINE HEADACHES

I was transferred to the Philippine Islands from Fort McKinley, Maine, in the summer of 1936. I proceeded to New York and got on the *U.S. Grant*, an Army transport. From New York we went to Panama, where we discharged some newly assigned officers to the Panama command. Then we traveled through the canal to San Francisco, where we picked up some people destined for Hawaii and discharged others who were going to the West Coast for duty. We picked up additional individuals who were going to Guam or the Philippine Islands. At Honolulu, we dropped people off for duty in Hawaii, proceeded to Guam and then to Manila.

As is the custom in the Philippine Islands, on the morning of your arrival in Manila on a transport, there is a party at the Army-Navy Club known as a *despedida*. A *despedida* is something like an *aloha*, and means hello and goodbye. At least, that was the interpretation of it in the Philippines at that time. It welcomed the newcomers who just got off the transports to join their regiments, whether it was field artillery, coast artillery, infantry, or cavalry.

In any event, it's a big day, and it also says farewell to those people who are going back to the States on the transport which just came in.

Now this gets to be old hat with some of the old timers who had been there for a couple of years, i.e., to go to these *despedidas* every quarter. Consequently, they get rather blase about them, and here follows a typical scenario.

When the transport docks at 7:00 A.M., each newly arrived officer is met by a fellow officer from his unit. He is escorted to his quarters immediately, and in my case it was the Army-Navy Club, because I was a bachelor, and that's where I was to live for the next two years.

Once you have been shown your room, you are taken by your escort officer to the tailor. There a miracle happens. You are measured, and that night a couple of uniforms of suntan (summer khakis), a white uniform, some outdoor shorts, sport shirts, and practically everything else that you've been advised to order is delivered to your room. How they do it all in so short a time is beyond me. A newcomer can proceed to work the next morning wearing a brand new uniform, freshly starched and pressed.

From the tailor, you're taken to the various places for check-in—the provost marshall, the bank, and the post exchange for identification cards and driver's licenses. Finally, roughly around ten o'clock, you are led to the *despedida*. The main purpose of your escort officer is to get you drunk so that he can join his golf foursome by twelve-thirty or one o'clock, so that the *despedida* doesn't spoil his day. To his credit, my escort, Lt. Gordon Cusak, was very successful in that objective, because he had a system that he had used successfully to get newcomers drunk early. It had to do with toasting. It seems that the 31st Infantry, where I was assigned, has a very interesting history of service in the Far East, in that it served in Peking after the Boxer Rebellion. While there, the officers had designed an enormous ornate silver bowl, beautifully embossed. It was accompanied by individual silver cups with names on them. Well, Cusak kept telling me that tradition demands that you drink toasts from the bowl which was an Artillery punch, or something equally lethal, or you had to fill the cup with scotch to toast the regiment, each battalion, each company, and if you lasted, each platoon. I had never had a drink of scotch.

I came from Fort McKinley, Maine, where prohibition was in effect at the time, and nobody could afford scotch. All we drank up there was rum run in from Puerto Rico, or alcohol we made into gin with juniper berry juice or grenadine.

In any event, Cusak was very successful, because he kept saying, "It is tradition to toast these units which served with great honor. To empty this cup you can qualify as a 'Thirsty Firster.' " (That was the nickname of the members of the Thirty-First Infantry.) So, lo and behold, at 12 o'clock, right on target, he and a couple of fellow officers laid me on my bed in my room at the Army-Navy Club. I was out like a light, and Cusak went to join his foursome, congratulating himself all the while on having been assigned such a patsy.

Although this was at noon, I didn't wake up until the next morning, and when I did, I had a severe "migraine" headache. I knew what it was because I had recently been to the Fort Banks, New Jersey Army Hospital for an operation on a deviated septum in my nose. Across the hall from me was a captain who groaned all night long and screamed and hollered because he had migraine headaches. During periods when he was rational he would describe to me just exactly where and how severe the pain was. On my first day of duty I was AWOL, lying in the sack and desperately ill, so I thought. One of the company officers came over with ice bags and aspirin.

He offered, "Maybe it will just go away." Of course, I had come from Maine, which is cold country compared to the tropics, and the officer suggested, "Sometimes people have problems coming from winter climate to the tropics."

Well, I lay in my bed and nearly died that day, and the next morning I couldn't go to work again, as I was still suffering. I went to the Army hospital emergency room, and the doctor there gave me a thorough examination and asked me a million questions. I told him about my experience at Fort Banks and that I had never had migraine headaches before, but I had them now. He then asked me to describe my arrival and participation in the *despedida*. He gave me a prescription and told me to get it filled and take two of the pills every two hours.

He said, "You know, Lieutenant, I have some good news for you. You do not have migraine headaches, but you do have one of the damndest hangovers I've treated since I've been in the Islands." And he laughed like hell.

But to me, it wasn't funny then.

11

John Gunther

In 1937 I was given command of the Military Police Company of the 31st Infantry, located in the old city of Manila, Cuartel d'España. The company was composed of about 60 or 70 highly trained military policemen. Some of them had detective backgrounds in civilian life. It was a very competent force.

As a result of this particular job, I got to know the City of Manila. I wouldn't say as well as the back of my hand, but I did know how the city worked, where the problem areas were, who was in charge and why. Because of my responsibilities to the troops, I had to know the prostitution situation as well as the *binabae*, which I'll discuss later.

One day I received a call from the office of the commanding general of the Philippine Department, Major General Emerick. I was told to report to him immediately. I didn't know what the hell I'd done. I had seen the General, but had never met him, because he commanded all the American forces in the Philippines, and I was assigned to the 31st Infantry Regiment and only a first lieutenant, way down the pecking order.

I reported somewhat shaking and was ushered into

the General's office. He told me to sit down, which I did. He said, "Quinn, I have here in my hand a message from the War Department in Washington, which states that the writer John Gunther is coming to the Far East, and his first stop will be the Philippines. He is going to do a book on the Far East comparable to his recent book, *Inside Europe*. I have been ordered to extend to Mr. and Mrs. Gunther all of the courtesies and assistance available to the military here; to provide them with escort and transportation, and with no prohibitions as to what they are to do or see, regarding the city of Manila and the military establishment. Now, I'm going to loan you my Buick (which was the biggest thing on the Island at the time) and a chauffeur. You will escort Mr. and Mrs. Gunther wherever they wish to go. In addition to that, I want you to develop an itinerary which will cover the city of Manila and environs regarding any subject on which he inquires and be able to drive him to the places and explain to him those things. If you can't answer his question, find someone who can."

"Yes, sir." I replied.

"I'm depending on you to carry out these instructions, and I'll be expecting a report from you subsequent to their departure as to how things went."

"Yes, sir. Can I have the chauffeur's name, and how can I contact him?"

"Don't worry. He will be assigned to you the morning the Gunthers are due to arrive. He'll be at your call from then on."

Well, I met the Gunthers on their arrival and took them to the Manila Hotel to get them settled in. As it was lunchtime and nothing had been said about expenses that might be incurred in this exercise, I was happy when Mr. Gunther invited me to have lunch with him and discuss the general program. We had a delightful luncheon. John Gunther was a dynamic kind of person, full of vim and vitality, and interesting. To me, he was really a macho, gung-ho type of guy—at least, he was at that point in time.

I outlined the things I thought might be of interest to him and then left it somewhat open as to what were his main areas of interest. He said, "My interest is in Manuel Quezon and the Philippine people." He was not necessarily interested in the economic structure, statistics on agricultural production or steel output, or things of that description. He covered those points in general, but what he wanted was an insight into the man on the street, what made him tick, who he was, what he thought and how he acted. In other words, he wanted a feel for the Islands which would give him a base for his forthcoming interview with President Manuel Quezon. Gunther appeared to be sociologically oriented, rather than economically or politically. As a matter of fact, Mrs. Gunther inquired into the latter areas.

Mr. Gunther said, "I would like to follow exactly what you have outlined as to where we will go this afternoon and what we will do in the next two or three days. You know my objective, I need a feel for the environment. I need a foundation upon which I can justify my questions to Quezon. I may have some ideas as we go along, but right now I'm going to leave it to you, Lieutenant."

So that afternoon we did an historical tour. I must say that from the time the General told me Gunther was coming, I had "boned up" on the Island. I had reconnoitered the routes and the places I planned to take him that were of historical interest, like Estada Mejor, Malacañang Palace, the Cathedral in the Old City, some of the old Spanish ruins, the river, the markets, and various institutions. This was to be a sheep dip in Spanish culture and heritage and not Filipino.

I told Gunther several stories about the attitude of the people, one of which he found very interesting. It was the result of a conversation I had with Mrs. McLean, a colonel's wife. She told me of a Filipino girl named Rosita, who came to apply for a job as a maid. The Colonel's lady asked, "How much are you expecting me to pay you a month?"

Rosita answered, "Thirty pesos."

Mrs. McLean said, "Well, I noticed on your reference that you worked for the Rodriguez family."

"Yes, I did work for them."

"Well, how much did they pay you?"

"Oh, they paid me 15 pesos a month."

"Well, I don't understand it. Why should you ask 30 pesos from me and only 15 pesos from the Rodriguezes?"

"Oh, you see, the Americans are our equals, but the Rodriguezes are Spanish, and they are our masters."

John (we were on a first name basis by now) thought that was a pretty good insight into the Spanish influence, and how Spain had operated in the area.

That evening he said, "I'd like to see some night life." It turned out to be quite an evening. I took him first to see the Santa Anna cabaret on the outskirts of Manila. The Santa Anna cabaret was, and probably still is, one of the largest cabarets in the world. It was a monster. It was so big that they used two bands, one band at one end of the cabaret, and one at the other end, with no conflict. I knew the manager, so I took John to his office, and he gave us a fine briefing on Santa Anna. The girls were all "ticket" girls, in that soldiers and sailors or merchant marines from all over the world paid to dance with these girls. Of course, some, maybe most, were prostitutes, but not all.

Gunther was fascinated by this operation, almost a hundred Filipino girls, some extremely pretty, dancing for 15 cents a dance and not getting much more for their bodies.

From the Santa Anna cabaret we went back to the Manila Hotel and called it a day.

The next morning, John and his wife worked on their notes and had lunch with some friends they knew in Manila. Of course, they had other contacts besides the Army. In the afternoon he had his long interview with Quezon. That night I invited them to have dinner with me at the Army-Navy Club, and at dinner, John said, "I would like to see how you operate in your position of Provost Marshall. Could we monitor some of the police activities in the city tonight?"

"Yes. First we can go over to the Lunetta Police Station and talk to Captain Torres, who is the Chief of Police of Manila."

We did that and got a briefing by the captain, after which we went to my office in the Cuartel d'España. Arriving there, we found all hell had broken loose. A couple of GI's assigned to the 31st Infantry had just arrived. They didn't know the workings of the Philippines, and on their first night they went out on the town and found their way to the red light district. They had picked up two beautiful girls strolling arm-in-arm down the street, and off they went to the girls' place. Where the girls took them was actually the house of the *binabae*, a house where gays, deviants, and transvestites holed up.

When the GI's were stripped and ready for action and the "girls" disrobed, the GI's realized they'd been taken, for the girls were not girls but transvestites. These GI's were so damned mad that they beat the hell out of the two queers. The gays screamed, and a score of the *binabae* came to their rescue, beat up the two GI's, and drove them out on the street in their drawer tails without their pocketbooks or identification.

Fortunately these two soldiers were not too far from their barracks in the Cuartel d'España. They made it home somehow without getting arrested and ran to their barracks in Company L where they told their story. After hearing the tale, about 15 or 20 GI's put on some pants and charged down to the *binabae* joint and literally cleaned out the place.

Now this is when John Gunther and I came into the act. The two GI's didn't report this incident to the MP's, only to their buddies in Company L. So when we heard about all this fracas and the noise of Company L moving out, we got an MP patrol and arrived on the scene just in time to see the end of a *mêlée*—a real rhubarb with blood all over the place, queers scattered around, knocked down and out, and the *binabae* house deserted except for those who were unconscious or incapacitated.

It was a real humdinger. John said later, "Wow! What an exercise! I'd like to explore this a little more."

"Well, tomorrow night we'll do just that. If you'll have dinner with me again, we'll go down to one of the parks." The Gunthers accepted.

Now, I had and still have a theory about Filipino people because both men and women are very affectionate. The next night as we sauntered through one park, we could see men holding hands or walking along arm-in-arm, or walking with their arms around each other's shoulders. John asked, "Are these people homosexuals?"

"No, they're not. I don't think we're seeing homosexuals at all. I think we're just seeing demonstrations of affection."

"Well, it's very feminine."

"Yes it is, John. Let's look at it this way. In most Western societies, male and female are distinctly different. I'm not referring here to the sexual organs *per se*, but rather to the inherent characteristics which we normally view as masculine and feminine. Stereotypes, if you will. Let's take some examples. The occidental woman exhibiting extremely feminine traits is usually gentle, often sweet in disposition, maternal, demonstrative, affectionate, and not usually prone to physical pursuits or violence. She's sensitive to the degree that the old story of the 'princess and the pea' would apply to her. On the other extreme, there's the 'manly' woman, deep-voiced, physical in disposition, aggressive, fearless, and quick to defend her views or rights. The same extremes apply to the occidental man, from the most 'macho' to the most effete.

"Now, these extremes that I've just outlined are not as extensive in most Asiatics, and there appears to be a commensurably closer spread between normal Filipino masculinity and femininity—the differences are just not as evident or obvious as they are in feminine behavior among the male population here, with widespread hand-holding and walking arm-in-arm."

"Well," John said, "that's a pretty good explanation. I never thought of it that way before, but it has a lot of merit."

"Yes, it does. Because of what you've seen, you can understand why there is a higher proportion of homosexuality in the Philippines than probably in any other of the Asiatic countries." I could be wrong on that, but it certainly was high in Manila.

When I first became provost marshall, I conceived of a naive plan to locate and identify all of the *binabae* houses and all the whore houses in Manila. I ran into twenty-five just outside the barracks, just five or six blocks away. So I quit, because they moved around just like nomads, and the Cata is loaded with prostitutes and homosexuals.

Now, the homosexuals in Manila tend toward transvestism, and then the strip, or red light district, is continuously patronized by transvestites, and they are unbelievably pretty.

At one point in our discussions, Gunther asked me about the incidence of venereal diseases. I told him that V.D. was the biggest morale problem with the Philippine command, that it was rampant. Any soldier contracting it was subject to court martial, a six month rap. Usually, two or three soldiers from each company would pick it up each month—in most cases these were new arrivals from the States.

I related to him one story about how one company defied the statistics for months, that is, not one case reported. The company commander was applauded, commended, and interrogated as to his success. He confessed that it was just good luck. He did, however, claim to have lectured on celibacy and the use of prophylactics.

The reason for this success was due to the initiative of one of the platoon sergeants, who carefully selected a house of prostitution not far from the barracks in the Cuartel d'España. He worked out a deal with the madam whereby several selected girls were medically inspected. If free of V.D., these girls were reserved exclusively for members of his platoon. Soon the word got around, and the whole company took advantage of the situation, less those who had regular girl friends. Periodically, a Filipino doctor would check the girls out.

This worked for over three months, until two of the girls went "extra-curricular" and became infected. A few days later and after a payday, ten GI's from Company L were treated at the U.S. Army Hospital in Manila for gonorrhea.

Well, the Gunthers were about to leave, and I was to put them on the plane the next morning for Hong Kong. They invited me to have a nightcap with them over at the Manila Hotel. In reviewing their visit, they were profuse in their thanks and indicated they planned to write a commendatory letter to the Commanding General and the Secretary of War on my behalf. I don't think they ever did. If so, I never saw the letter; but it could have been somewhere in my record or my 201 file.

At the end of the conversation and before we said goodnight, I said, "You know, you've really been around; you've done Europe, and you've been in practically every country there, so incidentally, how do you rate the morality aspects of the Philippine Islands with anything you've ever seen? Don't you think the morals are looser here than anywhere?"

"No," Gunther replied, "So far, I would class this as number two—from a morality standpoint."

"Number two? Then you must have a number one."

"I do." He said, "and that is Munich, Germany."

The Gunthers left the next day. That was the last time I ever saw them. But I was satisfied with my contribution to his interview with President Manuel Quezon, which appeared in Gunther's next book, *Inside Asia*.

12

wOw

While in the Philippines, I dated the daughter of one of the colonels in the 31st Infantry Regiment. At that time I was a first lieutenant. This was a wonderful girl, and she and I became very close. She was such a fine person that on many occasions I damned near asked her to marry me. But something happened to throw water on that particular idea.

It happened at Christmastime in 1937. At that time, monogrammed items were inexpensive and hence very popular. People loaded up on monogrammed items. We were exchanging Christmas presents, and the young lady's present to me was a navy blue necktie. My initials are *WWQ*, and this lovely girl had the embroidery people put the *Q* in the middle and a little larger than the two *W*'s on either side. The initials made good symmetry, and although not too high, they were in a conservative position and could still be seen.

What had happened was that the seamstress did not really know how to make a *Q*, and the little curlicue that changes an *O* to a *Q* was so small that you had to get very close to see that it was a *Q* and not an *O*. From a distance, the tie said, "wOw." Well, I thanked my girl when

62

she gave me the tie, but before I had a chance to wear it, I went out to play golf with Joe Anderson, a friend and fellow officer. Joe was in the class after mine at West Point, and he and his delightful bride, Nanie, kind of adopted me as a bachelor over there, so we became close friends.

Well, while playing golf the day after Christmas, I said, "Joe, you know, I got the damndest present." I didn't say who it was from, but explained how the tie said "WOW." He thought that was hilarious.

"You should wear it all the time."

That was the end of it, or so I thought.

Two nights later we were at a cocktail party, and I had my girl with me. Joe and Nanie were there, and we were in a circle, and Joe said, "You know, Bill Quinn got the damndest necktie for Christmas that you would ever believe. Somebody actually gave him a tie that says 'WOW' on the front! W-O-W! How stupid can somebody be?"

The girl who had given me the tie listened to all of this and then absolutely froze. She turned to me and politely said, "Bill, I would like to go home." I took her home, and that was the last date we ever had. *WOW.*

13

A JOURNEY THROUGH THE JUNGLE

While in Manila, a first lieutenant and serving as provost marshall of the city, I was called in by the G-2, the intelligence officer of the Philippine Department of the U.S. Army, Lt. Col. Henry McLean. He told me that the Department would like to send me on a mission to the island of Mindanao. Mindanao is one of the largest islands of the Philippine Archipelago and is inhabited mostly by the Moros, who are Moslems. Colonel McLean said, "If you will go, it will not count against your leave, and you can stop over in Zamboanga to visit your friends."

"Well, sir, what is it?" I asked. (Mind you, this was before Pearl Harbor.)

"We have reason to believe the Japanese are surveying, presumably for a rail line, across the island of Mindanao from Budkidnon to Davao. This rail line, we assume, would be for economic exploitation should Japan take Mindanao, or have other plans, in the event that there are hostilities, and the Philippine Islands came under the jurisdiction or the command of the Japanese. We would like you to find their survey party, if it exists."

"I'd like to do it."

I was then briefed on the topography of the island and given a map and told that when I got to Zamboanga I should check in with the Philippine Constabulary, which is like our National Guard except they are on active duty all the time. There I would be given a guide and equipped for the trip.

So, I went on the mail boat to Zamboanga, which was an interesting trip in itself. I slept out on deck of the ship with a helluva lot of other people, as there were no staterooms. It was a kind of a ferry. When we got to Zamboanga, I went in to see some friends of mine, former classmates from West Point who were stationed there, and spent a couple of days with them. I did some snorkeling in the Straits of Zamboanga. The thousands of multicolored fish swimming in and around the coral beds were spectacular. I spent most of a week in Zamboanga and environs and also went to Lake Lanao before I took off on my assignment.

Lake Lanao in Mindanao is one of the most interesting places on the island. There I paid my respects to the Sultan of Lanao. I called on him in his tent, something like an Indian wigwam, or a bedouin tent. We got along very well. He asked me what my hobbies were, and I told him I liked to fish, hunt, and play golf. He asked if I played chess. I said, "Yes."

"Well, I will play you tomorrow morning."

"Fine, I'll be glad to play with you. Where do you want to play?"

"I will call at your quarters."

I told him that would be fine, but nothing was said about the time.

After leaving the Sultan, I went up to the northern end of the lake in a bus to visit a place where they made sarongs and beautiful daggers, sabers and machete-type weapons. I bought several of the most beautiful steel blades I had ever seen. I watched them do some of the forging and tempering. Before I left the area, as I went down to the bus stop, there were some children playing along the way. I had quite a number of pennies, nickels, and dimes in my pocket, and I tossed most of them to the kids. They raised all kinds of hell, screaming and scrambling to get at the coins.

The bus finally came, and I got on to ride. A bus ride in the Philippines is quite an experience. You may be sitting by a crate of chickens or next to a woman with a goose in her lap, or a man holding on to a squealing pig for dear life. The buses were kind of ramshackle and open, but they were transportation and entertainment, if you like that sort of thing.

The bus took me back down to Lanao, and when I stepped off, half the kids in town were there, shouting for pennies. How they knew I had thrown money at the other end of the lake, I've never found out. There were no telephones or other known means of communication, but when I got off the bus an hour later, all these kids knew what I'd done in a little barrio north of Lanao. Then I had to throw these kids quarters or half dollars or whatever I had. To this day I've never figured out how they learned what I had done unless they had drums or smoke signals or something else.

The next morning, just after sunrise, I was awakened by my Filipino orderly at the Army billet where I was staying. It was a very small one-bedroom cottage which was maintained by the U.S. Army for visitors, and the orderly went along with the house. He woke me up very excited, and said, "The Sultan's here."

"The Sultan of what?" I asked.

"The Sultan of Lanao, and he has his chess set with him, and he told me that you were going to play chess with him this morning."

"Yeah, but my God, it's hardly daybreak."

"Well, he's out on the front porch."

I got dressed as fast as I could and without even a cup of coffee, I went out to the porch. The Sultan was sitting on the floor cross-legged with the chess board all set up. We started to play. That Sultan beat me so damn bad that I was almost ashamed to say I knew how to play the game. He had me wrapped up in knots in just about five or six plays. I found myself completely on the defensive from beginning to end, and of course, he won every game. After three games I realized he knew he had no competition and that he wasn't having much fun, so I told him I had to leave for Bukidnon. I guess he was happy to go, too. I had thought I was a pretty good chess player until then. Live and learn.

Now I began to review my instructions in connection with the mission. It was nearly time to take off. I unfolded the map of Mindanao and drew a line across the center of the island from Bukidnon southeast to Davao. The Penang River splits the southern part of the island, goes up to the eastern part of the island from the south. I was to find that river, which would have intersected or crossed the Japanese survey party's route, and go on down to a junction of the main road from Zamboanga to Davao, from which point I would take a bus into Davao. There I had some other intelligence missions to perform.

The interesting part of this whole operation was the fact that the entire center of the map was blank with the word "unexplored" written across it, and I was to proceed through that area so identified. The last town named on the map to the west before entering the unexplored area was Maylay Baylay. Between Bukidnon and Maylay Baylay, there was a constabulary station where I met the Filipino constabulary sergeant. He had two *carabaos* (water buffalos) and a Brahma bull, and four young men who were cargadors. They guided and took care of the animals which carried our packs, food, utensils, water, weapons, etc. When we camped at night, they also built a fire and helped prepare dinner. So the Filipino sergeant, two carabaos, a Brahma bull, four cargadors, a cur dog and Quinn took off into the unknown, in search of a Japanese survey party.

We headed southeast and soon found a trail. Somebody had been going our way before us. We were alternately going through open areas and jungles and following this trail. Later in the afternoon, we came upon an opening about the size of a football field in a grassy area. One sensed that somebody had cleared this field many years before. On each end of the field, we spotted a herd of cattle. I guess there were about 40 to 50 head of Brahmas in all. When they saw us, they turned in our direction and began what looked to me like a stampede roaring towards us like a bat out of hell. As we were pretty well into the field, I said, "Sergeant, we'd better run for it.'

"No," he said, "don't run. We'll just stand still with our animals, and they will stop before they run over us."

"I don't understand. It looks like they're going to stomp us to death."

And here they came. But sure enough, as he said, once they got within about 20 yards of us, the front runners put on the brakes and came to a halt, and the herd began to encircle us at about ten yards' distance.

"Sergeant, this is miraculous. How come?"

"They think that we have salt. There's very little salt in this grass, and from time-to-time the owner will come with a box of salt or a big salt lick and leave it in the field for them." As we didn't have any, we pushed our way through them. They followed us until we left the field and re-entered the jungle.

The second night we were in the middle of the dense jungle and were no longer following a path, just animal tracks. Now we were relying on our compass and the sun for direction. Naturally, we had to blaze our trail for a return trip if we either found what we were looking for or had to return for any other reason. I decided that because of reptiles and wild boar, I would sleep in a tree. I scaled up a small coconut tree and lay in the branches. Of course, it was the sleep of the damned, because I was afraid I'd fall out of the tree. Then there were also all kinds of noises in the jungle. It was not exactly the environment I had left in the Army-Navy Club in Manila and therefore not conducive to good sleeping.

In addition to a sleepless night, I felt sick after we had stopped for the day. It had been unbearably hot, and I was dehydrated. The cargadors had picked a number of coconuts and opened the tops. I was so thirsty, I began to drink the coconut milk like it was going out of style. If you have consumed any coconut milk, you know it's sweet and a person cannot take too much of it. But I did. On top of the milk we had some dried beef and wild *comoties*. A *comoti* is a kind of vegetable that looks like a Jerusalem artichoke. It tastes something like a cross between a sweet and white potato. They're good with salt and pepper, but are naturally semi-sweet. So after I ate the *comoties* and the beef and half a gallon of coconut milk, I became completely nauseated and had to let it all hang out. And I mean everything.

The next morning we took off with Quinn a little weaker. We walked another day in the jungle and spent another sleepless night. This was our order of march. After being given a general direction the cargadors would lead out with the animals, and the sergeant would follow them with a rifle. The jungle there was not dense undergrowth but generally clear. We were mostly walking under a canopy or umbrella of tall tree branches. We were hardly ever in the sun. I would bring up the rear with a shotgun and a .45 pistol. It actually didn't matter where we were in the order of march, because we were all concerned with pythons dropping on us from the limbs of the banyan trees or other arboretum in the jungle. It really was kind of hairy, because the rattan was so thick, hanging from the tops of the trees down to the ground, that it took on the appearance of snakes. Rattan sometimes grows to be as thick as a python. Of course, if a python drops on you, with that tremendous weight, from any height, you're going to have a broken shoulder or back or arm or something, and if it isn't broken, you're driven to the ground anyway and probably knocked out. This constant concern becomes wearing.

About the third or fourth morning out we were still going to the southeast, right through the middle of the "unexplored" territory. I knew that if we kept going to the southeast, we were bound to run into the Penang River. That morning we found a small spring, which looked to be the headwaters of a stream. This water was trickling to the southeast, meandering sometimes to the east and to the south. I estimated that this particular stream was going to run into the Penang eventually. Consequently, with an occasional look at the compass, we started walking down this stream bed. Now, this was really tortuous because it began to get rocky, and we were stepping from one rock to another. Eventually boulders came, and as we walked through the day, more springs added to the volume of water, so that eventually we were walking in water and on stones. This was really rough on the animals and all of us, but we had no choice. The sides of the stream were so thick with foliage that it was almost impossible to walk along the banks and follow the stream.

While we were moving down this stream, about two or three o'clock that afternoon, we were exposed to the sun, which was over my shoulder. I was leading the way at this point, and the bough of a tree overhanging the stream was blocking my path. I pushed it aside, and as I did, I saw right in front of me on a large rock a small man about four feet tall, poised to throw an upraised spear. He wore only a loin cloth. His skin was glistening bronze. Even though I was petrified, I thought at the time that I had never before seen such a perfect confirmation of humanity. I froze. For a second, he just stood there eyeing me, then jumped off the rock and disappeared into the jungle. I called the sergeant, who was back in the rear, and said, "Sergeant, let me tell you what I just saw."

After I told him, he said, "Well, there are rumors that there is a tribe which lives in the center of this island. Only a few people have ever seen them, and they are reported to be extremely small. They're not exactly pygmies, but they're of very small stature, and no one knows anything about them."

"Well, I do now. I just saw one."

In explaining, he said, "My guess is that he didn't expect to see you. What he thought was coming his way was a wild pig. We assume they live on coconuts, wild fruit, and such animals as are available in the jungle to catch and eat. I'm sure pork is their main meat staple."

I thought no more about the incident until later when

we eventually got on the river, and I talked with some of the people who lived on the fringes of the "unexplored" area. They said, "Yes, there are some people who live back up in the jungle and the hills. They have been seen from time to time, but they are scary and timid. Consequently, it is almost impossible to find or contact them."

Later on, in 1983, I recall, perhaps one of the Rockefellers ran across this tribe and there was quite a bit of publicity about this find and these little people. Based on that report, I realized that the location described was almost exactly where I had been, according to my own estimates, in 1937. I made no such report, because I saw just this one little guy. I have to admit that I read the Rockefeller report with a great deal of interest and a little nostalgia.

About noon one day there was the river! We had finally found the Penang. I was sure it was the Penang because it was flowing very fast in rapids toward the south. At that point the river was about 30 or 40 yards wide. Later I was able to estimate that we were then practically in the middle of Mindanao, maybe somewhat south of center.

As I mentioned earlier, we had blazed a trail, because we could only guess that we would eventually run into the river, or the Japanese. We had plenty of food, there was plenty of water everywhere, and we had no problems. Except that we didn't know exactly where we were. I forgot to mention that we did have to wait, from time to time, to forage the animals, to make sure they were rested and watered properly.

Speaking of water, one day we came upon a pool of water, and since I was very thirsty and the water looked clear and good, I reached down and scooped up a cup. I was about to drink it when the sergeant knocked it out of my hand. I said, "What the hell?"

"Poison." He replied.

"How come?"

He explained it was poison because of a plant that was in the pond, the name of which I don't recall. These plants were poison and any water you saw them growing in, you should not drink.

The dog traveling with us was very watchful at night, and I'm sure he saved us from injury from time-to-time by scaring off wild animals or snakes or other creatures.

As I said before, we'd blazed a trail because we had to assume that we might have to return if we didn't find the river. Not only that, but if we did find the river, we would not be able to take the livestock or the cargadors along. The cargadors, the sergeant and I pitched in and built a large flat bamboo raft. It was amazing how, with one little hand saw from the kit we had, we sawed the bamboo logs, which float like anything. With the thongs we cut by stripping bamboo, we produced a string-like cord which was as strong as a leather thong or rawhide. It took us the better part of a day and a half to build the raft. When finished, it measured about 12 by 15 feet.

The next morning after we loaded the raft with our possessions, the dog, and some food and water, I paid off the cargadors and they launched us.

So we took off. Fortunately, the depth of the water and the current was such that we could guide ourselves with bamboo poles. We had made several of them just in case we lost one or two overboard. We had stripped down all of our stuff, because we knew it was going to be rough in the rapids. We even had a kind of a double loop to put the dog in so he wouldn't fall overboard. We had made handholds in the center of the raft for ourselves. Whenever we entered a rapids, we naturally lost control. There we just let nature take its course and became flotsam. The river really moved.

It was early morning when we took off, and about noon, traveling fast, we came to a place where the river leveled out, but the flow continued to be very fast. We covered a large number of miles in one day, and by night-fall, arrived at a small *barrio* on the right bank of the river.

Just before that, the river had widened, and for a while we were in an area which reminded me of the Colorado River. I guess at one point the palisades must have been nearly one hundred feet high. I recall that in our talking to each other, our voices would reverberate across the canyon walls. It was rather eerie, and the river was in-fested with crocodiles.

In anticipation of an attack on our raft, I had my .45 caliber automatic pistol in hand. The sergeant said, "Don't let them bother you. They can't climb aboard be-cause they can't get their forefeet up over our railings. Moreover, we don't have enough ammunition to kill all the crocs in the river."

In building the raft the sergeant had constructed a foot-high railing around the perimeter, mainly to prevent stuff from rolling off the raft going down the rapids. However, this also took care of the crocs.

When we finally came to the first *barrio* on the river, we pulled over to the bank, and the sergeant went ashore. This village was occupied, not by aborigines, but by people without any education or skills. They just lived on the edge of the jungle and survived by its bounty. Their shacks were on bamboo poles about six feet high and constructed of bamboo with palm leaf roofs. But they took us in.

In walking down this gully on the stream bed, I had rubbed a blister on my heel. I was wearing the shoes I had been wearing for the whole trip, but my feet had been dry. When I entered the water, naturally, my feet got wet, and the top part of the shoes rubbed a blister at heel level. Consequently, my foot became swollen and red, and I guess I had blood poisoning when I arrived at the *barrio*. The natives took me in and put me on a cot on a thatched bed and propped up my foot. One of the villagers kept my head cool with cold water, and another got some dung from either a *carabao* or some animal that had just dropped it. They brought this in and made a poultice to put on my heel. They kept changing it every hour or so— always hot dung. The next day about noon, the festering had subsided, believe it or not, and I was able to go bare-foot with a bandage, still keeping the stuff on. I had brought some iodine which I used as well, but this crap prescription just clobbered the infection. In any event, when we departed, I left them some pesos. They were happy that we came and visited with them, but not happy to see us go. They were natural human beings.

We left the raft there with them. As a matter of fact, I paid them to canoe us down to the bridge, which crosses the Penang River not too far from Davao. When we got to the bridge, the three of us got off and climbed up on the road. Our canoeists started back up the river. The bus usually stopped at the bridge because of natives arriving by canoe. The bus would stop anywhere along the road to pick people up.

Now we were about to enter Davao, and still no Japanese in sight. We found a place to stay and settled down for the night.

One of the other items I was supposed to provide to the Philippines Department was my estimate of Japanese infiltration into the province of Davao and also the city it-self. At that time, and it may still be true, the Philippine government did not allow foreigners to own property in the islands. The only way outsiders could control private property was to marry a Filipino woman. And this is what the Japanese were doing. The town was not filthy with Japanese, but they were in evidence practically all over the place. They'd move around town in small numbers or in twos.

I, of course, did not speak Tagalog, but the sergeant did. I'd ask him to go in civilian clothes and get the answers to questions I would give him. He would talk to the natives, bartenders, prostitutes, etc., and find out what was going on. We learned that almost a hundred or more Japanese men had arrived in Davao that year with a lot of money and had married Filipino women who then purchased, in the woman's name, a piece of property which was strategically located in the city. In some cases the woman was thrown out by the man, but in other cases, they lived as husband and wife. A lot of the women were prostitutes, and after they had bought a house, they merely went back to their own business and settled with the Japanese man for a bundle.

I asked if there was a place where the Japanese gathered, a club, some place—and yes, there was. On the outskirts of Davao was a large plantation which probably had been the home of a copra plantation owner—copra being a product of the coconut. The house was quite large and had a long lane guarded by steel gates leading up to it, and fences all around. So, I went up to this place, and as the gate was ajar, I just went in. I got almost up to the big house, when a couple of Japanese rushed out to block my path, but didn't grab me. In confronting me, they wanted to know what I was doing there. Now, I had heard that the plantation was an arsenal and that some of the natives and one of the Filipino women who had been there had indicated that the place was filled with all kinds of munitions and weapons. Hence, if the Japanese ever attacked the Philippine Islands, they had an immediate supply of weapons and a group of people who could be instant guerillas against the Philippine army.

Well, I told these two Japanese that I was looking for a friend. Some people had told me that he lived there, I was calling on him, and I wanted to see him. They indicated that there was no such person there. They then firmly escorted me to the gate and snapped the lock. I sketched the place and identified it. I never did get in to know what was there, but it was obvious that the Japanese were in Davao and in town with muscle—*four years before Pearl Harbor.*

I had crossed the line, I don't know where, a line that would be drawn from Bukidnon to Davao, in which the rumor indicated that a Japanese survey party was surveying this area for a railroad. I found no evidence of it at all. It could have been true, and we just missed it. Maybe it was before a Japanese crossing of the island, for if they had passed, they left no trace.

I saw no human, felt the touch of no other human, from the time I left Maylay Baylay until I saw the small golden man on the rock.

So, I returned to Manila. My heel got well. I was debriefed by the Intelligence people there, as to what I had seen.

I can recall the experience as if it might have been yesterday. When a person lives in complete fear of life for days on end—not fear of a known and identified enemy, vis-à-vis the other side of a battle field, but from an unknown predator, an unpredictable predator—one doesn't soon forget.

P.S. I'm told that P.S.'s are for letters only. So be it.

But this P.S. tells you that when the Japanese hit the
Philippines, their well-armed "boys at the lodge" came
storming out and took over Davao in a matter of, not
days, but hours.

14

LUCY CHERIKOVA

While in Manila I lived at the Army-Navy Club, and it was my habit to drift down to the bar each evening before dinner and have a drink. There were two bars. One was a men's bar, and the other was a cocktail lounge bar adjoining the veranda, which was open but covered, where dinner was served. This was a beautiful veranda, and the Army-Navy Club was considered one of the best places in Manila to dine—it and the Manila Hotel across the *Lunetta* from the Army-Navy Club. It seems that practically every night this beautiful girl was being ushered to the dining room by mostly Navy officers. It was curious to me, that she was always with somebody different and that it was never the same person twice. She was an absolutely gorgeous creature, and I've hardly seen anything like her in my life except for Bette Quinn *née* Williams.

In any event, I became so obsessed with this girl that I would go down to the bar just to watch her come in and be seated and have dinner, and then I would go up to the card room and play poker.

One afternoon I was on my balcony on the third floor

of the Army-Navy Club, and down below my room, which faced the harbor and looked westward, was the Club swimming pool. There, down by the pool, stretched out on a chaise lounge was this apparition. Her name was Lucy Cherikova. I had, of course, inquired as to that piece of intelligence. Her body was incredible, and at that moment I kinda came unglued and decided, "I've got to meet this woman soon."

Well, I didn't want to go down to the pool, walk up to her, and say, "Hi, I'm Bill Quinn." I didn't think that was the way to do it. So I went down to the cloakroom where there was a Filipino girl attendant. I said to her, "Do you have Miss Cherikova's belongings here?"

She said, "Yes I do. I have her handbag."

"Would you put this note in it?" The note I wrote said, "Dear Lucy. I am Bill Quinn. I'm in Room 305, and I would like very much to have dinner with you some evening."

Well, that was about five o'clock. When I went back up to my room, I looked down at the pool, and Lucy was gone. About an hour later, my telephone rang, and a voice said, "This is Lucy. I'm absolutely thrilled at your note. I think it's one of the nicest things that ever happened to me. I would love to have dinner with you. When would it be convenient for you?"

I said, "Tomorrow night."

"That would be fine. I'm at . . . ." (which I knew, also).

I picked her up. I was absolutely beside myself. Here was this gorgeous thing on my arm as I breezed into the Army-Navy Club. I had called the maitre d' and had an orchid corsage for her, and boutonniere for myself, and orchids on the table. I noted a bunch of bachelors watching us, obviously very envious of me. It was a real first-rate operation.

We had a good dinner, and afterwards we took a drive around the harbor of Manila Bay. Then I took her home.

The next morning I received a call from the office of the G-2 of the Philippine Department, which was run by Lieutenant Colonel McLean. The voice said, "The Colonel would like to speak to you and would appreciate your coming to the headquarters."

So I went to his office. I had served with Colonel McLean up in Maine, so we knew each other. I walked in. He said, "Quinn, I want you to go with the Lieutenant here and read about Miss Cherikova. She's a Japanese agent, and I think you should know this." So I went in this small reading room where the officer pulled out a book, and here's Lucy, full-face photograph, and her story.

Lucy was a White Russian from Shanghai. Her parents were victims of the Bolshevik Revolution, as were an awful lot of Russians who came from Siberia and from all over Russia, seeking, if you will, security from the Bolsheviks. Lucy had been recruited by the Japanese. That's why I saw so many Navy types with her all the time. Her mission was to marry or become engaged to, or otherwise shack up with a Naval officer, and when he went to sea, she was to go to San Francisco and observe the Navy yard and all the Navy ships that left the harbor. She was to associate with officers' wives to find out where their husbands were, on what ships, and what their missions were.

After my reading was over, I went back to see Colonel McLean. He said, "Bill, I guess you understand now why you won't see Lucy any more."

"Sir, I do. I've been puzzled over the fact that she's always with a different person."

He said, "We have a steady stream. Every morning of life, practically, we provide this briefing for some officer. Now you're a member of the club, but there are no dues."

15

Around the World

After living in Manila approximately eighteen months, I was ordered to Fort Benning, Georgia, to attend the Infantry School. When I received those orders, I found that George Bishop and Tommy Thompson, classmates of mine at West Point, were on the same orders. We decided that we should continue from Manila around the world, returning to New York from Europe, having left the U.S through that port. Having so decided, we conferred in the early evenings, planning our itinerary. We searched out travel companies and organizations, but found that by doing our own scheduling, without going through a tourist company, we could save approximately $1,000. We decided to go to Shanghai first, but soon found that we were not allowed to go there because of the war between the Japanese and the Chinese, which was in full bloom at that time.

We settled on Hong Kong, which of course was a British crown colony and an open city. We proceeded to Hong Kong by boat—a freighter, to be exact. We spent several days in Kowloon, and one day decided we would pay our respects to the American consul general. We sought his permission to proceed to Canton, China, which we had heard was also off limits. He indicated that he did not have authority; that because of the state of war between China and Japan, Canton was off limits for Americans, and that he couldn't give us permission. Well of course, Hong Kong is not too far from Canton, so we decided to hire a taxi and go anyway.

We got into China okay, and I guess we were probably about halfway to Canton, when all of a sudden we saw hordes of Chinese coming the other way. We learned that on that morning, just a few hours before, the Japanese had bombed Canton for the first time in the war and that consequently, the refugees were pouring out of Canton and heading for Hong Kong.

We immediately turned around and hotfooted it back to Hong Kong in our cab. As we did, we periodically paralleled a railroad. Box cars and flat cars and every other kind of car on the tracks were completely loaded with people—refugees hanging on for dear life. It was an unbelievable sight to see this mass of humanity covering every inch of the boxcars and fighting to stay aboard. There were wagons and bicycles and motorcycles and rickshaws and everything else with wheels on the main road. We were in the middle of this melee as we returned to Hong Kong.

Nevertheless, we got back into Hong Kong okay, and the next day we picked up the paper at breakfast in our Kowloon hotel to learn that Hong Kong was saturated with 300,000 refugees from China in 24 hours. Later in downtown Hong Kong we found the streets hardly passable because of refugees. Some of them were lying in the gutters, some were actually dead, and in two or three cases, babies were being born on the sidewalks. It was an incredible sight.

As a result, we decided to move on. The situation more-or-less marred our interest in Hong Kong, because we couldn't get anywhere. Traffic was tied in knots. We hopped a ship to Saigon, the *Hong Kong*. This was a very interesting trip because we had little money and were in "steerage class." Incidentally, one can find some interesting people in steerage. At meals, for instance, passengers sit around the standard kind of picnic table with no chairs, just benches, as in one's back yard. We sat at a table for two days and watched a Chinese family. They were obviously grandmother, grandfather, their two sons and daughter, and their *kinder*. What was so unique about them was the affection that they showed for each other, children to children, and children to their parents and grandparents. We watched the children particularly; they would take a morsel or the best of the food, and with their chopsticks, get up from the table and go around to give it to their grandparents, who accepted it and patted them on the back or head and thanked them. It was absolutely the warmest thing I ever saw, and I marveled at the kind of a tradition in which the old were revered to such a high degree. This is something I guess we don't really have in America, in that our older people usually have to fend for themselves.

When we arrived in Saigon, we stayed at a hotel which turned out to be so brand new that things didn't work, the beds were hard and lumpy, and it was hot. There was no air conditioning. It was summertime. So we only stayed in Saigon a night or two.

The three of us, Tommy Thompson, George Bishop and myself, still together, decided to hire a taxi to take us to Phnom Penh and then to Angkor Wat in Cambodia.

We stayed at Phnom Penh, a beautiful city at the time, for a couple of days, and then with our cab driver still with us drove to Angkor Wat, which is beyond description. It was a civilization that had a very mysterious ending, and although I will not attempt to describe it to those who know it, a short background might be appreciated by those who don't. Angkor Wat is considered one of the world's archaeological treasures. It was constructed during the rule of one in a long line of Khmer kings during the 12th century, when Cambodia included large parts of modern day Thailand, Vietnam, and Laos. In the 15th century, the capitol of Cambodia was moved, and the temple was gradually taken over by the jungle, until it was rediscovered by the French in the 1860s.

One of the interesting aspects of Angkor Wat is the fact that its occupants deserted it practically overnight. An entire civilization disappeared. The sudden departure apparently was not caused by pestilence or natural disaster, but by a threat or an insurmountable fear of remaining there.

So much for Angkor Wat.

We proceeded from there by taxi to the Siamese frontier, where we discharged our driver and went through customs to get on a train for Bangkok. This was an interesting and slow wood-burning train which serviced the Malayan Peninsula from the Cambodian frontier to Bangkok and further south. Tommy, George and I started through customs. They were not challenged; nor were hundreds of young students and other travelers. However, I noted that two of the customs guards looked at each other, then at me, and then called me over to the side and had me open my suitcase. The two of them went through my clothes until they came to a point where they stopped, looked at each other, and nodded. They told me to close up my suitcase and move on through, which I started to do. However, my curiosity took over. I didn't know why they'd picked on me and not anyone else in that long line. I couldn't resist asking one of them, "Why did you select me out of all those people, to open my suitcase?" (From the time I left New York, going around the world and returning to New York, that was the only place in the world where I was asked to open my suitcases.) The customs official became rather embarrassed and turned to the other one. The other one nodded, as if saying, "Yeah, go ahead and tell him."

The first then said, "Well, we just wanted to see what kind of neckties the Americans were wearing." That was the end of that, and we boarded the train.

The cars were filled with young people. They were on their way to Bangkok, Kuala Lumpur, or Singapore to go to boarding school or college. The cars were fully loaded with kids, and of course, there were no bunks. We slept on boards—some were placed on the seats, and a second level was placed for upper berths on the backs of the seats. We used our knapsacks or suitcases or anything we could for pillows. There were no sheets or coverings, because we were in the tropics. Well, the kids played all night, and they had a great time, so we didn't get much sleep. Anyway, we were on our way to Bangkok.

Before starting the trip, I had written a Siamese friend, a graduate of West Point named Johnny Khambu, who was in the Class of 1932, a year ahead of me. When we located him in Bangkok, he was working for the Martin Company, trying to sell Martin bombers in the Far East. I said, "Johnny, we heard that you were in jail."

"I was," he said. "When I graduated from West Point, I was assigned to the Royal Engineers, which was an organization you might call the King's Own engineers. We were very loyal to His Majesty.

"Now, before joining my regiment, I spent a month or six weeks touring Europe, and on the day I arrived home to join my regiment, there was a revolution. I had already signed in; the revolution was, of course, successful, and the King was overthrown. All the troops loyal to him were incarcerated or shot, and I was summarily put in jail because I belonged to the Royal Engineers. Well, I didn't know anything about the situation until I was arrested. That is, I knew about the revolution within hours after I signed in, but it was too late.

"So, I was in jail for approximately two years, and then the powers-that-be, in re-examining my case, realized that I was not a co-conspirator or a conspirator, nor had I done anything in any way to stop the revolution, because I wasn't there. Consequently, they released me from prison.

"Well, there I was two years in jail and it was very difficult to get re-oriented into military or civilian life. Then I decided I'd be a Buddhist monk. I went up in the mountains to a Buddhist retreat monastery and stayed there for about a year and a half."

I asked, "Why did you leave the priesthood?"

"To tell the truth, the food was so lousy that I couldn't stick it out. I had to come back to Bangkok to get a square meal."

When he came out of the priesthood, he landed this job selling Martin bombers. He was great to us; showing us around the town and dance halls he knew so well. So much for Johnny Khambu, a great little guy.

We found, like everyone else who goes to Bangkok, a fantastic type of city. It is really bizarre from our standpoint of architecture, and the tinkling of the bells throughout the city is truly something to enjoy.

From Bangkok we proceeded down to Kuala Lumpur and spent a day or so there, and then on to Singapore. In Singapore we found an inexpensive hotel only three blocks from the famous Raffles Hotel. So we would hole up in this hotel and go over to the Raffles in the late afternoon for a Singapore gin sling, which was invented there about one hundred years ago. From there we would retreat to some joint for supper, and thence back to our dive.

The second night in Singapore, we went out shopping. There had been torrential rain, a real tropical downpour. In those days, in some parts of Singapore, the gutters were about eighteen inches to two feet deep and about a foot wide. In crossing a poorly-lit street, I stepped off the curb into one of those gutters, and as I went down, my shin hit the opposite edge of the gutter and raked a big, three or four inch gash right on the shinbone. Bleeding like a stuck hog, I first thought of getting to a doctor.

Inquiring at the hotel, we were given the name of a British physician; I went immediately to his home, and he patched me up and gave me some salve and antiseptics to preclude an infection. Then for three days, I was holed up in my hotel room with my leg stretched out. Even so, I was able to hobble to a rickshaw which took me over to the Raffles Hotel for a couple of gin slings before dinner.

We left Singapore for Ceylon. Unfortunately, it was the height of the monsoon season. Being poor lieutenants, naturally we were in the lowest accommodations of the ship, and we were right next to the engine room. Due to the fact that the ship was rolling from side to side, the portholes were closed. The three of us were in a four-bunk room, and our fourth roommate was an Armenian. His concept of a bath was to use a very heavy perfume. With the rolling of the ship and his perfume, I found it

impossible to stay in the room even to sleep. Consequently, I spent the two days from Singapore to Ceylon in
a step-well leading up to the deck. I just sat there in unbelievable torture, dozing from time to time, but waking
up with cricks in my back and a sore side from sleeping on
the steps. Though I had taken a pillow from the bedroom
for a cushion, it was not nearly enough.

The docking in Ceylon (now Sri Lanka) was like the
relief that follows pain. We spent a lot of time at the
docks watching the packaging and shipments of tea and
all kinds of other things. We were fascinated by the activities of this unusually active port.

From Ceylon we sailed to Bombay, which, like the
other cities in that part of the world, was fascinating. The
most interesting and memorable place we visited in Bombay was the Towers of Silence. Certain religious sects,
among them the Zoroastrians, if I recall, do not bury or
cremate their dead, but place them instead in areas where
vultures can take care of the flesh. At the top of the Towers of Silence, we discovered the rooftop of a round
building completely covered with bones of cadavers. It
was a depressing scene. We saw vultures still soaring and
waiting for new bodies to be placed on the top of the
tower. This was something I had never seen before, and I
still have no plans to return.

We went to Agra from Bombay to see the Taj Mahal
and then to Jaipur, where I bought an emerald for my
bride-to-be, who was still unknown at the time. That was
quite interesting. The jewel merchants put you in a tent
where you sat cross-legged on the floor. They had all
kinds of tea to serve, and they took bags of gems and
spread them out in front of you, and you couldn't help
buying something. So I bought a pretty good-sized emerald.

At Agra we had an interesting experience in social customs. When we arrived, I went to the Hotel Agra to check in. This transient hotel also served as the Officers' Club of the British regiment stationed in the Agra area. Shortly after I arrived, and as I was signing in, a British lieutenant came up to me, clicked his heels, saluted, and said, "Are you Leftenant Quinn?"

"Yes, I am."

Very British, he said, "Compliments of the Colonel, sir. This being Saturday night, we are having a party on the hotel lawn, and the Colonel has directed me to give you and your two friends, Leftenant Thompson and Leftenant Bishop, a cordial welcome to join the circle of officers and their ladies. There will be cocktails, a buffet, and native dancing. I think you'll find the evening most enjoyable. The Colonel observed that you have some kind of celebration on this date (it was the Fourth of July), and he wishes to compliment you on your holiday."

I responded, "My compliments and thanks to the Colonel. We accept with pleasure. What time?"

"Between half-past six and seven. I shall come and fetch you; where might you be?"

"We'll be either on the porch here or the patio."

The porch was an extension of the dining room and bar, a cocktail-lounge effect, overlooking the lawn and swimming pool. The lawn was well-groomed, about half an acre or more.

I asked what the dress was and he suggested jacket and tie, but the officers of course would be in uniform. I thanked him and off he went.

I told Tommy and George what had happened and said, "Well, we can get some shut-eye before we go to the party. Let's meet at the bar some time around five-thirty."

At about five-thirty, the three of us met at the bar and

ordered three beers to be served at a table on the veranda. We could see the preparations being made on the lawn. A large circle of chairs, a bandstand, dance floor, and a bar were being readied. A moment later a very nice-looking man took a table almost next to ours. We began to discuss our trip and our plans to visit the Taj Mahal the next day. As we talked, I glanced up at the gentleman, and as I caught his eye, I said, "Why don't you join us? Come on over."

He had a beer in his hand and said, "I'd be delighted." He introduced himself, explaining that he was a British citizen and a traveling salesman. He had been in Japan and all over the Orient representing a British firm that sold machinery for making cloth. I think his name was McGrath. As we had another beer, he began telling some of his experiences in Hong Kong, Japan, and Peking. Because the war was going on, he hadn't been able to return to China; if he dared, it was at his own risk. He had been all over French Indochina. Of special interest to us, he had been in Manila trying to sell the Filipinos some of his machinery. We established a fine rapport with him. As he was very interesting, we were all enjoying ourselves.

At about 6:45 P.M., up marched the British lieutenant. He snapped his heels and said, "With the Colonel's compliments, gentlemen, will you, Leftenant Quinn, Leftenant Bishop, and Leftenant Thompson, accompany me to join the Colonel and his company?"

I got up, called the lieutenant aside, and said, "Lieutenant, we have just been joined by a gentleman by the name of McGrath." I told him who he was and what he did and that we would like him to accompany us to the party.

The British lieutenant did not hesitate. "Leftenant, I am sorry, but that cannot be done. You see, Mr. McGrath is a 'commercial.' "

I said, "I'm not too sure what that means."

"Well, actually, he's not really in our class."

"I see. Would you ask the Colonel to make an exception in his case? We've gotten to be good friends in a short time, and he might think us rude to desert him at this juncture. I can assure you that he is a gentleman."

"I'll have to speak to the Colonel."

"Okay. Thanks."

When the lieutenant returned, he called me aside and said, "The Colonel regrets very much that he can't accept Mr. McGrath at this party for reasons which I think you will understand." (The implication was that McGrath had a caste mark and was not acceptable in the military class.)

So I said, "Well, please give the Colonel our compliments, and tell him how much we appreciate his thoughtfulness in inviting the three of us to join his company, but we have now committed ourselves in a way, by befriending Mr. McGrath, and now he's one of us. Consequently, we'll have to decline the Colonel's kind invitation."

"Oh," he said, "the Colonel will be very upset."

I replied, "Well, lieutenant, actually, I'm a little upset myself, because in America we don't have the same kind of caste system you have. I mean, it doesn't matter to us whether you're a president or a shopkeeper, you're an American, and there's only one rank in our society."

"I'm sure he's going to be upset at your regrets, but I'll report your sentiments."

In a very short time the lieutenant was back. He called me aside again. He said, "Leftenant Quinn, the Colonel is going to make a very big concession to you by virtue of the fact that it is your holiday; Mr. McGrath will be invited to join the company. However, as we all sit in a circle watching the performance, it will be necessary for him to sit in back of the three of you. He cannot join the circle."

"Well," I said, "let me talk to McGrath about this."

I told McGrath and he was not really embarrassed. He said, "Look, fellows, the hell with it! This is no big deal as far as I'm concerned. I've been treated royally everywhere I've been in the world, but I'm back home now, and I know where I fit."

"Well," I asked, "would you be willing to join us even if you have to sit in back of us in the second row?"

He said, "It's up to you guys."

"Then let's go."

I called the lieutenant and nodded my head and off we went. We met the Colonel, who, with grace, greeted McGrath and welcomed him. But sure enough, our three seats were in the front row of the circle, and McGrath had one chair in back of us. Even so, we all had a fine evening.

After the performance there was dancing, and as everyone got liquored up, McGrath's charms emerged. The first thing I knew, he was the center of attention, particularly among the ladies. It seems the caste marks don't hold up when everybody is half stoned.

The next day after visiting the Taj Mahal, we went to Jaipur, primarily to see the Palace of the Maharajah of Jaipur. It was a fascinating palace, ornate and elegant. One of the unusual features was the pavilion on the palace grounds by the lake. The guide who took us through told us that the pavilion was used primarily for the execution of the enemies of the Maharajah. He pointed out the throne and a seat of honor on the right, which was for invited guests. If the invited guest was to be eliminated, he was seated in this chair. The whole area to the right of the Maharajah was a trap door, and when a lever was pulled, the unfortunate guest was dropped into a lake filled with crocodiles. The guest/victim was wined and dined, honored in the pavilion, and dropped to the crocs and consumed—no fingerprints, just gone.

I walked down some steps leading to the lake. The water level was down, and I could walk under the pavilion and actually see how the system worked. I walked the narrow beach to the water's edge, and there were actually crocodiles floating around. I began to photograph them. A couple of them took out after me and came up out of the water onto the shore. I barely got the hell out of there in time. I never knew crocodiles were that fast! But I did breathe a sigh of relief when I got back to the steps and off of the beach.

After seeing these sights we proceeded to New Delhi by train. As we stopped at small towns on the way, we saw groups of monkeys at the stations. When a train pulled in, the monkeys climbed all over the train, inside and out (the windows were open) to find banana peels, orange peels, peanuts, or anything else they could find on the floors to eat. They were real scavengers, but kept the trains clean of refuse.

We spent only a day in New Delhi. It was a rather new city and not too interesting in 1937, except for the ivory carvers and the guys with the cobras.

From New Delhi, we walked into trouble. We decided to cross the Sind Desert by rail, taking three days and two nights. George Bishop had decided to return directly to the states; and Tommy and I remained to continue our voyage. The rail ran from New Delhi to Karachi, and this was one rough trip. We were in open cars with windows, but no glass. The wind and sand blew continuously. At each oasis, there were little men who would come in and shovel out the sand in the cars. At every oasis where there were wells, we stopped for water for the steam engine.

The sand accumulated on the seats and floors up to three inches deep. We ate only fruit with skins, due to the fact that there were vendors trying to sell food at the oases, with flies all over the biscuits or meat, or whatever they had. The only safe foods were bananas and oranges, and of course, bottles of soda water. We dared not drink any of the local water.

The wind and sand were torturous. We had to put our handkerchiefs over our noses and mouths to breathe through; we had to wet them down with soda water to make sure the dust didn't get into our lungs. When we woke up from naps, our hair and eyebrows and everything else was white. We looked like snowmen, with our bodies and hair covered in fine white sand.

Finally, we arrived at Karachi. We immediately went to a hotel and checked in. We had arrived about seven in the morning. Tommy and I agreed to get cleaned up and to meet in the dining room for breakfast. I went upstairs. I filled the tub three times. I took three full baths. I washed my head three times. By the end of the third bath, I finally felt clean. I put on fresh clothes and went down for breakfast.

We were seated at a table for two, and I said, "Tommy, you hungry?"

"You know, I could eat two breakfasts."

"Why don't you? I'll get two myself."

We ordered four special breakfasts, consisting of the works—hash brown potatoes, biscuits, jam, et cetera. When the waiter took our order, and we asked for four special breakfasts, he said, "Thank you; may I suggest that you move over to this table which will seat four?"

We said, "We don't have to move."

"But aren't there four people coming?"

"No."

"*Each* of you wants two breakfasts?"

"Yep. and we'll sit right here."

I could see him shaking his head as he went back to the kitchen to place the order. But he brought the four breakfasts, and we consumed every bite, along with a couple pots of coffee.

After a day or two in Karachi, where we saw the sights and spent a lot of time at the Yacht Club, we flew to Basra in Iraq.

We had nowhere in our entire trip seen anything like the heat in Basra. No matter where you walked it was so hot that the heat waves were bouncing up and everything looked like it was crazy. We were in a hotel near the airport. Of course, the planes were coming in periodically, and that didn't help. There were no fans and no air conditioning in the hotel. Only an open window with the flies coming in and out. I lay there in deep perspiration all night long. That was a real toughie.

Arriving in Baghdad we researched the things to see in Iraq. I'd heard that the Um-Altouboul, the third most important mosque in the Moslem world, was located near the outskirts of Baghdad.

The next morning I asked the hotel manager "How do I get out there?"

"You can't go out there because no infidels are permitted in that area."

"Well I just came here to see things." Then I went out and asked a cab driver if he could take me to this mosque, and he said, "No. I can't."

"Why?"

"I'll be arrested or beaten up or hurt or maybe killed."

"You can't mean that, you've gotta be kidding. How far can you take me?"

"Well," he said, "I'll drive you to this shopping area, the marketplace, and that is about a half or quarter of a mile away from the mosque, but that's as far as I'm going to take you."

"Okay, let's go." So we got in the cab and I made it to the marketplace.

"It's right up there on the right," he said.

I started walking. Nobody bothered me at all, I had my camera slung over my shoulder, and I went up to the gates of this thing, and here was a monstrous gate with tremendous heavy camel chains hanging down to preclude the camels from either coming or going out because the chains hit them in the throat. I looked across the street and there was an empty, adobe-like house about three stories tall. I thought, "Now, if I can get up on top of that empty house, I might get a real good photo." So I went to the house, climbed up the steps to the second floor, and found a ladder leading up to the roof. I climbed up this ladder, and I was looking right in the courtyard and had a great view of the mosque itself. I started to take a snapshot and the first thing I knew I was flat on my back, my camera scattered over on the rooftop, and there were two guys holding me down, and one of them had a knife right at my adam's apple. My lord! I said, "Wait— wait a minute, what's going on? What happened?" Well, they didn't understand English, but they understood that I was not supposed to be there and now I did, too!

They pulled me up, and forced me down the ladder and out on the street, and they each grabbed me by an arm and marched me about two blocks into a house, or rather kind of a shack that looked like it was an office. There was a desk and a telephone, some Arabic things on the wall and a couple of photographs. I didn't believe it was the police, because no one was in uniform. And as I look back on it, I suspect they were security people for the mosque itself.

The head man there could speak a little English and he said, "You know, you could have been killed, and they had a right to kill you. So you're going to have to go to jail."

"I want to call the American Ambassador," I replied.

"That won't do you any good."

"I demand as an American citizen to call the American Ambassador or his representative. And I believe that your country, Iraq, requires you to do this."

I continued, "Listen, I'm a dumb American tourist. I don't know anything about this country, and I've probably made a mistake, but if you came to the United States and couldn't read the signs and you walked into something, wouldn't you expect the Americans to understand that you didn't have any designs or desire to hurt Mohammedanism or the Mosque? I was not going to attack it. I'd like to call the Ambassador."

This guy began to speak to two or three other people, and they were talking up a storm. Finally, he said, "You're very lucky. We're going to take your film. You can have your camera. But we want you to know that you should have learned a lesson today. Don't do this any more, either here or anywhere else that would antagonize a Mohammedan or criticize him or his environment."

"You've gotta believe it; I won't do this any more." And I sure as hell didn't.

Well, from Baghdad we got back on the Orient Express and went into Aleppo and from Aleppo to Sophia in Bulgaria and then on to Budapest.

Budapest at that time was equal to Paris from the standpoint of gaiety and fun. I remember one night I went to a cabaret on Saint Margaret's Island in the middle of the Danube. I had quite a number of drinks and a band there was playing American music and American songs. They had a singer who wasn't very good. He stumbled on a couple of words, as he hadn't memorized the song. So I went up to the band leader after the music had stopped and said, "Listen, I am an American and that song you just played, if you ever play it again, give me a call and I'll come up and sing it for you." Well, I didn't know how to sing because I had no voice, but by golly, they repeated it, and the guy waved to me, and I went up there and sang this damn song and got quite a hand.

So be it. That was quite an evening.

What I loved about Budapest more than anything else were their colorful restaurants. I remember one in particular that was arbor covered. There was bougainvillea, it was open around the sides, and the top was open except for vines, bougainvillea, grapes, and you name it—very, very colorful. The food and the service were elegant, and the paprika dishes and the goulash and a thousand and one other things, particularly paprika, I remember vividly. I was very impressed with that place.

16

VIENNA

After we left Budapest, we went to Vienna and stayed at a hotel in front of which was a square and monument. It was a small hotel, but very nice, and it had a patio which extended out toward the square with tables for cocktails and luncheons. On the right side of the patio were several large bushes and evergreens.

In any event, after dinner Tommy and I decided that we would go to the famous and beautiful St. Stephens Cathedral and say a prayer or two. The cathedral was only about seven or eight blocks from our hotel. We entered, and after saying our prayers, we spent some time looking it over. There was no service going on, but the doors, of course, were open. After leaving the cathedral, we decided to return to our hotel, sit on the veranda or patio and have a beer before we turned in. On the way back I sensed that we were being followed.

I must mention that this was in the spring, and it was just a month or so after the Anschluss, the German takeover of Austria. Consequently, the Germans were everywhere to be seen. And of course, one of the sad things we observed was the Germans had immediately begun to work over the Austrians who had resisted the takeover, as well as the Austrian Jews. We saw Jewish stores which had been broken into, swastikas plastered all over the city, and businesses owned by Jews or carrying Jewish names, in shambles.

Coming back from the cathedral, however, we passed some store windows that were not touched. I stopped and looked in one store window and immediately turned around. In the direction of the Cathedral, there were two characters who were obviously following us, because as soon as I turned around, they stopped and began to look in a window, also. I did this another time, and sure enough, these guys were obviously a couple of Gestapo types, and they were tailing us.

I found it humorous. Here we were, a couple of everyday lieutenants, no threat to anybody, being followed by a couple of German Gestapo. When we arrived back at the hotel, we took a table on the patio and ordered a beer. I knew that these characters were somewhere near us, and I suspected that they were in the bushes off to our right rear. After the beers were served, I took a draft and said, "Tommy, let's have some fun or get into trouble."

I got up and left my table, went down the steps, went around to the right and into the bushes, and there they were. I said to them in German, "Come with us. *Kommen Sie mit mir für ein Bier.*" They were visibly shaken and embarrassed. They just stared at me, l left the bushes, and they began to walk down the street. And that's the last we were tailed in Vienna; though we stayed another day.

From Vienna we went into Paris. We stayed two or three days and did the sights, the Louvre, Napoleon's Tomb and what have you. While in Paris, Tommy Thompson decided he didn't want to go to London and Ireland, so he left me there.

I went on to London alone and did the Tower and everything else according to Baedecker. We had done a lot of planning in Manila before we began our trip. Baedecker's tour book was the popular one at the time. It listed the sights to see in our itinerary, and we saw practically everything we thought worthwhile or had time for—mosques, churches, cathedrals, statues, ruins, parks, plazas, and you-name-it. We had seen an awful lot, so much so that what happened in London was no surprise.

I decided to take the Ely Cathedral Tour; so I got on a tour bus which arrived at the Cathedral about eleven o'clock in the morning. We got off the bus, the tourmaster with us, and went into the edifice. We formed a little circle, and he said, "We are now in the Ely Cathedral. The Ely Cathedral was built in 1382," or some such number, I don't recall. All of a sudden, I realized that I had arrived at my capacity to absorb anything more and as a matter of fact, I became nauseated. It didn't matter what it was, if it was statistical, or if I had to absorb a date or some philosophy, etc., there was no way I could handle it. So I left the cathedral and got back on the bus, and sat there until we returned to London.

Well, I did go to Ireland, but not to see any statues. I went to Ireland because I wanted to see where my forebears had come from, and as I'd never been there, I wanted to see the beautiful land of my ancestors. I was not disappointed.

17

IRELAND

When I left England to go to Ireland, I went through Wales and took a ferry boat from Wales to Dublin. Arriving in Dublin about ten o'clock that night, I got a cab and told the cabbie to take me to a hotel, which he did. But he said, "I'm gonna wait for you, because we're gonna do some touring."

"Why?"

"Well, the horse show is on."

"What horse show?"

"The Irish Horse Show. This is the week of the show, and there's probably not a hotel room to be found."

So I went in to the clerk of this hotel. He asked, "What can I do for you?"

"I'd like to get a room."

He laughed. "You can't. There's not an empty bed in this hotel or any other hotel in this town tonight."

"Why?"

"It's the horse show."

When I came back out, the cab driver was still there. I said, "What am I going to do, sleep in the back seat of your car?"

"No, we'll find a pension, a bed-and-breakfast, but it

may take us some time."

So we started touring the city—up and down the streets, block after block. There were signs everywhere, but every sign read, "No vacancy." Finally we saw a sign that said "Vacancy." I inquired, and the lady had an attic room unoccupied. so I took it. This was about 11:30 P.M. We'd been going around town for an hour to find this damn room. I paid the cab driver off and went up to my room to bed.

The next morning I slept until about nine or nine-thirty; I guess I was tired. I drifted downstairs for breakfast. This was a standard row house, with the front or living room used as a dining room, and one could look out on the street. The dining table was nicely prepared, and there were two couples sitting there. I sat down opposite these people, as they were all sitting side by side. Finally, an elderly gentleman said, "May I introduce myself?"

"Yes sir."

"I'm Sergeant McGuire of the Irish Guards, retired, and this is my wife Dorothy, and this is Mr. and Mrs. Malone. I take it you're a Yank."

"Yes, I'm a Yank. I'm Lieutenant Quinn of the United States Army, and I'm on my way back home."

"What brings you to Ireland?"

"A matter of curiosity and interest, I guess. my family has been in America for a good number of years, and I have no roots here any more; I just wanted to see the land of my forebears."

"That's good of you."

I began to work on my bacon and eggs, and at one point looked up to see the sergeant winking at me, so Mrs. M. couldn't see it. I didn't know what the hell to do about this, so I didn't wink back. I just watched him. Then he winked again and continued talking, "Not having been here in Ireland before, I guess you've never been told about the great Guinnesses and the stouts and the ales and beers that we have in Ireland."

I still didn't understand the winking, but replied, "Well, I've heard of them because I was in the Philippines, and we used to drink Guinness beer and also Schwepp's ginger beer, but I've never had a taste of your stout or ale."

"Oh, this is terrible. You know, I think I'll take you down to Mooney's to give you what you might call a little bit of education." Now I got the message.

Mrs. McGuire spoke up, "Oh, no you don't McGuire. I know you're up to your old tricks. You're not going anywhere. You're going back to Belfast as soon as we can pack up."

"Oh, Dorothy, it's a shame, the young man came all the way from the States and might never know of the customs of the Irish and their favorite drinks."

I interjected, "Will you please, Mrs. McGuire?"

She said, "Well, it's against my better judgment but okay, if you both promise me you'll be back by noon."

I promised her and off we went to Mooney's. As we went down the street, McGuire said, "You know, Lieutenant, you're a good actor."

At Mooney's Pub we took seats in a booth overlooking the bar. McGuire asked the bartender to bring two bottles of ale. After discussing the quality of the ale, the subject turned to India, where he had spent most of his service. Then it was time for some Guinness stout. I didn't like it, but I kept him company, and he talked more on the British in India. McGuire then ordered a bottle of John Jamieson's Irish Whiskey. It was eleven forty-five, and we were feeling no pain, when I said, "Listen, Sergeant, we'd better leave. I promised Mrs. McGuire we'd be back at noon."

He replied, "Never you mind. I'll take care of her."

When it was about quarter to one, we were both completely drunk and agreed that it was the hour to head home. We walked back as it wasn't too far, but the house we were staying in was on a slight slope, and we had to walk up this incline. It was not a big grade, but it seemed as if we were climbing the Himalayas. We were arm-in-arm, holding each other up, and it was a very tough climb for us. When we finally got up to where we could see the house, there was Dorothy, standing on the steps, elbows stuck out akimbo. As we approached, McGuire said, "Now, Lieutenant, this is the time for you to do your greatest performance. You must understand that you don't have to live with this woman, but I do. So consequently, I want you to take the blame for this operation on your broad shoulders."

"You know, Sergeant, I tried to get you out of there at twelve o'clock."

"I know all of that, but you can do a great favor for me if you'll accept the blame."

So when we got up to the pension I said, "Mrs. McGuire, it's my fault that we're late."

"I don't believe it. I don't believe it, Lieutenant, not for a minute!"

"Oh yes, it's my fault, please believe me."

In any event, McGuire was off the hook. As we parted, he whispered, "You're a great actor, Quinn; you'll go far."

At one point during my breakfast with the McGuires, he had asked me if I had ever been to a Irish horse show, and the answer, of course, was that I never had. "Well," he said, "we're going to Belfast this afternoon, and we have a box that seats four people. You're welcome to the tickets because we won't use them. We've been here three days."

"Well, Sergeant, I appreciate that. I'd like to pay you for them."

"No, no; they'd go in the wastebasket. We're happy you can use them, and take any of your friends that you might have in Dublin."

"I don't have any friends in Dublin, but in any event, I would like to go."

So that afternoon after I'd sobered up a little bit, I went to the Horse Show. That was a great experience—one incident impressed upon me the great affection and love the Irish have for horses.

I'd heard about it, and now I was about to witness it. That afternoon in the military jumping class of the show there was a beautiful horse of the Canadian team. In making its rounds, it made a jump, and its forelocks hit the top bar. The bar didn't fall; for some reason it held; so the horse went over the hurdle and landed on its head, throwing the jockey clear. After the horse landed, it didn't move. Within seconds an ambulance came rushing on the field with a veterinarian and crew. The one I assumed to be a vet placed his hand on the horse's heart and throat; for a second he crouched there by the horse. Finally, he looked up to the booth where the judges were, and I saw him shake his head as he pointed to the horse's neck. The stadium of over twenty thousand people were as quiet as an empty church. The announcer spoke over the loudspeaker with a quivering voice: "This horse has a broken neck and is dead."

Now, I don't know whether you've ever heard twenty thousand people moan, but it's the most solemn, unbelievable sound I have ever heard. When twenty thousand people said, "Oooohhh!" chills ran up my back. Even today, after many decades, whenever I hear that sound in my mind, I understand the love of the Irish for their horses.

From Dublin I went back to Longford in County Longford where, my Uncle Lorie Quinn told me, the Quinns had originated. I went to the graveyards, and there were Quinns all over the place. Since I couldn't identify any of them, the exercise was meaningless. They had been buried a hundred years before more or less. So I decided to see if I could find a live one. I went to the hotel cashier or registrar at my hotel in Longford and asked, "Are there any Quinns in this town that you know of?"

"I don't know. I'm new here. I'm from Dublin. Sorry I can't help you. But why don't you go down to the square in the middle of the town and ask a peeler. He might know."

I went downtown to the square and found a policeman, and trying to show my Irish way of talking, I said, "I beg your pardon. Are there any Quinns about?"

"Now that you asked, I don't know. I can only tell you what happened two months ago. There was in town a Paddy Quinn who started a pub three blocks from here and to the left on a side street. He never opened it, but as I understand it, he came into a little inheritance and decided to open a pub. Well, he rented this place, had shelves and a bar put in it, and stocked it with all kinds of whiskey, ales, stouts, and so forth. While all this was going on, I dropped in one day. I wanted to know what was going on, because it could be a source of trouble. Paddy said to me, 'Peeler, wouldn't it be terrible on my opening day or any day thereafter that someone would come in here and get a drink and be poisoned?'

" 'Well,' I said to Paddy, 'you know, you're right. But are you talking about food or about whiskey?

" 'Oh,' he said, 'not the food. No, no, the food will be fine, but I don't know who the bottlers are. So I think I'll be the devil's advocate, the court jester, as it were, and test some of these beverages before they go into the stomachs of my customers.'

"Well," the cop said to me, "now, that was two months ago, and this I know: Paddy Quinn never opened his pub. He drank everything in it to make sure that no one got poisoned. He drank his inheritance, and if you're looking for a Quinn in this town, it would be Paddy. And if you find him, he'll be in the gutter."

So much for my heritage.

After that, I returned to England and went to South-hampton to take passage on a ship for New York. I was in a stateroom for four, again practically in the steerage, and my three roommates were all Irishmen on their way to New York to seek their fortunes. They were fascinated with the trip I had just made.

We arrived in New York, and one of the Irishmen said, "You stay with us because you won't have to go through customs."

I said, "What do you mean?"

"You don't have to go through customs. We know the head of the customs service in New York, he's arranged to have us met and take us right off the boat and right on through. And your name being Quinn, you can be one of us."

Sure enough, when we arrived, I stayed with them. I took my suitcases; they took theirs. We got down the gangplank, and by God there was this man there.

He said, "O'Grady?"

"Yes, that's me."

"Then follow me."

Well, hell, the first thing I knew we were out on the

street. So in about three minutes I was in a cab headed for the train to take me home to Crisfield.

They had real connections, those Irish did, in those days. Some still do.

I finally got home and made preparations to go on to Fort Benning, Georgia, for a course at the Infantry School.

Lesson Learned: Maybe the Army recruiting posters should paraphrase the Navy's pitch of "Join the Navy and see the world" to "Join the Army and go around it."

PART IV

FORT SCREVEN, GEORGIA

18

Meeting Bette Williams

In 1939 I graduated from the Infantry School at Fort Benning, Georgia, and was assigned to the First Battalion of the 8th Infantry Regiment at Fort Screven, Georgia. With war clouds brewing that summer, a large number of newly trained commissioned second lieutenants from the Reserve Officer Training Corps (ROTC) were called to active duty. They were mostly from Southern colleges and universities and were called Thomason Act Officers, from an act of Congress directing them to report to various posts of the Army. The young officers who reported to Fort Screven were assigned to one of five companies. I had two in my company, Company D.

The Post and Battalion Commander, Lt. Col. Robert O. "Tubby" Barton, later became the Commanding General of the 8th Division, one of the divisions that went into Normandy at Omaha Beach. The Colonel was socially inclined; he felt that with all these young officers—including myself, a bachelor at the time—it would be appropriate for him to arrange for his young officers to meet some young ladies in the environs of Savannah or Savannah Beach.

As in most large towns, there is one person who is in charge of debutante parties. Col. Barton located one such lady, told her the circumstances, and asked her to arrange for a group of selected young ladies to be his guests at a tea dance on the 4th of July in the Officers' Club at Fort Screven. Col. Barton also offered transportation. The lady thought this was a pretty good idea and issued invitations to about twenty young, eligible ladies in Savannah.

On the Fourth of July, these girls came unescorted. The protocol was that under the circumstances there was no requirement for escorts, since the escorts were the young officers waiting for them at the Club. Formal introductions, in this case, were unnecessary. I stood in the background watching these young ladies arrive. I also watched the hungry bachelors size them up, and as a matter of fact, I did a little sizing-up myself. I missed Bette Williams, however.

Shortly after the ladies arrived and the pairing had taken shape, I went to the bar to get a drink. Seated at the bar on a stool with her back to me was this girl. I couldn't see her face, but I saw her legs hanging down from the bar stool, and they were beautiful. I guess I was a leg man at the time. In any event, I decided that I had to find out who she was. I went around to her side and spoke to her, assuming that she was one of the group. I said, "Could I have this dance?"

She answered, "I'm sorry, but we haven't been formally introduced."

It seems that she was not one of the invitees but had come with a date whose roommate at Auburn University was one of the Thomason Act Officers. "Oh," I said, not knowing this, "there's no requirement that we be formally introduced. The very fact that you've been invited here as a guest of the Commanding Officer satisfies the requirement of a formal introduction."

"Well," she said, "I don't know about that. I've never been on an Army post before, and I don't know how the Army works. But in Savannah, you just don't dance with anybody who comes up and asks you unless you've had a formal introduction."

"Well, if that's the way it works in Savannah, so be it," and walked off.

However, the more I thought about this gal the more I admired her stand. I thought, well, maybe we can have some fun here. I went up to Col. Barton, who had a great sense of humor and, still believing her to be one of the group, I told Col. Barton what had happened.

"I'd like to have some fun meeting this girl. I don't know her name yet, but when I meet her, I'm going to bring her up to you, and I'm going to say, 'Colonel, this is the one.' "

The colonel said, "Fine. Let's do it."

So I found somebody who had met Bette Williams officially, one of the other officers, and said, "I'd like to break in on her, and you can introduce me during an encore of one of the dances."

So he did, and we were formally introduced on the dance floor. I danced with Bette Williams but didn't utter a word. I didn't open my mouth, nor did she. When the music ended, I said, "The colonel would like to see you."

"What for?"

"Well, I think you'll find out when you see him." She seemed apprehensive as to what this was all about, but I led her up to the colonel and said, "Colonel Barton, this is the one."

He said, "Lady, you know we have a guard house here

on the post for prisoners, but I see no reason why you should have to go there for a breach of protocol. What do you think, Lieutenant?"

All of a sudden, I saw that Bette Williams was a little shaken, and I winked at the colonel. He just laughed and reached out, put his arm around her and hugged her, and said, "We're just having some fun. And you have just met one of my finest officers. I hope you'll have fun together."

Well, Bette Williams didn't think that was very funny, but I did. We have talked about it many times since then.

On that day, however, she had a date, Ben K. Armstrong, waiting for her outside. Ben later became one of my best friends, but then, off she went with him.

Ours was a very brief courtship, because shortly after the Fourth of July, I was ordered to Camp Perry, Ohio, as a transportation officer in connection with the National Rifle Matches which took place annually. I was gone most of the summer. When I got back around Labor Day, Bette and I started dating and had seven dates between Labor Day and Armistice Day, when I proposed. We were married a month later on December 16th in the Independence Presbyterian Church on Bull Street in Savannah.

That is how I met Bette Williams, who has, I'm sure, been sorry ever since.

19
GENERAL VAN HORN

After Bette and I announced our engagement, we attended various social functions at Fort Screven together, and one day the Post had a visitor, an officer who came to make a routine call to the Commander's Office. His name was General Van Horn. That night there was a dinner party in his honor at the Officers' Club, and I took Bette. She was introduced to General Van Horn as a forthcoming bride. He said, "I'd like to talk to this couple; maybe I can give them some advice about Army life." So Colonel Barton placed Bette and me at his table, and the general was very fatherly and gave us some advice about Army life and what to and what not to do.

When we were about to depart his table, he said to Colonel Barton, the post commander, "Tubby, when this young couple returns from their honeymoon and comes through the gate, I want you to give them one of my guns."[1]

---

[1] In those days a brigadier general was entitled to a salute of eleven rounds of ammunition blanks to be fired from cannon whenever he entered an army post. A major general got twelve guns, a lieutenant general thirteen, and a full general fourteen. The President gets twenty-one guns, as Commander-In-Chief.

Colonel Barton said, "Yes, sir, when they come back, I'll give them one of your guns."

And the General said, "Good, the next time I come to Screven, give me only ten, understand, Colonel?"

"Yes, sir, I do." We thought it was very nice of the General, a white-haired old man. I thought he must have been as old as Methusalah at that time—probably 58 or 59.

We went on our honeymoon, and we had prearranged to meet the adjutant of the post at a special time regarding our return and arrival at the gate. It was traditional in those days that an honor guard meet an incoming bride and groom at the gate and escort them to their quarters or elsewhere on the post. In my case, I had command of Company D, 8th Infantry, a machine gun company. In 1939, machine gun companies were mounted, i.e., they had mules pulling the caissons that contained machine guns; some caissons contained thousands of rounds of ammunition, and others carried spare parts, first aid, etc. All the caissons were drawn by mules, and the officers were mounted on horses.

When we arrived at the gate at the precise time, here was my entire company lined up with all the mules and horses at the gate. After Bette and I had parked our car, we were escorted to one of the caissons and seated on one with a driver. What got to me was the fact that here to greet us was my whole company with all these mules and horses and a hundred men.

As our caisson passed through the gate, the retreat cannon roared just one time, and we went on then to the Officers' Club where we were greeted by Colonel and Mrs. Barton. They had organized a small reception to welcome Bette to the post and into the folds of the Army and to welcome me back from my leave.

What's so interesting about this is that, sure enough, around the turn of the year, General Van Horn came back to visit Fort Screven on an inspection trip, and when he came through the gate, he got only ten guns instead of eleven because I had already had one of his.

At that time we were still in what you might call the old Army. We lived a very formal kind of life. At night, after six o'clock, if we left our quarters, except to go into Savannah, we had to be in black tie. This was true even if we were going to the post movies. After Bette and I were married we moved to the post and proceeded to call on all the other officers in the post or to leave our cards if they were not at home. In return, each of the officers and their wives returned the call to our quarters, always all in black tie. This tradition and custom has gone by the board, but there was something very warm about it. It was also good in the sense that when the major came to a lieutenant's house, there was a certain relaxation from the day's issues or pressures, a kind of armistice if conflict had prevailed. There was the sense of social equality, even though the rank was different.

This tradition permitted you to really get to know your superior or junior officers, because you would always be having a drink or two, and your callers would stay maybe fifteen or twenty minutes, or a half an hour, and then leave. You were never bored, because the protocol dictated the standard call to be fifteen minutes. If for instance, we'd call on the Colonel, and the Colonel would say, "Quinn, we don't necessarily have to abide by protocol tonight. Why don't you and Bette stay for another drink," we were allowed to stay. Or maybe, "Would you and Bette stay here and have dinner with us?" That's the way it worked. In practice, where people had things to do and other calls to make, they would just stay fifteen minutes and leave their cards on a tray in the hall or under the door if you were out, and then take off.

As I say, there was something meaningful about those traditions, because the troops looked up to the officers with more esteem than they do now. The standards of conduct among officers were higher. There was not as much fraternization with the enlisted as there is today. The decorum and formality of the officer corps and their ladies had a great impact on the enlisted ranks.

I remember one night I was ordered to referee a boxing match. Believe it or not, the Colonel instructed me to wear my tuxedo. That was the way it was. And it was, after all, a rewarding way to live.

20

THE INSPECTOR GENERAL

Each year in the thirties and early forties, all Army posts received an annual visitation from an Army or Corps headquarters, i.e., an annual inspection. The officers who conducted the inspections were from the several offices of the Inspector General of the various headquarters. This year at Fort Screven, we received our visitation in the Spring of 1940. Bette and I had moved on the post and were assigned to a set of quarters. This particular year the Inspector General was a full colonel, Colonel Robinson from army headquarters in Atlanta.

Through a series of meetings with our post commander, Lt. Col. R.O. "Tubby" Barton, we were instructed to sharpen up the post, to make it look good, and to go over all of our equipment, our barracks, our supply rooms, etc. Assignments were made to monitor the parade ground, the post exchange and the post headquarters. Every officer had a specific task to perform in getting ready for the annual inspection. The day arrived.

The night before, Col. Robinson had arrived at Fort

Screven. Col. Barton, a very social-minded officer, decided to have a dinner dance in honor of the I.G., which was not only protocol, but good public relations. The dinner dance was held at the Officers' Club, and Bette and I attended.

Through some set of circumstances, Col. Robinson danced with Bette. Now, Bette was a new bride and had no concept of what the Army was all about. We had only recently moved into our new quarters, and she was like a raw recruit. While dancing, Col. Robinson asked her how long she had been married, and he found out that she was indeed very, very new to the Army. He asked her, "Now that you've been here for a few weeks, what do you think of the Army?"

"Well," she replied, "Colonel, I am more impressed with you than I am with the Army."

"I don't quite understand what you mean."

"Colonel, you have no idea what these people have been doing to get ready for you. They have whitewashed everything on the whole post. I have never seen it this clean before. Everybody, including my husband in Company D, has worked night and day. He has polished or helped polish everything in sight, and as a matter of fact, only this morning, I told him that I wanted to meet this Colonel Robinson, because whoever he is, he can really turn the troops on."

"Is that so?" Col. Robinson said, "That's very interesting."

"It's something to behold. And, incidentally, my husband has Company D, and I understand that you will go to his company, so I want you to give him good marks."

"Well, I will go to Company D, I'm sure, and I can only assume that your husband is doing a very fine job as its commanding officer. But you know, you're asking me to do something, to do you a favor; so what kind of a favor could you do me in return?"

"You could come to our quarters tomorrow morning for breakfast; I just received some Statesboro sausage. We received five waffle irons for wedding presents, so I'll make you some waffles and fix you some eggs with this Statesboro sausage. It's the best in the world."

"Good. Would seven thirty be okay?"

"Yes, seven thirty would be fine. I'll expect you then."

After we went home from the dance, I went upstairs to get ready for bed, knowing nothing of this conversation, but realizing that tomorrow was the day of reckoning. Bette was downstairs fooling around, and I called, "Bette, why don't you come on up and get to bed? We've got to get some sleep. We've got a big day tomorrow."

"I have to get ready for breakfast."

"What's the big deal about breakfast?" I asked.

"Oh, Col. Robinson is coming."

I nearly dropped my front teeth. "You're out of your mind—the I.G. coming to a lieutenant's quarters?"

"Yes, and he's going to give you good marks."

"What the hell are you talking about?"

She said, "Yes, he promised, if I would give him some Statesboro sausage."

I flipped. "You asked him to give me good marks? Good Lord!"

I could hardly sleep. I woke at five o'clock in the morning and began to go over the house to see if everything was just right. Bette was up cheerfully getting the sausage ready, and sure enough, here came Col. Robinson for breakfast.

I had problems swallowing. I was scared to death. I'd seen only a few full colonels in my entire life, and here was one at my table—not only a full colonel, but the Inspector General! Man Alive!

Colonel Robinson went through the post very me-
thodically. He came to my Company D. He went over it
with a fine-toothed comb. Would you believe it? He did
give me good marks. He commended me. As he left my
company area, he said, "Goodbye, Lieutenant Quinn.
That *was* great sausage."

21

TOUGH GRAVY

Early in our marriage, while Bette and I were living at Fort Screven, Bette knew how to cook Swiss steak with onions, and hamburgers. Period.

She was trying hard, however, to improve her culinary arts, and she was hardly ever seen without a copy of *A Thousand Ways to Please a Husband*. None of them related to sex, however, just to the kitchen.

Once settled, our evening meal rotated between Swiss steak and hamburgers.

As Bette once said, "We were so poor at one time, we only had money for one hamburger. Bill got the hamburger and I got the gravy."

Well, this one evening I came home for dinner. Swiss steak smothered in onions, mashed potatoes, and green beans were on the menu. I should mention here that Bette was an expert in opening cans, since we had received an electric can opener as a wedding present—hence the vegetables. So this evening I started to cut the steak, but the gravy was rubbery and stringy. I had to cut the gravy along with the meat. I said, "Bette, what the hell did you do to this steak?"

She said she didn't know what had happened, that she

had used the same recipe for years.

I said, "The problem is these onions. Where did you get them?"

"They're spring onions. I always use them. Sometimes I use dried onions, sometimes regular onions, but I've been using spring onions too, and that's what I used tonight."

"Well, where did you buy them?

"Oh," she said, "I didn't buy them at all, I just got them out of the back yard."

"We don't have any onions planted back there."

"Yes we do," she said.

"Well, show them to me."

So we went out back and looked at what she had pulled up for onions, and they weren't onions at all, they were daffodils. What a lousy gravy they make.

22

CAMP BEAUREGARD MESS AND COLONEL SAUNDERS

In the summer of 1940, large Louisiana maneuvers were held. Col. Barton and the First Battalion of the 8th Infantry at Fort Screvin, Georgia, were given the task of housekeeping or otherwise adminstering the headquarters and umpire system of the maneuvers. The maneuver headquarters was located at Camp Beauregard, near Alexandria, Louisiana. Each company had a specific task. Company D, of which I had command, was given the job of running the messes. I had Sgt. Crest, one of the finest mess sergeants in the United States Army. I was to run the official mess, in fact two messes: one for the general officers, which was a special mess for the maneuver director and certain of his key officers, and an officers' mess for the umpires, maneuver staff personnel, visiting officers, etc. We took over a former mess hall at Camp Beauregard. It was a World War I standard-built mess hall. We remodeled it as best we could without any funds. It was still somewhat primitive. It certainly was not the Ritz Carleton.

Col. Barton called me in before we went to Louisiana and said, "Quinn, you've probably got the most delicate, the most difficult, and the most responsible job, and that is to feed a bunch of prima donnas. I am going to let you do what you want, because I believe you have sufficient imagination to organize and run the best mess in the history of the United States Army. Now, you will be able to select anybody in the 8th Infantry Regiment to help you conduct this operation. You have your pick of any of the cooks or mess personnel. Maneuver headquarters will determine mess hours, but it's up to you to select the menus, purchase the food, and so forth. Go to it."

Well, I went back to my company orderly room and called for Sgt. Crest. He was Greek, and I have never in all my life met a more loyal person or a more dedicated soldier. As a matter of fact, I think Bette loved him as dearly as she loved me. I said, "Sgt. Crest, sit down and relax, because you and I are going to go through an experience for the next several months which is going to be demanding, but important to the regiment. It's going to put us very close together, as we're going to be mutually responsible for a job."

Then I told him of my orders and conversation with the Colonel. I continued, "Now let's brainstorm."

Sgt. Crest said, "Right off, Lieutenant, I can tell you we need only six cooks, no matter how many we have to feed in one mess hall. I don't want any more than that. I just want enough cooks to go on shifts, like three cooks and a pastry cook on one shift and three on the other. The reason I want two shifts is that I want one shift to be called A and the other B. And I'm going to tell them that there will be a prize for the team that has the best reputation, the best food, and so forth." He added, "I'd like to get Sgt. Alexander (who apparently also was Greek) from Fort Moultrie."

"Now," I said, "we know how to prepare the food. What kind of food are we going to get?"

"Do we have to stay in the Army Commissary system?"

"No, we can buy food anywhere in the world."

"That's fine. I've always wanted to have my hand in lobsters, in Texas capons, in frog legs if we're down in Louisiana, as well as top Omaha steaks and fine foods of that nature."

"The world is ours. Now, are our cooks really chefs?"

"No, they're not."

"Okay then," I answered, "here's my idea. Let's take this whole group with you in charge and go to one of the leading hotels in Savannah or Atlanta and have our cooks instructed not in basic cooking, but in sauces, use of herbs, gravies, salad dressings, garnishes, pastries, or anything that has to do with professionalism and a gourmet approach to food."

"I happen to know the chef at the Savannah Hotel, who is French, and he is probably (in my mind) one of the best chefs south of Baltimore."

I said, "Okay, I'll go to the manager or owner of the Savannah Hotel and I'll tell him what our problem is and ask him if we can bring our people in on shifts so the kitchen won't be completely crowded."

The idea would be that our cooks would, after a few days of observation, actually assist the chef on the preparation of orders. Our pastry cooks could monitor the pastry chef there as well. I made the call, and the manager was very flattered that the Army would come and seek his assistance in the preparation of food. So he said, "The hotel kitchen is yours."

I took Sgt. Crest into the Savannah Hotel kitchen, and he said, "I'm sorry, Lieutenant, I will not bring my cooks into this kitchen. It is absolutely the most filthy place I have ever seen in my life. Soot is all over. Cobwebs are hanging between the ceiling and the stove chimneys. We would have to clean this place up before I would let any of my cooks work here."

So I went to the maitre d' and told him the problem, "You're close to the chef—I don't want to insult him by having my people come in here and clean up his kitchen, but they won't come under the present circumstances. Can you talk to him?"

"That's no problem. I can just tell the chef that we need to get ready for an inspection of the Health Department, and these Army people said they'd be happy to help him get the place in order. No problem at all." So our cooks went in there one day and spent all day cleaning up the kitchen. They made it damn near immaculate, and not only that, they came in with some paint. The kitchen was spotless when they finished.

In any event, the cooks came to work in alternating shifts. They were on from breakfast through dinner each day. The A shift came on one day, the B shift the next. We were there about three weeks, and when these cooks came out of that hotel, they really had most of the culinary arts down to perfection. Since they were smart basic cooks to begin with, it didn't take much training to learn the gourmet aspects and the ways of making food look appetizing. They learned more about parsley, lettuce, and green and red things for garnishes than they'd ever thought possible. So off we went to Camp Beauregard and opened up this mess.

It turned out to be quite a mess. I sent to Texas for capons. I sent to Maine for lobsters to be air-shipped in. I got local frog legs. We had beef from Omaha, great steaks, and wonderful local fresh vegetables.

We served the officers at their tables as they entered and were seated. We prepared the plates at the counter. Waiters served seconds. We also had great soups.

In any event, the mess was a huge success. (Col. Barton and I have a commendation to prove it.) As a matter of fact, Bette and I sponged off the mess. I ate my meals there. We had rented a room in Pineville, outside of Alexandria. Bette and I had a room and bath for which we paid two and a half dollars a week. The lady of the house took such a liking to Bette that she brought her breakfast in bed every morning at no charge at all. Then at night Sgt. Crest made sure that there was something left over from dinner, so each evening we had a monstrous doggie bag to take home with us: fried chicken, or sliced turkey and dressing with gravy, or frog legs, or a lobster. We ate very well on so-called leftovers from the mess.

But now I'm coming to the part about Colonel Saunders. Col. Saunders was in my estimation the meanest man, the meanest Army officer I ever knew. He was a full colonel and as rough as a cob. One afternoon he came in the mess to get a cup of tea. None of the cooks were there at the time, only a kitchen police on duty. Unfortunately, the k.p. used a cold cup, one of those handleless, big ceramic white mugs that was used in the Army at that time. He poured in some hot water, which apparently wasn't too hot, and gave the colonel a tea bag along with it. The colonel, after taking a swallow, literally raised hell. He said to the k.p., "Listen, when I come in here and ask for tea, I don't want lukewarm water or dishwater, I want hot tea." He then got up and stormed out, calling over his shoulder, "I'll be back tomorrow afternoon, and I want this deficiency corrected. I'm going to speak to your mess officer."

When I was told what happened, I reported to him to apologize before he called me. He took me apart. He also criticized the mess for having frog legs, lobster, capons and turkey during the week. He said, "They are all meat substitutes. You should serve only beef, pork, or lamb. That's the food for fighting men." That stopped me, as I had never thought of fowl and seafood as meat substitutes. He was apparently in the minority, however, because most of the officers seemed content with a whole two pound lobster from Maine.

The next day we were braced for his arrival at the mess. What we had done in preparation for this visit was to take one of the white mugs and put it in a 400° oven awaiting his arrival. And here he came. The cup, of course, was white hot. He walked in, sat down, and said, "I'd like to have my tea."

Sgt. Crest reached in the oven with forceps and pulled out the cup, put in on a saucer, poured in some boiling water, put a tea bag on the side, and delivered it to Col. Saunders. Then Sgt. Crest and I cleared out of the kitchen and went into a storeroom which had a peep hole to the mess area. Saunders picked up the tea bag, dunked it in the hot water until it was just the right color. He didn't put in sugar or cream, just reached down and picked up the cup. He got it four or five inches off the saucer when he screamed like a stuck hog. *"JEEZ-us!"* He jumped up, the cup dropped on the floor, and he ran out the door to the dispensary, where he had all four blistered fingers and blistered thumb treated and bandaged. That night when he came in for dinner, his hand was in a sling.

And he never said a word. I'll say this for the old buzzard, he was no crybaby, he took his whipping like a man.

23

TOMATOES CAN TAKE
A BEATING

Annie was from Texas and was about the toughest woman I ever saw. When she and her shrimp-sized husband came to our house to work, she had just left a job in a carnival as a lady wrestler and motorcycle rider in the show's motordome.

When she moved her stuff into our servant's quarters at Fort Lewis, Washington one Saturday afternoon, she brought her worldly possessions with her on her back . . . literally . . . in the form of an old fashioned roll-top trunk. Her diminutive husband carried the suitcases. On observing this unusual variety of pulchritude, I was immediately impressed with the fact that here was one gal I did not want to tangle with, but somehow I knew I would.

A description of Annie would be incomplete without emphasizing her sloping neck muscles, from her ears to the point of her soldiers. Her upper arms were like the sections of an old fashioned stovepipe. She was the only woman I ever knew who was completely musclebound.

In all fairness, I must admit that she had a *few* feminine characteristics. She often crocheted ... when she should have been washing dishes. Pillow covers were her specialty, with inscriptions neatly worded, "To My Everloving Sister," and other sentimental salutations.

My wife came to hold her in great awe. Although Annie was not belligerent, she had an air about her of complete self-confidence and determination. Naturally, my wife had great respect for those bulging muscles and ape-like hands, for with one back hand slap by that Amazon, she could quickly have left me a widower. But let's get on with the story.

As we were living in the verdant State of Washington that year, we decided to have a vegetable garden. So, in late March I planted a variety of seeds and set out twelve or fifteen tomato plants. The latter did very well, and after the proper time had elapsed, they came into blossom. One evening, on my way through the kitchen from the garden, I was intercepted by Annie who asked, "When are you going to beat your tomato plants down?"

Although somewhat shaken by this weird question, I quickly recovered and with a (losing) poker face, answered, "Soon now, I guess." I beat a hasty retreat to the shower to ponder over this peculiar development. Besides being musclebound, had she lost her marbles as well? To have a mad gorilla running loose in one's kitchen could be disconcerting, I thought ... or was she pulling my leg?

I dismissed the whole thing from my mind until the next evening, when she gave me the same routine. I asked if her suggested form of agricultural mayhem was absolutely necessary here in Washington, confessing I was not too familiar with this revolutionary angle of botanical philosophy—being an Easterner.

She said, "Why, you're dern right. Many's the time my old man gave us young'uns some sticks and took us out to the tomato patch. When plants are in blossom you just *got* to beat 'em down."

I was sure she was nuts. However, later on when I recalled the convincing and demanding manner in which she spoke, the thought occurred to me that maybe there might be something to this screwy advice. In any event, maybe it might be judicious to humor her.

The next day I ran into Johnny Guthrie, my next door neighbor, who also was an amateur gardener. I decided to have some fun with him. I asked him casually if he had beaten his tomato plants down yet.

"What are you talking about?" he asked, with a wide-eyed look.

"I'm talking about beating your tomatoes down when the plants blossom," I answered, as seriously as I could.

"I never heard of such a thing," he snapped.

"Why, everyone knows you have to follow that procedure to make a good crop," I argued. "Even the Amazon we've got in our kitchen will tell you that. Why, her old man is the biggest tomato planter in the South, and he always does it at blossom time."

"Then you're both nuts. Too bad. However, they say the State Insane Asylum is very nice," he cracked as we parted.

The following night I came through the kitchen and there she was, arms akimbo. "You still haven't beaten the tomatoes down," she charged. I was braced this time and told her that wasn't necessary here ... maybe in Texas, probably, but not here.

"It *is* necessary, Mister," she countered, "and you'll have to do it."

The chips were down. To preclude her pulling one of my arms out of its socket, I agreed to work over a few of my plants. So later that evening when the dinner dishes were finished and all was quiet, I slipped through the kitchen to the backyard, grabbing a broom on the way.

Near the steps to the back porch were three beautiful, tender, and innocent tomato plants. After looking in all directions to insure I was not observed, I gave those three plants the beating of their lives. I beat them all the way down, after which I sneaked sheepishly back into the house, feeling something like a sadistic moron. I returned to the reading of my evening paper as if nothing subnormal had happened.

Well, believe it or not, those three plants out-produced any six of the others. The vines practically took over the back porch and the size of the tomatoes were unbelievable. By this time, however, Annie had departed our house for other climes and never did see the results of her forced advice.

About a year later, Johnny and I had gone off to war and were fighting together in southern France. One night during a breathing spell, we were sharing a bottle of liberated wine and reminiscing. For some reason or other, I recalled the image of Annie lecturing me about those tomatoes.

I said, "Johnny, I have a confession to make to you. Do you remember the girl who worked for us back at Fort Lewis ... that musclebound character we had in our kitchen?"

"Yes, I remember her."

"Well, that stuff about her father being a big tomato planter, and so forth, I was just ribbing you."

"You were?"

"Sure. The whole idea was hers ... and you probably won't believe this, but that woman practically forced me to beat up three of my prettiest tomato plants. I actually sneaked out one night when no one could see me and really worked them over."

"The devil you did!" said Johnny.

"I sure did. Remember how big some of my tomatoes were?"

"Yes, you had some whoppers."

"Well, they were from those plants. I still don't understand it and I wouldn't have told you this if they hadn't turned out so well. I guess you think I'm touched in the head."

Johnny looked at me and smiled. He said, "I've got news for you, friend. Some of my tomatoes turned out just as good as yours. All of the big ones came from two plants."

"Which two?" I inquired.

"The two I beat the living hell out of," he confessed, with a simpering smile on his guilty face.

PART V

WORLD WAR II

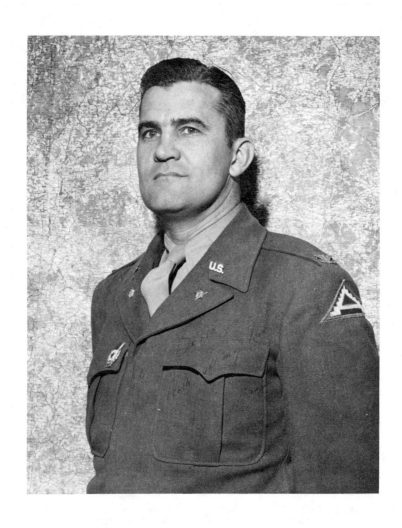

The author, 1945

24

INVASION OF
SOUTHERN
FRANCE

In March, 1944 Lieutenant General Alexander M. "Sandy" Patch, Commander of the IV Corps, then at Indio, California, was ordered to go to Algiers and report to British General Alexander, the Commander of Allied Forces in North Africa (AFHQ). General Patch was authorized to bring only seven or eight officers with him. He chose Col. A.A. White, Lt. Col. John S. Guthrie, Lt. Col. William A. "Billy" Craig, Lt. Col. Eldon "Bud" Larecy, myself and his aide.

On the way over we had a rough trip. We were flying in a C-54 with bucket seats. After leaving the Azores and a few hundred miles out from Casablanca, the ship ran into an incredibly rough area of turbulence. It was so rough in pitching and lurching that a large airplane motor strapped down in the center cargo section of the plane began to strain its bindings. It was obvious that if it came loose from its moorings it would go through the side of the plane, in which case the war would have been over for us.

As the co-pilot and a crew member entered the area, General Patch yelled, "Okay, sailors, let's get to the ropes." All of us, including the General, surrounded the motor, and every time it would shift over to each side, we would tighten the ropes a little more. Finally, we got the motor stabilized, landed safely in Casablanca and then flew to Algiers.

The staff was billeted in hotels, and General Patch was assigned a villa. For several days we hung around town wondering what had happened to the General. Finally, one afternoon his aide contacted us and said, "General Patch wants you to come to his villa this evening for dinner and to give you some news." We could hardly wait to get the news that we were going into action.

He didn't say anything until we had a drink in our hands. Then he said, "My friends, I have the greatest news ever, and I can't begin to tell you how much of a thrill it is. I have been given command of the Seventh Army, and we are going to invade Southern France."

Wow! Somebody dropped his drink. There we were, fresh from the desert, and now we were going to be in the front row, tackling jobs that are now history.

The General proceeded to brief us on what he had learned about the operation, which was fragmentary. The timing of the landing had not been set because of a continuing difference of opinion between the British and the Americans as to where the landing should take place. Winston Churchill believed that it should be in the so-called "underbelly" of Europe, preferably somewhere in the Balkans. He felt that the Normandy Invasion was going to be so successful that there was no need for a sec-

ond landing in France. The American position was conservative and one of caution, i.e., to make sure that all of
France was secured and not make an assumption that the
Normandy effort was going to do the job. Furthermore,
there were two German Armies in Southern France
which at any time might go north to attack the Normandy
forces from their southern flank. After Roosevelt got in
the act, the American philosophy prevailed.

Now that the dust had settled, the new Seventh Army
staff took over a school complex called *L'École Normale*
outside of Algiers. Besides our group from the IV Corps,
there was also a nucleus of a staff under the command of
Brigadier General Garrison H. "Gar" Davison. Gar was
the engineer for General Patton in the Sicilian Campaign
and had remained in Algiers with a small staff after the
Seventh Army had been inactivated on Patton's departure for command of the Third Army in England.

At this point in time (March, 1944) we had no combat
troops assigned, hence were in a planning mode only for
the invasion to take place on August 14, 1944. We had a
tentative troop list for planning purposes, i.e., the 3rd, the
45th, and the 36th Divisions, then in Italy under the Fifth
Army. We also had to plan for the landing of French
Army B, commanded by General de Lattre de Tassigny.
All personnel, operations, logistics and intelligence problems had to be solved and plans drawn for execution.

As the Intelligence Officer for the operation, I was
supported by AFHQ. (In Part VI of this book I will describe my relationship with General "Wild Bill" Donovan's O.S.S. and the storm that resulted.)

Immediately prior to D-Day, our headquarters moved
to Naples. Landing craft, naval combat ships, paratroops
and glider units were stationed throughout the Mediter-
ranean. We boarded the *U.S.S. Cococtin*, Admiral Ile-

witts's flagship, on August 14, 1944.

On August 15, 1944, at dawn, all hell broke loose on the Riviera. Under aerial bombardment and naval gun-fire, the underwater obstacles and gun emplacements on the beaches at St. Maxime, St. Tropez, and St. Raphael were pulverized for a highly successful landing by our troops. Even Churchill was on hand as he sailed around the *Cococtin* giving us his V sign.

As there are scores of books written on this campaign, I'll not attempt to duplicate them. I would make reference to a fine biography of General Patch by William Wyant which also covers this very successful operation.

Prime Minister Winston Churchill, Under Secretary of War Robert Patterson and Lt. Commander J. Rylands of the British destroyer Kimberly *watch the D-Day landings in southern France.*

HEADQUARTERS SEVENTH ARMY
Office of the Commanding General
APO 758   US Army

20 August 1944

ORDER OF THE DAY

TO: All Officers and Men of the Seventh Army.

Due to your courage, resourcefulness, zeal, and aggressiveness, we have achieved a great initial victory. The enemy in our area are perplexed and stunned. Except for his coastal defense forces, he is in full retreat.

I, therefore, call upon every officer and every man, regardless of fatigue or possible shortages of food and equipment, for an uninterrupted continuation of their maximum energy and endurance so that the enemy may not have time to recover. Reject every temptation which could possibly interfere with this crucial duty. The opportunity for decisive results is in front of us and we must and will move with the utmost speed and effectiveness.

The Secretary of War, Mr. Stimson, has asked me to convey to you his appreciations and congratulations for your initial victory and sends you his best wishes for continued success. My own admiration for your achievements to date is beyond expression. I am proud and greatly honored to command such magnificent troops.

A. M. PATCH,
Major General, U.S. Army,
Commanding.

25

OPERATION NORTHWIND

On Christmas Day 1944, the U.S. Seventh Army was in Alsace, butting up against the Siegfried Line, or West Wall, the shield the Germans had erected to defend their western frontier. The Seventh Army, for which I was the G-2, had been on the attack since we invaded southern France on the Riviera on August 15, pushing steadily northward through France. We had pushed through the difficult terrain of the Vosges Mountains and taken Strasbourg, the leading city of Alsace-Lorraine. By November 25 we had reached the Rhine River and were on the German border.

The Seventh Army command post was in the picturesque village of Saverne, about 30 miles west of the Rhine. We were facing east and northeast into Germany —some units had actually penetrated into German soil. We were the southern, or right flank of the Allies' western front, which ran 450 miles as the crow flies from the North Sea to Switzerland.

The Battle of the Bulge was still raging in the Ardennes, about 100 miles to our northwest. On Christmas Eve, the big German thrust, the Nazis' last great spasm of the war, a vain attempt at capturing the Belgian port city of Antwerp, had made its deepest penetration. It had fallen far short of its goal. General George Patton's Third Army had begun counterattacking the southern flank of the German salient on the 22nd, and Bastogne would be relieved on the 26th.

Things were comparatively quiet on the Seventh Army's front, but we had no reason for complacency. We were still on the attack when the Germans opened their offensive in the Ardennes to our north. In fact, my boss, Lieutenant General Alexander M. Patch, commanding general of the Seventh Army, and Lieutenant General George S. Patton, Jr., the aggressive and flamboyant commander of the Third Army, had tried to sell General Dwight D. Eisenhower, the supreme Allied commander, on a plan to cross the Rhine north of Strasbourg, which might have altered the course of the war. On the day after Thanksgiving, however, Ike decided to stick with the original plan of breaching the Rhine further north, near Worms.

All this became moot when the Germans struck in the Battle of the Bulge. The Seventh Army's lines had been stretched dangerously thin when Patton's army was pulled away from our left flank and sent north into Belgium to counter the Nazi thrust. We were covering 84 miles of the front with six divisions and faced the German 19th Army, which was part of Army Group Oberrhein. It was commanded by no less a personage than Reichsführer SS Heinrich Himmler himself. Because of his exalted position in the Third Reich, Army Group Oberrhein was, in effect, a tactically independent theater command.

On Christmas Eve the U.S. Sixth Army Group, made

up of the Seventh Army and the First French Army, warned of intelligence agents' reports that the Germans appeared to be concentrating in the Black Forest, on the German side of the Rhine River across from Strasbourg and Colmar. This was opposite the Seventh Army's southern sector and that of the First French Army, which was on our southern, or right, flank. In addition, I saw something on Christmas Day which confirmed my growing suspicion that the Seventh Army was about to undergo a major attack.

Military intelligence is gleaned from a number of sources—information from subordinate units and superior headquarters, from patrols, from prisoners of war and refugees, from aerial reconnaissance, and, in this case, from the highly secret and closely guarded ULTRA signal intelligence system. In 1939, British and Polish cryptographers, unbeknownst to the Germans, had solved the Nazis' secret cipher machine and its codes, which we called ENIGMA. ULTRA obviously was enormously valuable because it allowed the Allies to decode the unsuspecting Germans' most sensitive and secret communications.

From August 15th, the day the Sixth Army Group waded ashore in southern France, to December 16, the day the Germans launched their Ardennes counterattack, we had had a daily flow of tactical intelligence. After December 16, though, it seemed as if all our intelligence sources had dried up.

The ULTRA traffic fell off to nearly nothing as the Germans shut down their radios on our front as part of their security arrangements. Bad weather shut down our daily reconnaissance flights. No refugees were getting through. Patrols sent out to get prisoners ran into superior strength, which prevented them from capturing Germans and bringing them back for interrogation. We couldn't penetrate, even though there was supposed to be nobody out there. There was a void of positive intelligence keeping me from learning the German order of battle—the identification and location of enemy units and their commanders.

In view of this void, I began to suspect we were in for a big surprise. *It was just too quiet out there.* As there were 22 German divisions, panzer and infantry, which couldn't be accounted for, it occurred to me that they might well be on our front. In any event, our patrols indicated that

French woman rejoices over liberation.

we had enemy strength in front of us. The almost absolute negative input of information was to me a *positive* sign that something was going to happen.

On Christmas Day there was a partial break in the weather, and our tactical aircraft were able to get some serial photos of the areas around the town of Bitche, about 20 miles north of Saverne, where the Germans had dug in a strong defense position in a complex of the French's Maginot Line forts. The photos revealed newly dug enemy artillery emplacements, forward of the normal reserve unit positions. They were empty. This triggered new suspicion in my mind.

I took the photos and a map to the Artillery Section of Seventh Army Headquarters. I asked them what the photos indicated. They responded that freshly dug but empty positions indicate a plan to occupy them, and if so, a possible intention to initiate an offensive operation.

That settled it. The morning after Christmas, I went in to see General Patch. Just the two of us were in the meeting. After exchanging greetings and formalities, I said, "General, we're going to be hit. We're going to get clobbered."

"How do you know?" he asked.

"I don't know positively, sir. There's a lot of gut feeling in this."

"When?"

"New Year's Eve."

"With what?"

"I don't know. Let me tell you what has gone on since the Bastogne breakthrough." I explained in detail my suspicions, the gut feeling due to the void in intelligence information, the cessation of the ULTRA radio traffic, and the radio silence.

"I think you're right," he said when I finished. "But

why do you pick New Year's Eve?"

I replied that the German concept of American New Year's Eve activities is comparable to their own Fasching, where a spirit of abandon reigns. Only a short time earlier, we had overrun a German division command post, and among the documents we found was a treatise entitled *The American Soldier*. It described the American male in both flattering and unflattering terms. One section, however, was devoted to the actions of the average American on New Year's Eve. A picture was painted of Forty-second and Broadway in New York City. I explained that the Germans would logically expect us all to be drunk and would therefore attack.

"Okay," Patch said in his direct and decisive manner. "I go along with what you have outlined." With that, he picked up the telephone and called his immediate superior, Lieutenant General Jacob L. Devers, commanding general of the Sixth Army Group. He asked if Devers and his staff could come to Severna for a briefing on the situation that evening.

Devers could. He brought along with him Brigadier General Eugene Harrison, the Sixth Army Group intelligence officer, Colonel Russel Vittrup, and others. We went over a number of key questions:

What was out in front of Seventh Army? What should we do with French General Jean de Lattre de Tassigny, the temperamental commander of the French First Army? What could be left of German western forces outside of Bastogne? Could the radio silence to our front mean there was nothing there rather than being a security tactic? Where would the attack come from? And when?

These latter two were obviously the big questions.

General Patch turned and asked me to repeat the conversation we'd had in his office. "Colonel Quinn, get up to the map and tell us where it's coming from."

I told them: New Year's Eve, main effort in the Bitche area. And with no doubt in my voice, I said, "We are going to be hit."

"I am supporting this conclusion," General Patch said, and there was no doubt in his voice, either.

Devers responded, "Sandy, I have the French on my hands. all I can say is do what you think is necessary to save the Seventh Army. If you are convinced, go on the defensive."

It is important to note that at this meeting General Devers and his Sixth Army Group staff had no intelligence information, ULTRA or otherwise, on an impending attack, even though they had warned of the buildup in the Black Forest, 50 or 60 miles southeast of Bitche, on the other side of the Rhine River.

After Devers and his staff had left, Patch picked up the phone and called his three corps commanders, Major General Frank W. Milburn of XXI Corps, Major General Wade H. Haislip of XV Corps, and Major General Edward H. Brooks of VI Corps. He ordered them to meet with him the next morning at Haislip's XV Corps headquarters.

Haislip's HQ was in a schoolhouse, and the room was packed with the three corps commanders and their staffs. The commanders sat in the front row. Patch and I walked in with Patch carrying a map of the Seventh Army's front. After the map was set up, he turned to me and said, "Tell 'em, son."

Whew! Talk about tall cotton! There were more stars and eagles in that room than I had seen all at once in a very long time. So I told them, wondering all the time: how in the hell did a web-footed Chesapeake Bay crabber get himself into this kind of a situation?

The corps commanders gave me a tortuous interrogation, but had different reactions. Haislip was the most skeptical and gave me a hard time. Brooks and Milburn seemed to take it in stride and would do what had to be done.

At the end of the session, Patch gave the orders. Seventh Army would go on the defensive on a crash basis immediately.

This put an enormous strain on the engineers, who were commanded by Brigadier General Garrison H. "Gar" Davidson, for whom I had played football at West Point. It meant re-positioning infantry, tank, and artillery units for defense and counterattack capabilities. It included digging fortifications, laying mines and barbed wire, and preparing bridges for demolition, all of which involved an enormous amount of work. The engineer officers would look at me and say they hoped I knew what I was talking about. I assured them that the attack would come.

"It's my neck," I said. "You'll be the ones to pull the rope of the guillotine if it doesn't happen." All the time, I was thinking to myself, this *is* your neck that's out on the line, boy. You're the one out there swinging in the wind. I sure hope you're right on this one.

• • •

I was.

However, there were subsequently a couple of controversies over my intelligence estimates. One was that my written estimate, "G-2 Estimate of the Enemy Situation No. 6" dated December 29, listed the possibility of a major five-to-eighteen division enemy attack south from the Bitche-Sarregue-Mines area, which was what I alerted

General Patch to, as the second most likely course of action. The most likely, according to this estimate, was a less ambitious series of limited attacks with forces "currently in contact and in immediate reserve," which would contain the Seventh Army and be the most economical use of the enemy's forces.

The reason for this was quite simple. We had captured a number of enemy spies in our area, and I didn't want to put my estimate on paper when it might wind up in enemy hands. No matter what was said in the estimate, the Seventh Army was on a *crash* defensive effort.

The other controversy involved the role of ULTRA. The Seventh Army G-2 officer who handled ULTRA intelligence was Captain (later Colonel) Donald M. Bussey. After the war Bussey contended that ULTRA intelligence had not dried up and that, while not spelling out the Germans' intentions, it had provided information on their order of battle that would make such an estimate as mine possible.

All I know is that I didn't see any such information, nor did General Harrison at Sixth Army Group which was also served by ULTRA.

In any event, Seventh Army was ready for the German offensive, which came at the time and location I predicted. We converted ten percent of our support troops to infantry. Sixth Army Group closed its forward command post at Phalsbourg. Seventh Army secretly pulled back some of its forward units and registered mortars and artillery on their positions, which made them free fire zones for the surprised Germans. All New Year's Eve parties were cancelled. Seventh Army command post moved 50 miles to the west, to Luneville.

Major General Arthur A. White, Patch's chief of staff, recorded in his diary entry for January 1, 1945. "German offensive began on Seventh Army front about 0030 hours (12:30 A.M.). Krauts were howling drunk. Murdered them."

26

THE SEARCH FOR A COMMAND POST

While the 7th Army was about to end the war down in Bavaria, the German Army was in full retreat. A lot of the officers and the hierarchy of the Third Reich were trying to get through Bavaria to Switzerland for obvious reasons. The G-3 Section of the German Army was under the control of Brigadier General Heusinger. He was head of the planning and operations staff of the German Army, the OKW. His section had agreed to meet with other sections of the German High Command at a certain location south of Munich. They never got there.

The reason I know this story is that in later years when I had business in Fort Benning, Georgia, I was introduced to and had lunch with General Heusinger. Until then, I had not realized that he had been captured south of Augsberg and had been in my prisoner of war stockade. Much later, after his release, he was recalled to the new German Army. He had been sent to Fort Benning by the German Army for an orientation course in infantry tactics. This is the story he told me at lunch.

When his operations section was north of Munich, he realized that the Americans were closing in on them and that they had no chance to get to the Bavarian Alps. So they pulled off the Autobahn, the superhighway, and proceeded with their convoy up a long lane for a half a mile or so to a very large farm complex. Not only was there a big farmhouse, but attached to it were several big barns forming a quadrangle, a typical German farm establishment with one entrance into a square. Once you entered the courtyard, you felt like you were in a Yale Bowl.

As the establishment was ideal, he had his men billeted in the barns and the officers in the house, which had been vacated for one reason or another. That night he heard tanks rolling down the Autobahn and realized that he'd been bypassed and was soon to be captured; whereupon, he called together his officers and men and said, "The war is over for us and for Germany. We shall act like good soldiers at our surrender."[1]

He continued, "I want every man to do the best he can to clean himself up, and when the Americans come, as they eventually will, we'll surrender in formation and in good grace and form. We will bear no arms; so after this meeting, you will stack your arms in the courtyard and subsequently surrender in accordance with established military protocol. I will extend the hilt of my saber to our captors. Dismissed."

Two days passed. The American tanks were still rumbling south down the Autobahn. Aircraft were still overhead, and it seemed that no one was about to come up the lane and take them into custody. Finally, from the top of one of the barns serving as a crow's nest, a soldier observing the lane yelled out, "Here come the Americans!"

The Colonel immediately ordered his section to form

---

[1]These were not SS troops; these were German Army troops.

up in the courtyard as planned. He went to his room and retrieved his saber. He then took his position in front of his section with his saber in his hands, the hilt towards the forthcoming Americans.

In a few minutes, a vehicle roared into the center of the courtyard. It was an American jeep carrying a driver and a young captain. The driver drove the jeep to the formation. The captain looked around, ignoring the saber, and said to the Colonel, "Okay, you got here first; looks like a good command post." And to the utter amazement and chagrin of the Colonel, the jeep drove off.

Apparently, the captain did not appreciate the circumstances; maybe he did, but was too busy to take a bunch of prisoners in tow. Two days later an American patrol came in and took the surrender.

27

NATIONAL REDOUBT

One factor in Eisenhower's strategic decision, although not the major one, was the possibility of a last-ditch Nazi holdout in a position rumored to be under construction in the Alps of southern Germany and western Austria—a National Redoubt. This idea had been planted by Goebbels' propaganda machine and had been espoused by several influential Germans. This Alpine area was in front of the operational area of the 6th Army Group, which commanded the U.S. 7th Army and the French 1st Army.

Most Allied intelligence officers discounted the probability of any significant fortress in the area, partly because of the region's limited industrial and agricultural resources. However, there was the possibility that some army and SS units would make a final suicide stand there. This caused some of Eisenhower's staff to worry that future generations of Germans could claim that National Socialism and the Third Reich had never surrendered.

I thought that many of the reports were exaggerated, but concluded that there was some evidence that Hitler was contemplating a final stand there. Even though there might not be a National Redoubt, the Alps constituted such a natural fortress area that it seemed prudent to attack into the area to prevent a major concentration of German forces from retreating there from Eastern, Western, and Italian fronts. I therefore prepared a study which indicated a capability which might prolong the conflict.

The Sixth Army Group's primary responsibility at this point was to protect the right flank of General Bradley's 12th Army Group. However, General Eisenhower contemplated reinforcing the army group to enable it to *"prevent Nazi occupation of a mountain citadel."*

On April 3, the SHAEF G-3, our operations officer, Major General Harold R. Bull, read my special report on the redoubt and recommended expanding our operations into the western Austrian Alps to seal off the area to the Nazis. When Field Marshal Sir Harold R.L.G. Alexander, the Allied Commander in Italy, who was advancing on the Alps from the south, indicated that he would welcome a linkup in the Alps, General Eisenhower approved the expansion of operations.

The 7th Army made a three-pronged drive east to the Austrian border. XV Corps was on the Army's left, or northern flank, XXI Corps was in the middle drive through the rugged, forested Odenwald, and VI Corps was on the right flank. The French 1st Army was on 7th Army's right flank, fronting the Black Forest.

XV Corps' attack took it through Nuremberg, the site of many Nazi Party rallies and a shrine of National Socialism, and then on to Munich and the infamous, ghastly Nazi death camp at the nearby town of Dachau. Seventh Army troops liberated Dachau, the Nazi's original concentration camp, and its 30,000 surviving inmates, on April 27, 1945.

One factor behind the 7th Army's timing was that the Allies had a special intelligence mission called ALSOS, with the assignment of getting data on German progress on atomic weapon research and development. The AL-SOS Group was to accompany VI Corps, then make a dash for the town of Hechingen, about 50 miles southwest of Stuttgart, where German scientists were reportedly conducting nuclear experiments. ALSOS wanted to capture these scientists before they were taken by the French.

*Lt. Gen. Ferdinand Neuling after surrender,
with Maj. Paul Kubala and Col. Quinn.*

On May 4, Salzburg, a town famous for its music, surrendered. General Patch then ordered his XV Corps to attack Hitler's mountain retreat at Berchtesgaden from the rear. The only thing that delayed the capture of this Nazi shrine was congestion—every unit in the 6th Army

Group wanted to get into the town!

With the capture of Salzburg and Berchtesgaden, the last passes into the Austrian Alps were sealed, and along with them, any prospect of a National Redoubt. There was no longer any place for the German Army to retreat, regroup, or hide. All that waited was the formality of the Nazi surrender on May 8. For the Americans, the shooting war in Europe was over.

That the National Redoubt did not come was due to its predictability in my assessments, whereupon steps were taken to prevent it. Such is the function of intelligence.

As of the end of May in 1945, my prisoner-of-war camp contained (besides thousands of German Army and SS troops) over 250 field marshals, generals, and high ranking government leaders. The latters' goal had been to enter the Redoubt and eventually make their way into Switzerland.

28

THE FINAL DAYS— HITLER VS. GOERING

On May 8, 1945, Reich Marshal Hermann Goering surrendered to the American forces south of Munich and was subsequently confined in a prisoner of war compound in Augsberg, Germany, operated by the 7th U.S. Army. The preceding two weeks saw the dramatic deterioration of the relationship between Hitler and Goering, with Hitler ordering the latter's assassination.

It is not my intent to cover all of the events that transpired between Goering's departure from Berlin on April 20 and his surrender. Any numbr of excellent books have been written covering those details.

My purpose is to shed light on the following points: first, to fill in some of the voids in those books or to augment them; second, to address some misconceptions; and third, to correct the record as to the activities and handling of the Reich Marshal while he was a prisoner of war under the control of the Seventh Army Headquarters.

The following documents, describing the disintegration of the German High Command structure, were captured by elements of the 7th Army, or procured through radio intercept.

Prior to actions reported in these messages, Goering had bid Hitler farewell at the Fuehrer's birthday ceremony on April 20, 1945, and had started moving his small staff to Berchtesgaden to await word from Berlin as to the situation there.

The first of these Messages is a report by a Lt. Volck, who was General Major Christian's adjutant.

V o l c k , 1st Lt. Res.   HQ., 25 April 1945
Adjudant Air Corps Command Staff

Staff matter
Through officer only !

Report on Fuehrer briefing on 22-4-1945
Beginning of briefing: appr. 1530 o'cl.

Before the briefing Generalmajor Christian presented me to the Fuehrer as his adjudant.

After representatives of the different branches had finished making their reports the Fuehrer withdrew for a short time. Subsequently, all officers present at the briefing were ordered before the Fuehrer. I personally had occasion, after General Christian had called me over from a room adjoining the Fuehrers shelter to hear the following expressed by the Fuehrer:

This essentially is what he said:

I consider the war lost and I feel that I have been lied to and cheated by those, who had all my confidence. I have resolved to stay in Berlin, the great German city committed to war against Bolshevism. I have also decided to take charge of the defense of this city (Berlin).

All attempts by those present at the briefing - as well as Reichsfuehrer SS (notified by phone) Grand Admiral Doenitz (notified by phone) - to cause the Fuehrer to modify his resolution, were useless.

Reichsminister Dr. Goebbels also was present when the Fuehrer stated his decision. Reichs Foreign Minister von Ribbentrop, who had also made his appearance at the Fuehrer's shelter, was not given a chance by Hitler to voice his opinion on this occasion.

On our trip back again to Kurfuerst General-Maj. Christian confirmed the words of the Fuehrer which I was privileged to hear. Gen.-Maj. Christian, in the course of our discussion of the events, called this briefing the historical event of our times. He also pointed out that for the first time the Fuehrer admitted the hopelessness of the war situation and accompanying it Europe's hopeless stand against Bolshevism.

signed V o l c k ,
1st Lt., and Adj.

Covering this same meeting, General of the Air Corps Koller dispatched the following report to Goering.

Chief of General Staff Air Corps
    KOLLER
General of the Air Corps

Nr. 6/45 top secret

Staff matter !

Only through officer !

To

the Fuhrer

Report on the main points of the events on the 22.4. and my message to Herrn Reichsmarschall on the 23.4.

(Report made from personal notes.)

I. During the late afternoon of the 22.4. the following was told to me over the phone by General Christian following the Fuhrer's briefing.

"More freedom of movement to be expected for Air Forces Supreme Command". Then the following telephone message came in at night: "Historical events; I am coming to report personally".

Christian reported to me personally at 20.45:

"The Fuehrer has collapsed, he considers further resistance useless, refuses to leave Berlin, insists on remaining in the airraid shelter, defending Berlin and taking the consequences as a last resort. All present (Keitel, Jodl, Bormann, Himmler, Goebbels, and the Grand Admiral over the phone) have tried to sway the Fuehrer and coax him into leaving Berlin, pointing out that the city was no longer suitable for command functions and that he could ill afford to surrender the leadership to anyone else. Everything was in vain. The Fuehrer has released his personal files for destruction, he has ordered Goebbels, the latters wife and their 6 children to join him. They are all sitting there with him in the shelter. Fuehrer said he would remain there, the others should leave; they may go wherever they please. The Reich Foreign Minister had repeatedly tried to engage the Fuehrer in discussion; the Fuehrer however refused to listen.

Now the OKW (Keitel and Jodl) wants to assume the Fuhrers command, it intends to have forces, disposed along the Elbe, turn around facing the East. OKW abandons Berlin, will reassemble in Krampnitz tonight. The Fuehrer refuses to go there. The atmosphere in the shelter depressed me greatly.

To my question, whether I was to act independently or whether the Fuehrer had ordered that we move and where, Christian said: "That I don't know myself, the Fuehrer has given no orders whatever, he only said, the others should go wherever they please".

My reply to Christian: "I can't do anything with that. I desire orders or an objective report on the situation. I must definitely speak to Jodl." Christian shared my views.

II. In spite of repeated efforts, nobody could be reached at OKW up to past 2300, neither Keitel, Jodl, Bucch, Bruchmuller nor any other official.

III. Phone inquiry by Koller with Below at 21.20 o'clock, whether situation described to me by Christian, still prevailed:

Below: No change in the situation, we are still trying to sway the Fuehrer.

To my question, whether a change of the Fuehrer's views could be considered likely, Below replies: "No, that can hardly be expected any more".

My question, whether there was still a chance that I could expect an order, was answered in the negative.

Below considered my move to the North as well as to the South as essential, so that the Reichsmarschall may be informed. We agree, that in any case I must at first get in touch with Jodl.   (Goering's aide)

V. Badly muffled phone conversation with Colonel von Brauchitsch, whom I told, that the Fuehrer had decided to stay at his present location.

To my question where the Reichsmarschall wanted me to go, Brauchitsch replied, that the Reichsmarschall had ordered me, to go South with the Operations Staff.

I have told him, that in any case I should have a talk with Generaloberst Jodl, the result of this talk would determine any further steps on my part.

V. As nobody could be reached by phone at OKW I personally went searching for Generaloberst Jodl. I met him in Krampnitz where he had arrived shortly before.

I have asked General Jodl, who was sitting in a room, giving orders to some officers, to grant me a personal interview, barring all witnesses.

Present at OKW on 23.4. between 00.00 o'clock and 01.00 o'clock.

The talk with Generaloberst Jodl took place within this period.

1. I have presented Jodl with the report of Christian, I asked him to either confirm it or inform me otherwise or issue orders. Christian had been in such an objective mood, that I found it difficult to convince myself that the situation was exactly as he told me.

2. Generaloberst Jodl:

"What Christian told you is correct."

Verbatim: "The Fuehrer has surrendered his command and has resolved to remain in Berlin, directing the defense and shoot himself as a last resort."

Fight, the Fuehrer said, he could not for reasons of health; he would refuse personal combat anyway, so as not chance being wounded or fall into enemy hands.

All of us (he gave the identical names Christian had mentioned) have tried wholeheartedly to change the Fuehrer's views. We proposed to have troops engaged on the Western front yet comitted in battle against the Russians. The Fuehrer however did not think much of this plan. He said, everything was going to pieces anyway; he could not favor it and that the Reichsmarschall should concern himself with this plan. To a remark which was made that no soldier can be found who will continue to fight under the

Reichsmarshall, the Fuehrer said the following: "There is not much more
to fight for, and when it comes to making peace, the Reichsmarshall can do
that better than I." The Fuehrer had been very much impressed by the latest
developments of the situation and he now speaks of treason from all sides, of
failure, corruption, and that the SS is now lying to him. The offensive
"Steiner" has not taken place, and the finishing touches were given him by
Sepp Dietrich.

   3. My question to Generaloberst Jodl:

   This cannot go on. What can yet be done? Are there no chances that
Hitler might revise his decision if more persuasion can be utilized, and
for example, through the Reichsmarshall?

   4. Comment by Generaloberst Jodl:

   That cannot be counted on. The Fuehrer has made his decision and is
grasping onto it so powerfully that no change in his decision can be expected.
The Fuehrer has said that the troops are not fighting, the road blocks are
opened, and are not being defended. He is most likely informed and aware
of the fact that soon we will have no ammunition and gasoline. Most likely
he has had knowledge of this for some time now, but hesitated to let us know.
After his birthday, the Fuehrer has told me that we will fight to the last.
Besides, he has always promised himself more success than was possible to
expect from weak forces.

   5. To my question as to what should happen and what the High Command
of the Armed Forces (OKW) will do, Jodl said the following:

   We will assemble our staff here in Krapnitz. We're turning the 12th
Army around to face the East and to attack the 3rd Guards Panzer Army on
its left flank, and will be completely indifferent to anything the Americans
may then do along the Elbe. It may be possible only by such a deed to show
others that we want to fight against the Soviets. Field Marshall Keitel is
already on his way to take care of the most pressing matters for this change
of direction.

   In the meantime the enemy has also broken through Vietinghoff. I have
ordered a withdrawal behind the Tessin and Po, if the breakthrough cannot be
stopped. This I have done alone and independently. After all, actions and
orders must take place.

   6. Question to Jodl:

   What can I do? I can't stay here any longer, and I've got to get out
of Werder. Shall I remain in the North? For all practical purposes there
are hardly any possibilities for command. All units in the North are under
the command of Airfleet Reich. These are to be under leadership of the
Grand Admiral, depending on principles laid down by the Fuehrer for the
crisis, and as was ordered by Keitel, who had just come to you before my
journey. I am lacking a prepared command post in the North. All attempts
to communicate have been in vain. In spite of that, I'll stay in the North
if the situation warrents it. But I want orders and don't want to do anything without the approval of the OKW. According to your description, Herr
Generaloberst, I think it most important that my Supreme Commander receives
knowledge of this. Rightly he would blame me, if this would not be done.
But I think it impossible to do this by radio.

   I recommend, that if you approve of my Supreme Commander's knowledge
of this, that a Liaison Force under General Christian and several General
Staff Officers be attached to the Supreme Command of the Armed Forces (OKW),
and that I and the rest go South and report to the Reichsmarshall on what
you have said. Depending on developments, I may come up again.

7. Generaloberst Jodl:

Completely agreeable. This is the only thing for you to do, and you must do it, as a matter of fact. This is very pleasing to me and when you do go South you can contact General Winter and transmit my order for him to break up his journey and consolidate all parts of the Supreme Command of the Armed Forces that are there.

Simultaneously, you will inform him of the situation here, transmit to him the Fuehrer's orders on the Alpine Fortress, and my order to Vietinghoff, which otherwise I myself may not be able to get through.

8. Furthermore I have asked Generaloberst Jodl just how the Supreme Command of the Armed Forces pictures the control in the South. What will happen in the Southern section of the Reich, once the fighting troops of the North who are now facing the West will be swung around to face to the East? I have expressed my doubts about such a simple maneuver as the Western enemies will undoubtedly follow up our withdrawal, cutting our command, communications, and supply routes, thereby making a fight in the East an impossibility.

Jodl answered as follows:

At the moment the urgency of this problem is not that great in the South where the fronts are yet far enough apart, but as time goes on, there too the same developments should take place. Besides, we'll have to wait and see what actions the Americans will take.

9. Then, following this, I took up a number of other matters with the Generaloberst such as the Liaison Force and its organization, matters of courier planes, and protection of the remainder of my Staff in Werder which, for administrative purposes, was attached to the Commandant of Sector "E".

VI. Approximately at 2.00 o'clock there was a telephone call from Colonel von Below to me.

It was asked whether I had spoken with Jodl. I answered yes, and that the Liaison Force will remain under General Christian at the OKW, and that I will fly South to report to my C in C.

Below answered that all is in order then.

VII. Landed in Neubiberg due to weather at 6.00 o'clock; after interior administrative matters had been completed took off at 3.30 o'clock from Gatow. Ride to Berchtesgarden. Arrival 12.00 o'clock. Begin my recital to the Herr Reichsmarshall approximately between 12.30 and 13.00 hours. After the briefing of the ground situation until my start from Berlin, I informed the Herr Reichsmarshall of the above report. I considered it the unquestionable duty of the Chief of the Air Corps General Staff to inform without hesitation the C. in C. of the Air Corps of all developments in the situation.

VIII. In the evening of the 24.4 General Schulz reported to me that 1st Lt. Volk has arrived here. Volk (until now unknown to me), claims to have been present at the Commanders briefing with General Christian and had to deliver a message to me. I am enclosing in this report a copy of the written message delivered to me by request.

It is assumed that Koller's report prompted Goering to dispatch the following historic message to Hitler. It is believed to be their last communication.

HQ, the 23. 4. 1945
22.00 hours.

My Fuhrer !

Is it agreeable to you that I as your second in command, as stated in your order dated 29. 6. 1941, take over the total leadership of the Reich with full freedom of action from within and without, now that you have decided to remain at the Command Post in the fortress of Berlin?

Should there be no answer until 22.00, then I will take for granted that you have lost your freedom of action. I will then look upon the pre-suppositions of your decree as given to me and will act for the benefit of the Nation and Fatherland.

What I feel for you in this, the gravest hour of my life, you will know, and cannot be expressed in words.

God bless you and may he let you come here soon.

Your faithful

Hermann Goering

There is reason to believe that Goering's message was delayed and the deadline had passed by the time of its receipt by Hitler. In any event, Bormann intercepted the message and convinced Hitler that Goering had pre-empted him and had, in fact, staged a *coup d'état*. Finally, Hitler was sufficiently aroused to order Goering stripped of his right to succession by a message written by Bormann, who sent an additional message to the S.S. Commandant in the Obersalzburg area to assassinate Goering.

On the 1st of May the following message was dispatched, whereupon Hitler was reported to have taken his life. In his press conference with allied reporters later, Goering indicated that Bormann issued the order instead of Hitler.

Fuhrer Headquarters
1 May 1945

Ass't. Chief
of the Armed Forces Operations Staff

Most honourable Herr Reichsminister !

I am herewith sending you the text of an order which Grand Admiral Donitz has received.

"The Fuhrer, instead of Reichs Marschall Goering, chooses you as his successor. Written authority is on the way. As of now you are entitled to take all measures, as resulting from our present situation, deemed necessary.

sign. Bormann
Reichsleiter

The wireless message was sent to the Operations Staff B via Naval Channels.

Heil Hitler !

Your devoted

Winter

The S.S. Commanders Frank and Bredow placed Goering under house arrest and separated him from his family, but did not kill him, although Bormann kept insisting that they do so. It is assumed that the S.S. saw no advantage in that course of action as Goering might emerge as the Fuehrer.

Subsequent to Allied bombings of the Eagle's Nest and Goering's home, Goering was permitted to make a peace overture to the Allied High Command; he dispatched letters by his aide-de-camp to General Patch and General Eisenhower asking for aid. The following chapter cites those communications and sees his surrender.

The view from Hitler's front room—Berchtesgaden

29

HERMANN GOERING SURRENDERS

On the 6th of May 1945, a white flag was seen in the enemy lines, moving toward our lines in the 36th Division area southeast of Munich. The vehicle carried, besides the driver, a Colonel von Brauchitsch who was personal aide to Hermann Goering. Colonel von Brauchitsch told the front line people to take him to their commander. They took him to the commanding general, or the G-2 of the 36th Division. Colonel von Brauchitsch, who spoke excellent English, indicated that he had personal letters from Reich Marshal Goering to General Patch and General Eisenhower and requested an escort to take him to 7th Army Headquarters.

General Alexander M. Patch was the commanding general of the 7th Army at that time, and I was his G-2 (intelligence officer). The military police brought Colonel von Brauchitsch to me in my office, and the colonel said, "I have two letters which are from the Marshal; one is to General Patch and the other to General Eisenhower. I have been instructed to give them to General Patch."

I told him to hand me the letters, and I would go in and present them to General Patch, which I did. General Patch read his letter, as well as the letter to General Eisenhower, both of which follow:

The Letter to General Patch:

THE REICH MARSHAL
OF THE
GREATER GERMAN REICH   6 May 1945

Your Excellency!

My personal adjutant and plenipotentiary, Colonel von Brauchitsch, is the bearer of a personal letter from me to his Excellency the Supreme Commander of the Allied Forces, General Eisenhower.

I beg you, Excellency, as a soldier, to forward this letter to General Eisenhower by the most expeditious means, by air or by radio, whichever seems more practicable to you. In that letter I requested General Eisenhower, and I repeat this request, to be placed, together with my family, under American protection in the area under your command until a decision has been reached by the Supreme Commander, General Eisenhower. Because of technical reasons, I suggested for this purpose my former Adjutant's office in Berchtesgaden, since my house there has been destroyed.

If this suggestion should appear impracticable to your Excellency, I request you to point out to my adjutant another, more suitable location within your command. It is understood that I will be at your disposal according to the decision of General Eisenhower.

I request you, Excellency, to read my letter addressed to General Eisenhower so that you can orient yourself on my position and on the reason why I was unable to take this step before today.

With my expressions of soldierly respect, I remain

Yours truly,

Hermann Goering

The Letter to General Eisenhower:

THE REICHMARSHAL
OF THE
GREATER GERMAN REICH   6 May 1945

Your Excellency!

On the 23rd of April, after I had tried for many months, unfortunately without success, to make my influence felt in this direction, I decided, as the highest ranking officer of the German Army, to place communication with your Excellency to do everything on my part to provide a basis for the prevention of further bloodshed.

On that day I was arrested with my entire entourage and family by the SS in Berchtesgaden. The order to shoot me and my household, including my family, was not carried out by my guards. At the same time I was expelled from the Nazi party. The story given forth on the radio was that I had been relieved of my command of the Luftwaffe because of a serious heart disease. Because of the close ties which bind me to the German people and its soldiers, this account was given little credence and the majority of the people believed that I had been forcibly removed from the scene. Because of my arrest, I am today still unable to understand fully on what basis the whole procedure against me was carried out, especially since I had right on my side being the decreed successor. Through recent developments and the arrival of some of our Luftwaffe units, I have just succeeded in regaining my freedom at the place of my arrest, after having previously been removed from Berchtesgaden together with my entourage.

In spite of all the events which occurred during my arrest, I submit to you, your Excellency, the same request, to receive me personally without any obligations on your part and to allow me to talk to you as one soldier to another. I request of you to grant me free passage for this interview and to place my entourage and family under American protection. Although my house there has been completely destroyed there is a sufficient number of rooms in the house of my adjutant's office.

Would you please inform me where we can meet for this

interview. If, for reasons of time or technical reasons, it is impossible for your Excellency to receive me in the near future, I would ask you to appoint a plenipotentiary to whom I could convey what I wish to tell you personally. My request may possibly seem very strange to your Excellency; nevertheless I make it, remembering the time when the Aged Marshal of France, Pétain, in a situation equally difficult for his country, asked me for a similar interview which then actually took place.

I wish to emphasize again that it would be an interview entailing absolutely no personal obligation on the part of your Excellency. It would be a conversation purely on a human and soldierly level.

I ask you Excellency to let me have your reply through my personal adjutant, Colonel von Brauchitsch, the bearer of this letter. If you agree to my suggestion, please inform the American commander in the Salzburg — Berchtesgaden area of my request to have my household placed under American protection at Berchtesgaden or at another locality within his command. Your Excellency will understand how I feel in this, my most difficult hour, and how much I have suffered through my disability, due to my arrest, to do everything possible a long time ago in order to prevent further bloodshed in a hopeless situation.

With the expression of my soldierly respect, I remain

Yours truly,

Hermann Goering

After General Patch read both letters he said, "Well, let's find out what Ike wants to do about it." He called General Eisenhower, and fortunately, he was in. General Patch said, "We've got a couple of letters here from the 'fat boy,' one is for you and one for me, and he wants to give himself up."

Eisenhower said, "Well, let him. Read the letter to me." After he read the letter, General Patch asked,

"What do you want me to do, Ike?"

"Sandy, just give him a safe escort through our lines,

because he would have been our prisoner in a few days, anyway." He ended by saying, "You know, Sandy, this guy's got to be nuts. When you do get him, lock him up and treat him as an ordinary prisoner."

Goering surrenders. Left to right:
von Brauchitsch, Goering, Quinn and Kubala.

Two days later, after the rejection of his plea, Hermann Goering came by with his aide, Colonel von Brauchitsch, a driver, and an orderly. He had surrendered to the 36th Division. He was in uniform but without decorations. I have a photo of him being turned over to me at 7th Army Headquarters, along with Colonel von Brauchitsch. Goering had with him his baton, the famous baton which is now in the West Point Museum. He carried, oddly enough, an American Smith and Wesson .38 revolver. He was wearing a dagger about eight inches long fastened to his belt, and curiously, it had written on it in ancient Runic, "To Hermann from Eric, forever." There has been some question as to who Eric was; he may have been a distant cousin, but no one really seemed to know. I gave that dagger to West Point. He also had a little Minox camera.

Now we had Hermann Goering in our camp, and I took pictures of his lodging and room. We put him up in a place in Augsburg which had been a workers community for a nearby factory. It was some kind of a housing unit where all the houses looked the same, an almost barracks-type place. Also quartered in the same area were Field Marshals von Runstedt, Kesselring, von Weichs, and Schoerner. For three weeks General Patch, myself, and Major Paul Kubala, who ran the 7th Army Interrogation Center, talked to him quite often. Some very curious and interesting things happened while he was there. One incident showed me the impact that our own propaganda had on us as Americans. One of the images we had of Hermann Goering was that he was often pictured or cartooned as being in a Roman toga with a velvet bag of gems and jewels which he carried on the belt of his robe. From time-to-time, these pictures had him pouring the jewels out on the table and just running his hands through them.

One day we received a call from General Eisenhower's headquarters, indicating that the General (and I didn't believe it, but this is what the message said) "General Eisenhower would like to see that bag of jewels." So I asked Hermann Goering where the bag of jewels was, and he just laughed. He laughed uproariously and said, "This is a perfect example of propaganda in wartime. I never had a Roman toga on in my life, unless it was at a masquerade party, and I never had a bag of jewels. I did rape the Louvre in Paris, and I took all the art the French and Austrians had. It's down here in Berchtesgaden. You've already found it, carloads, but I really wasn't that kind of nut."

30

HERMANN GOERING ANSWERS THE 64-DOLLAR QUESTION

Reich Marshal Hermann Goering was probably the most intellectual German we every interrogated at the 7th Army headquarters. He was absolutely brilliant—not only academically but technically. This was demonstrated very vividly to our Air Force interrogators and the scientists on our staff who questioned him and found him particularly knowledgeable about jet aircraft and other highly technical subjects. We had him about a week when General "Tooey" Spaatz, who was then Chief of the U.S. Air Forces, called General Patch and said, "Sandy, I hear you've got the 'fat boy' down there, and I'd like you to send him on up here, because I want to talk to him."

General Patch said, "Tooey, this guy is *our* prisoner. If you want to talk to him, come on down here to 7th

Army."

"Now, wait a minute, Sandy. This guy is an Air Force type."

Sandy responded, "Listen, his knowledge is not limited just to Air Force matters; so if you want to see him, he's here, and we'll make him available." So General Spaatz, General Hoyt Vandenberg, and a couple of staff officers and civilian technicians came to Augsburg.

Major Kubala, head of my interrogation unit, set up a little briefing room in one of the local schools on the premises. General Patch, myself, my executive officer Colonel Perry, and Major Kubala were in attendance.

The Reich Marshal was brought in and stood by the teacher's desk. Major Kubala stood beside him. Generals Spaatz and Vandenberg and the others began to drill him with questions. He handled them just as neatly as a surgeon and answered every one of them in a technical and brilliant fashion. Finally, Tooey Spaatz said, "Marshal, could we have won the war by bombing alone?"

Goering said, *"Nein."*

This answer was published in an article I wrote after the war for *American Mercury Magazine*, which follows:

Reich Marshal Herman Goering is dead and probably forgotten by many. I have not forgotten him, however, nor have I forgotten that day in May, 1945 when he astounded some very important people with his keen intellect and his unusual analysis of the Nazi defeat.

Goering had surrendered to our forces earlier in the month and was being questioned by our officers in the U.S. Seventh Army. General Spaatz, who then commanded the American Air Forces in Europe, on learning of Goering's status, requested us to fly him to London for interrogation.

We moved into a rather new and modern school building which served as the headquarters for the enclosure. We went upstairs to the principal's office, which was very well lighted and furnished with relatively new and modernistic furniture. We all took seats in a semicircle in front of an enormous desk which was almost black in color and bare on top except for a small, revolving globe of the world.

I had told the Reich Marshal of the impending visit of General Spaatz. He seemed delighted and I believe a little flattered that General Spaatz was interested in talking to him. He told me he would enjoy the visit as he was sure they had a lot in common.

It was interesting to watch Goering when he was ushered in and placed behind the big desk. One could assume that the maker of the desk must have had Goering in mind when he built it, for they went together like a picture and its frame. Goering bowed slightly in greeting and, upon the interpreter's instructions, sat down at the desk. He had on his favorite blue-gray uniform with heavy gold braid trimmings but without ribbons or medals.

Before the conversation began, Goering made a short salutatory statement to General Spaatz. He was very complimentary and said that he was extremely glad to be able to see and to talk to General Spaatz face to face as he held him in great esteem as an airman. However, he added that he wished the circumstances were just a little different and that he were not the vanquished. General Spaatz smiled at this and the conversations began.

General Spaatz started with questions about the "Battle of Britain," the technique and tactics of the air fight over the British Isles, i.e., Luftwaffe offensive tactics and the Allied defensive mechanisms. By Goering's dissertation on this comprehensive subject it soon became apparent to the whole party that his technical knowledge regarding aerodynamics, meteriology, and jet propulsion was amazing. Not only was he a strategist but he had a tremendous amount of basic knowledge of aircraft and the techniques involved in their employment; so much so that General Spaatz on several occasions turned to his advisors and looked at them quizzically. Without exception they nodded back affirmatively, indicating that they agreed with the particular observation or the statement involved.

Goering also gave quite a discourse on the B-25 and its role in the Allied air counter-offensive. He admitted that he was completely fooled and surprised by its extensive use. He went on to say that it was not the existence of the B-25 that came as a surprise but the fact that he had grossly underestimated the industrial potential of the U.S. to produce it in such numbers and to introduce it in combat with such speed and devastating effect.

This conversation continued for some time until finally General Spaatz said, "Now, Reich Marshal, I am going to ask you what we call in America the '64 dollar question.' I want to ask you: Could we have defeated Germany by strategic bombardment alone and don't you consider, from an airman's point of view, that the Normandy invasion was unnecessary?"

I remember the knowing smile that flashed across Goering's face when he answered, quite dramatically, *"Nein!"* (No!) I also remember General "Sandy" Patch's chuckle when he turned to General Spaatz and said, "Tooey, you asked for it and you sure got it."

General Spaatz countered with another question: "If you do not believe that we could have defeated you by strategic air and that we had to invade the Continent, will you please explain to me your reasoning?"

Goering slowly rose from the chair as the principal might have done when posed with a tough question from one of his students. He glanced out of the window and turned slowly back to General Spaatz. As he gave the globe a slow turn with his finger he answered, "I'll try."

"I'll try to show you precisely those reasons," he continued. "First you must understand this: that in the history of warfare there has never yet been an offensive weapon that has not been countered by a defensive one. Swords developed the shield, the submarine developed the destroyer, the bomber the interceptor, and so forth. Of course, offensive weapons destroy when the defensive ones are absent, but my premise is that defensive weapons or techniques have kept only a short step behind offensive weapons. Naturally, such evolution is based on a standpoint of sheer military necessity.

"For example, when the B-25, and then later Lancasters and B-17's, were giving us a going-over, we began to go underground. I might interject at this point, that if we had started at the outset to go underground, your B-25's would not have hurt us seriously nor would have your heavy bombers. However, we made great progress in our passive defense program, particularly with our industrial tools, other critical and strategic products and supplies, as well as the jet. And I tell you this, Herr General, if we had had one more year, at the rate at which we were rapidly building our jets under shelter and unmolested by your strategic aircraft, we would have driven you from the air. And since your people have captured and inspected our jets, I am sure you can have little doubt.

"Consequently, if there had been no invasion, if the Allied infantry had not stormed the beaches of Normandy when it did, we would not have been defeated from the West. There would have been no decision in the West.

"Now the reason that the invasion led to our defeat was the fact that it caused the clock to run twice as fast from a standpoint of time available to us. In other words, when the invasion came, our position became doubly worse, for besides running out of time, we were now confronted with loss of space.

"You see, we began to lose ground when we were unable to eject you from Normandy. The main reason was General Vandenberg's Ninth Air Force, I might add. This support was mainly responsible for the fact, and I believe Field Marshal Von Rundstedt agrees with me, that we could not shift our reserves to the beaches in time to throw you back into the sea. However, that was a part of the invasion. Yours was a concentrated air effort, in that it was completely localized and thereby you employed en masse the great power that you had. But that is beside the point. My point is that when we lost ground and continued to lose ground, there was entailed a loss of subsidiary plants, small-parts factories, civilian labor, and small component construction. Either they became a loss or had to be displaced further east. When this displacement took place, there was a simultaneous interruption in production in some particular item. A great number of these factories were dispersed throughout France and their loss retarded our jet production.

"We lost so much ground that eventually we had to take men out of the plants, put rifles in their hands and dispatch them to your front to try to hold back the tide to save this space and gain more time. And as we lost the men in the plants, our production decreased, so that our dispatch of a jet for combat was progressively becoming less frequent.

"Finally we came to the point where the production returns diminished to zero. We were overrun. We lost the war. So in answer to your American '64 dollar question,' Herr General, had you not invaded when you did, we would not be having this conversation today."

When the foregoing article was published, I was chief of the Army section of the Joint U.S. Military Advisory Group to Greece, and General Spaatz was Chief of Staff of the United States Air Force. He took great issue to the article and indicated that it never happened, that Goering didn't say it, etc. Fortunately, before I had sent it to the publisher, I had forwarded it to Major Kubala, who had been the interpreter at the interview, and asked him to "proof" it for me, which he did. He made some changes in my version and indicated that the resulting text was an authentic version of what Goering had said.

General Spaatz was so adamant about it that he asked Lieutenant General Arthur Trudeau, who was then the G-2 of the Army (military intelligence) to persuade me to write a denial of the article. As the article was true and still is, I wrote General Trudeau to tell General Spaatz that I wasn't changing a word in the article because it was the truth and that was what Goering had said. That was that. I never heard any more about it, and it went away like all things do.

Generalfeldmarschall Hermann GÖRING
erhält vom FÜHRER
die höchste Kriegsauszeichnung

Adolf Hitler (left) and Hermann Goering

31

HERMANN GOERING STOPS THE PRESS

At 1500 hours on the 11th of May, 1945, the cream of the Allied press was assembled. They came from all over Europe. Most came to interview and photograph, but some to badger the great Reich Marshal Hermann Goering, pride of the German Air Force. Only a few days before, he had surrendered to the United States 7th Army. Now he was to face 63 eager war correspondents and cameramen in his first contact with the Allied press since the beginning of the war. There were many who believed that Goering would not be able to withstand the intense questioning. They were to be disappointed, however, for he held the pack at bay like a master swordsman.

The scene was a garden in Augsburg, Germany. The correspondants were seated in a semi-circle facing a large arm chair which had been placed under a shady tree. Goering appeared with his guard and interpreter, Major Paul Kubala. Goering was wearing his usual blue-grey uniform, *sans* decoration. He was seated in the chair under the tree, ready for the interview to begin.

The press conference was actually held in my billet in Augsburg. It was a nice villa which had a good-sized lawn and garden and a large patio. Consequently, it could take care of all the cameramen and correspondents comfortably. Leading to the patio was the living room, and one could walk from the living room out onto the patio and then onto the lawn. In moving from the living room to the patio, one went through double French doors which were covered with curtains made of a silky, thin material, which allowed one to see outside without being seen on the inside. Just prior to the interview, Goering was driven from the compound where he was incarcerated to the villa and turned over to me in the living room. We walked over to the French doors and looked out.

As I had sat in on the interrogation of Hermann Goering for a week, practically every night—with General Patch or the interpreter—the Reich Marshal and I had developed some kind of a rapport. I thought he was a brilliant man. Based on that familiarity, we were at ease with each other.

Before this particular occasion, I had never heard him utter a word of English. I had heard, however, that back in the early days in Berlin he had spoken in English. I also knew through interrogations that he understood English. When he was being interrogated, he would say to the interpreter, after being questioned in English by General Patch, "I understand it, General." But he always responded in German. So, as I said, I had never heard him speak a word of English until this precise moment. I was therefore surprised as we were standing there looking through the French doors at the cameras being set up, the correspondents being seated and the hustle and bustle out there, when he said to me, in English, "Colonel, you will learn a lesson today about the press, particularly as it relates to utter lack of respect for confidentiality. Let me just pick out some of the people in the front row whom I know. Now, the girl in the red hat, I wager that before the war, we scrambled a hundred eggs or more in my apartment in Berlin at wee hours of the morning after parties many, many times. On several occasions, I confided in her of my trials and tribulations with the Fuehrer and several other topics which are very sensitive. Now, Colonel, I'd like you to listen to her questions, they will entail a violation of my trust in her. Now, there's Tom Jones of Y magazine in the center with a scarf around his neck. Next to him is Bill Wilson, Bureau Chief of Z Paper, and they'll hit me where they think I'm tender."

When the interview started, all who wished to ask questions raised their hands, and Major Kubala would pick the correspondent. When certain sensitive questions were posed, Goering several times turned to look at me standing nearby. He shrugged his shoulders and gave me an I-told-you-so look.

Here follows the full interview:

PRESS CONFERENCE AND INTERVIEW
WITH REICH MARSHAL GOERING

1500 Hours 11 May 1945

Q: Can the Reich Marshal give us a complete story on the Hess escape?

A: The flight of Hess was a complete surprise to everyone in Germany. I believe there were only about three people in Germany who know why Hess left and what he intended to do.

Q: Who were they?

A: It would be people who were very close to Hess.

Q: *While in Paris in 1940, the Reich Marshal was supposed to have stated, "On to England." Is this true?*

A: The Reich Marshal denies making any such statement and says he remembers well what he said. He explained that such a statement was impossible because they did not have sufficient air power to substantiate the making of any such statement.

Q: *Was the invasion of England ordered?*

A: It was in preparation but never ordered.

Q: *Was the start ever made?*

A: No, it was never made. Forces were not sufficient at that time.

Q: *What was the strength of German's air force at the beginning of the war in 1939?*

A: I believe it was the most powerful air force in the world at that time.

Q: *About how many aircraft?*

A: That has been approximately six years ago and I am not prepared to answer this question. I could not tell you how many planes there were available, but at that time Germany had four air fleets.

Q: *Do you believe Hitler is dead?*

A: I am completely satisfied that Hitler is dead.

Q: *How do you believe he died?*

A: He was a very sick man and I heard that there was something wrong. I also heard he had killed himself.

Q: *When did you last speak to him?*

A: On 20 April 1945.

Q: *Where?*

A: As I said goodbye to depart to the southern German boundary. Hitler was at that time in Berlin and intended to go down to Berchtesgaden that day.

Q: *Why did Hitler change his mind and stay in Berlin rather than go to Berchtesgaden?*

A: On 22 April certain things happened which convinced Hitler that the war had been lost and it was useless to continue in the southern area.

Q: *What area do you mean?*

A: The southern "Redoubt" area. Hitler realized then for the first time that the war was lost.

Q: *Who were the people who might have suggested to Hitler that the war was lost?*

A: His closest military associates were Jodl, Chief of the Chancellery, and other party members.

Q: *Why have they not found Hitler's body?*

A: The Reich Marshal believes that Hitler has been dead much longer than has been admitted and has been disposed of in such a manner that the body will not fall into the hands of the Russians.

Q: *When you began the large air attack against England, was that in preparation for an invasion? What did it have to do with strategic bombing?*

A: It is the chief order of an operative Air Corps to destroy the enemy's air forces and then the installations in order to have your forces free for other attacks.

Q: *Did you order Coventry bombed?*

A: I ordered it because Coventry was an industrial center and it had been reported to me that it was also a center of large aircraft production. I had heard that three large aircraft factories were located there.

Q: What about Canterbury?

A: Canterbury was bombed by orders from higher head-quarters for revenge because of the bombing of a university city in Germany.

Q: What city?

A: I do not remember.

Q: You had at the end of the war many aircraft; why were they not used?

A: Because of three things: (1) shortage of gasoline; (2) could not train any more pilots; (3) bases from which to operate were too badly damaged.

Q: Were the autobahns used as air strips because of the shortage of gasoline, or was it because of the attack upon German established airports by the Allies?

A: Its use as an airport had nothing to do with the consumption of gasoline. The autobahns were used as they provided longer air strips for jet-propelled planes and were consequently used for that purpose.

Q: How long has the Reich Marshall been familiar with the basic strategy of the American air offensive and its planes?

A: Very well acquainted with the strategical planes of the Americans; also well acquainted with their ability to construct planes with the exception of one: the long-range fighter bomber, which came as a complete surprise. The biggest surprise of the war was the ability of the American pilots to fly fighter bombers from England to Berlin.

Q: How about the German control of the air in Russia?

A: Never has Germany's Air Corps lost control of the air in Russia, except of course where there was no Air Corps operating. Otherwise, we have always had control of the air in Russia.

Q: When did you realize the war was lost, or when do you think it was lost?

A: Very shortly after the invasion and when the Russians made the breakthrough in the German defense. From that time things began to look bad and soon became so bad that we realized the war *could be* lost, but always had hope that we could come out from under.

Q: Who controlled the V-bombs?

A: The V-1 was completely under the control of the Air Corps, but the V-2 was not, being under control of a different organization. The two were subsequently placed under one control. The V-1 was invented by a German scientist and after the tests proved successful, was adopted by the German High Command. The V-2 was a complete surprise to me.

Q: Did anyone tell you the war was lost?

A: Yes.

Q: What contributed mostly to the loss of the war?

A: The uninterrupted air offensive of the Western front, in conjunction with the invasion of Normandy.

Q: Who told Hitler that the war was lost and what were his reactions?

A: Several military people pointed out to Hitler that the war *could* be lost from a military point of view. Hitler's reactions were absolutely negative and later talk about this matter was prohibited.

Q: Who prohibited it?

A: Hitler himself did. Hitler refused to accept this point of view.

Q: When was it prohibited?

A: When the people first began to talk about it, about the middle of 1944. In the later years the party became more and more under the power and influence of Bormann. It came more and more to the point of Bormann telling Hitler what to do.

Q: What role did Himmler play in this affair?

A: Himmler carried out the orders which were given to him. He, too, realized in the latter months that the orders given him could not be carried out, as it was then too late. Himmler was Minister of Home Defense and Bormann was the Secretary of the Party. There was always a conflict between the two.

Q: Do you believe Doenitz was appointed Fuehrer by Hitler?

A: *No.* (Emphatically.) The telegram appointing him Fuehrer carried on the bottom the signature of Bormann. There is nothing in writing that states that he was ever appointed as Fuehrer of Germany.

Q: Why did such a colorless personality like Bormann become such a powerful force behind Hitler?

A: He was behind Hitler day and night and thereby brought his will upon him and got to where he could rule Hitler's life.

Q: Who made the decision for the Russian campaign and why the defense at Stalingrad?

A: The war against Russia was ordered by Hitler himself. He was convinced that Russia was about to declare war on Germany, as Russia had also made war on Poland. I pointed out to Hitler the statement in his own book, *Mein Kampf*, which brought out the danger of a two-front war. I was convinced that Russia would not attack during that year, although Russia had attacked Finland. Hitler believed that he would soon have Russia on her knees and would then be able to finish the war against Russia with very small forces.

Q: *Did Hitler have any plans against America?*

A: Hitler tried from every point of view to keep America out of the war. I pointed out to him that never again should America enter into a second conflict. Hitler believed that because of the bad experience America had after the last war, she would never enter another World War.

Q: *Was Germany surprised when America entered the war?*

A: It was a complete surprise.

Q: *What was the cause of the failure of the German Air Force?*

A: It was a mechanical failure which kept them from manufacturing bombers equal to those of the Americans.

Q: *What firms were making the German heavy bombers?*

A: Hienkel was making the 177, and Messerschmidt was constructing the 264. If the war had lasted a little longer, this plane would have come as a complete surprise to the United States.

Q: *Has Hitler expressed any regrets about conditions in the concentration camps?*

A: If he had any regrets about matters that happened at concentration camps, I am unable to state because I was never that close to Hitler and do not know, as he never expressed himself to me—after the break-through of the Germans into Russia, I have knowledge that there were a million workers who came on their own free will westward to work in Germany. They were paid the normal wages that were paid workers of their particular skill.

Q: *Have you ever ordered the handcuffing of British prisoners of war?*

A: No. A number of our own people were held in English custody. Also, I am against handcuffing prisoners.

Q: *Who was responsible in the early part of 1944 for urging the Germans to lynch American pilots who were forced down?*

A: There was in Germany of course, much bitterness among the public against the low-flying aircraft. I had issued instructions that all American pilots would be turned over for questioning.

Q: *Give details of your quarrel with and arrest by Hitler.*

A: After Hitler's declaration on the 22nd (April) that the war was lost, he saw that the situation was hopeless and that he would remain in Berlin. I reminded Hitler that because of my position as second-in-command, I would take the Fuehrer's place if anything happened to him. I told him that I would take immediate steps to go into consultation with the Allied powers. Hitler was raging mad, and three hours later the SS troops placed me and my family under arrest in Berchtesgaden. Two days later they carried us to a small village in the Alps. The following day an order came from

Hitler condemning me to death.

Q: *What future did you expect for Germany?*

A: No matter what the outcome, the people of Germany will have to live. If no ways and means are found for the German people, I see a very black future for Germany and the entire world. I am no prophet and cannot tell what will happen in the world. Although everyone wants peace, it is hard to see just what will happen.

Q: *Did Hitler order the SS to the concentration camps?*

A: Hitler was personally responsible for orders at the concentration camps, and all people who had anything to do with these camps were directly responsible to Hitler. State organization had nothing to do with what went on in the camps.

Q: *What did he hope to gain by these concentration camps?*

A: Hitler never discussed these matters with me and talked only to those who were directly responsible for the camps.

Q: *Give details of the Reichstag fire—did you set it on fire?*

A: I can assure you I did not set the Reichstag on fire as I had very good use for it.

Q: *Who did set it on fire?*

A: I do not know but believe that the one who actually did set the Reichstag on fire had nothing to do with the party. That same night the Communists were primed for another uprising. The arrests of the Communists were absolutely separate from the fire and had nothing to do with it.

Q: *Why was the attempt to destroy the British air fields*

called off in 1940?

A: The correspondent is in error when he says 1940, as the end came in 1941 (The question was not answered further.)

Q: *Does the Reich Marshal have anything he wants to get off his chest?*

A: I have nothing else to say, but that I wish you to understand that I want Germany to be helped and I am very thankful to the German people who have stood by their guns during the past six years, even though they knew that the end was hopeless.

The press conference and interview came to a close at 1545. After the 50 minutes of the interrogation interview were up, I walked Goering back to the living room. I heard a correspondent in back of me saying, "Hell, they didn't lay a glove on him!"

32

HOW HITLER MURDERED ROMMEL

NOTE: This chapter is a verbatim report to 7th Army Head-quarters on April 29, 1945. It was written by Captain Charles Marshall of the VI Corps Headquarters, a unit in the 7th Army command. Here follows his report:

With the capture on Friday by the First French Army of Manfred Rommel, 16-year-old son of Field Marshal Erwin Rommel, Germany's most brilliant tactician of World War II, the story of who and why Hitler murdered Rommel can be told. The authority for the story is none less than the late Field Marshal's widow, Frau Lucie Maria Rommel.

On Wednesday April 25th Sgt. Thomas S. Greiner of New York accompanied me and assisted me in the inter-rogation of Mrs. Rommel in her villa at Herrlingen, sub-urb of Ulm. The following day I sent him back to return various documents we had taken which proved upon in-spection to have no military interest. All Rommel's offi-cial files had been removed to Berlin by the German High

Command immediately after his death.

In the conversation which developed on Sgt. Greiner's return, Mrs. Rommel compared the clothing and equipment of our Army with that of the German forces. She declared their inferiority made the war only a hopeless undertaking for the Nazis. Referring to the Russian campaign, she stated that the entire German High Command had advised against it and most vehemently Colonel General Halder who conducted the operations, "But soldiers," she said, "must obey orders."

At this point Sgt. Greiner turned the conversation to Field Marshal Rommel and the failure of his Normandy defense.

"My husband wrote a personal report to the Fuehrer," she said, "just the day before he was wounded by one of your fighter-bombers. In this report he bluntly stated that as commander of the forces opposing the Allied invasion, he felt it his duty to inform the Fuehrer that the overwhelming enemy superiority in air, armor and other material made further attempt at resistance futile. He urged Hitler to halt further bloodshed and destruction and initiate negotiations with the enemy immediately."

"What was Hitler's reaction?" asked Sgt. Greiner.

Frau Rommel trembled. There was terror in her eyes. Her son was still in Nazi hands. Would he give her his word of honor that he would tell no one until she knew that her son was either safe or dead?

"My husband did not die from a heart attack as the German press reported and as I told you yesterday," she sobbed. "Those who saw him know it. He was recovering from his wounds and his heart was all right. *He was murdered!* He was poisoned! Right here in this room. Now you know it."

"Because of that report?" asked Greiner, when he

could get his breath.

"That and something else too. You are familiar with the details of the attempt on the Fuehrer's life. My husband knew nothing about it, I am sure, but the conspirators decided he would be the best man to negotiate with the enemy. They knew my husband's opinion was that the war would end in total disaster for Germany should it continue, and they also knew that he was highly respected abroad. So they chose him and it leaked out."

"But how could they poison the Field Marshal in his own house?" asked Greiner.

Mrs. Rommel laughed bitterly. "They were after him ever since he returned wounded. They did not want to let him out of France. He had to use every influence he had. But the moment he arrived home here he was guarded and watched by the Security Police. He did not dare go out by himself, because he was sure that a "stray" bullet would hit him.

"Then they sent him a message to report to Berlin for a new assignment. Which was ridiculous, my husband could not travel; the surgeon forbade it. And what new assignment could they have had for him? No, I tell you, as sure as I am sitting here his train would have been blown up on the way. 'Victim of terror-bomber attack,' they would have said."

"What happened then?" Greiner asked.

"Well, when they saw that wouldn't work either, they had to resort to a cruder method. They sent two generals from the War Department to see him. One was General Maisel and the other General Bergdorf. My husband had not known them before. They arrived here on October 14th and were alone with my husband for half an hour. When they left, he called me in. He sat right here, in this chair, and bade me good bye. He told me he was going to die now. Fifteen minutes later he still sat there, but he was dead and his lips were drawn downward in a smile of contempt."

"But how were they able to get him to take the poison," said Greiner, "If he had not wanted to? They didn't apply force, did they?"

"No," explained Frau Rommel, "they didn't have to. They knew him too well. They knew he would obey the order. He was a soldier and all through his life he had trained himself to carry out orders without question. That is why he carried out the last order given him.

"But you see, up to the last minute he believed in the Fuehrer. He was sure that the Fuehrer personally did not know about it. And for a while I believed that too. But now I find it harder and harder to believe. No, I am certain now that Hitler issued the order personally. And to think that every evening, for years and years, I prayed for the welfare of that man—the murderer of my husband!"

Sgt. Grainer asked her if she believed other generals of the German Army would have been as obedient.

"What choice have they?" responded Frau Rommel, "Do you think von Rundstedt wanted to launch the Ardennes offensive? Do you think he did not know that he could not succeed and would only sacrifice thousands of lives in vain? He knew it very well. But his orders were to attack then and there. And he did his utmost to do the job as well as possible.

"I know that Colonel General Halder opposed the Russian campaign and so did Field Marshal List. Yet they had to do their jobs and they did them as well as they could. Halder is in jail now because they suspect he was involved in the July 20th plot.

"Do you think Field Marshal von Witzleben, who devoted his entire life to serving his country, is a coward and a traitor? Don't you think that a man like that thought a thousand times before he resorted to that desperate measure in an attempt to save his country from utter ruin? And then what? Convicted by a 'people's court' and hanged like a dog.

"If the Nazis cannot get the individual they will take his family. Take Field Marshal von Paulus. No man could be more honorable. I knew his wife and family well. They are all imprisoned now. Or how about the Commander at Koenigsberg? Do you think he would have surrendered had he seen a way out? Imagine the responsibility. Thousands of civilians in the city and all half-starved. And when he finally surrenders his family is thrown into prison like criminals.

"Now you must understand why I cannot talk freely. My son is in their hands and they keep an eye on him. They must be aware of the fact that I know how my husband died, that I know Hitler killed him."

33

JEAN BELIARD AND THE SIGABA

In connection with the invasion of Southern France and subsequent operations there and in Germany, the French Army B, commanded by General de Lattre de Tassigny, dispatched a team of French liaison officers to the Headquarters of the Seventh Army. One of the members of that team was Lieutenant Jean Beliard. Lt. Beliard was a very sharp intelligence officer. He served well, but on one particular occasion rendered the United States Army and Allied Forces a great service.

It so happened that near "Colmar Pocket" the 28th Division found it necessary to move its headquarters. In the move, the signal company of the division headquarters was responsible for moving and operating the division *sigaba*. It was at night when the move took place, and a two and a half ton truck filled with communications equipment was under the control of a driver and several of the signal corps operators of the *sigaba*. This machine was an encryption and decryption device, the most important piece of equipment that a division had. This item was never issued below a division headquarters because of its sensitivity and the security aspects associated with it. As a matter of fact, the *sigaba* was the main communication system for the United States Armed Forces in Germany in that most messages and all classified messages were sent through this system. On this particular night, the crew responsible for the *sigaba*, in moving from one area to the other to establish a new command, pulled into a French tavern and parked the truck outside, and all went in. No one was left to guard the *sigaba* or the other equipment. After they had dinner, they came out, and the truck was gone, along with its contents.

The theft of this truck with the *sigaba* caused an unbelievable degree of concern and anxiety on the part of the entire military forces establishment, to include General Eisenhower's Headquarters, for if the *sigaba* were in the hands of the Germans, it would entail a complete compromise of all communications that the Americans had.

As no one had any idea who stole the truck and equipment, I had a gut feeling that it was not captured by Germans but stolen by French troops who were also in our area, and who had a reputation for finding "lost items." I called in Lt. Beliard and told him what had happened. I said, "I would like you, if you will, to leave the headquarters, disguise yourself in any way, shape, or form, but find the *sigaba*."

We knew precisely where the truck was stolen in Selestat; so Beliard took off from that point. After a day or so, he found the truck because of its markings, in a French organization—but it was empty. Then he had to find the people who stole the truck, and he eventually found one of the soldiers responsible. It seems that two young French soldiers had been ordered by their commander to go find some wood for the camp stove. Now, these soldiers had no way to transport wood, even if they found some, so they "borrowed" the truck in question without having any idea what was in it. On the way to their camp or billet, they crossed a small river, Le Bruche, stopped on the bridge, and unloaded the truck by throwing everything, including the *sigaba*, into the water. Upon learning of its location, Beliard, with the help of a special detail from Seventh Army Headquarters, went into the river and pulled it out. The other equipment was later found ditched in the same river.

The relief was so great at this particular effort on Beliard's part that General Patch awarded the Bronze Star for his service, and General Patch personally commended him for doing an unbelievable piece of detective work and thus saving the sanity and career of the division commander.

Later on, after the war, I saw Jean at the French Embassy in Washington in connection with a visit of President de Gaulle to the United States. As I came through the line, Beliard, who was in back of the President, held me up and told de Gaulle something in French. Then de Gaulle shook my hand as if he were priming a pump.

Besides being an aide to President de Gaulle, Beliard went on up in the diplomatic service, and his last three assignments before his retirement in 1985 were as French Ambassador to Mexico, Brazil, and finally, Ambassador to Canada.

34

DACHAU

During the planning stages for the invasion of Southern France, intelligence relating to Dachau came to our attention, but we had no real concept of what went on inside the camp. I then took a special interest in Dachau and interrogated my German and Polish prisoners about the camp as well as the order of battle of the German forces.

When we were about to take Dachau, I sent instructions to the intelligence units that as soon as it was liberated, or about to be liberated, to please let me know through channels. On the eve of April the 29th, I received word that Dachau had been liberated, that is, the prisoners, and that the camp was under the control of the International Prison Commission. I think it was headed by a British major named O'Leary, if I'm not mistaken. When I received this information, I decided I would be there early the next morning.

I proceeded to Dachau with some of my officers in the Seventh Army, including our prisoner-of-war chief, Major Kubala. I had a representative of the OSS, the Office of the Strategic Services, which was headed by General "Wild Bill" Donovan. And I also had a group from my

counter-intelligence corps division that was operating under my jurisdiction as G-2 of the Seventh Army.

Our findings were published during the spring of 1945
in a compilation entitled *Dachau*. I published this because
I felt that this thing had to be documented, that the
world, or the future, should have something that was the
truth, and truth *then*, and not necessarily something that I
would write about in later life.

The forward, which I wrote in May of 1945, is as
follows:

> Dachau (1933 – 1945) will stand for all time as one of
> history's most gruesome symbols of inhumanity. There our
> troops found sights, sounds, and stenches horrible beyond
> belief—cruelties so enormous as to be incomprehensible to
> the normal mind. Dachau and Death were synonymous. No
> words or pictures can carry the full impact of these unbe-
> lievable scenes. But this report presents some outstanding
> facts and photographs in order to emphasize the type of
> crime which elements of the SS committed thousands of
> times a day, to remind us of the ghastly capabilites of cer-
> tain classes of men, to strengthen our determination that
> they and their works shall vanish from this earth.

At Dachau the only objective of the inmates was to
survive under the most primitive and cruel conditions
which constantly threatened their sanity and physical existence. Little more than this was humanly possible. As a
result of these abnormal conditions, this camp of thirty
thousand men cannot be compared to the structure of
any normal society, differentiated, that is, by social
classes, political, religious, or professional affiliations.
Hence, neither normal moral standards, nor normal political or sociological criteria are applicable to the Dachau
situation.

When I arrived at Dachau, I came in a jeep with others, and I came through the main gate. The main gate had a sign on it that work will free one—*Arbeit macht frei.* There was an MP there. There were bodies all around. The SS guards who had been shot were still lying by the towers and wherever they had fallen; some of the inmates had been killed by their fellow inmates for their cruelty and cooperation with the S.S.

And so, everything was status quo as it happened; so I saw it first hand very early in the morning following the night it was captured. The sight that probably impressed me more than anything else was the box cars and flat cars. I think there were thirty-five or forty of them, loaded with human bodies, and most of them Jews at this particular point in time. As I walked past, I could see inside the box-cars, nothing but naked human bodies.

As to the gas chamber—this was a very clever system that they had, in which they would herd the ones that were alive (and this was one of their basic systems of ex-termination), bring them into this place near the crematorium (I think it was even next door or adjacent), and hand these prisoners a towel and a bar of soap and tell them to walk in that room labeled "showers." Well, there were shower heads in there. The shower heads were on the ceiling, not on the wall like a normal shower room. But no water came out, just gas. Within ten minutes they could kill up to five hundred people. Then they were put into the crematorium where they were shoved, several bodies at a time, into the furnaces where they were cremated. I don't know how many or what the capacity was, but it was enormous. And then, of course, when it got so big and so many people, they had the inmates dig ditches, and they were murdered and thrown in the ditches, and were piled up. There's a marker, I believe it says ten thousand lay there.

Dachau and death were synonymous.
The cleanup is underway.

There was a controversy in March of 1981, where the assertion was made that Dachau did not have a gas chamber and did not murder people intentionally. However, I saw the showers the morning after the camp was liberated, and if the space was used for storage of bodies, as claimed, I doubt it would be that clean. My estimation is that the showers had been used for gassing very recently.

Of the approximately 32,000 inmates, the number of Jews in the camp on liberation was 2,539, including 225 women. The prisoner of war section of my entourage questioned some of the inmates, and their testimonies were published with our other findings. Some of the other evidence our men were able to discover was the fact that 25,000 Jews were murdered at Dachau, both by gassing and by being shot in the back of the head.

Our intelligence work at Dachau was done on the spot, and it was done within one week, roughly, maybe two weeks of interrogation. I'm not sure how long it took. There are no dates, you see, and I didn't date it as to when it was published. I probably should have. I published this in early June, or maybe late May, because I left Seventh Army with General Patch to go to the Pacific on the tenth of June. He was ordered to take an Army, but it didn't materialize because of the atomic bomb. I took a stack of the published documents with me; so it had to be done around the first of June or maybe earlier. I issued the study to the Seventh Army troops. This was not for circulation to the press. The press got copies of it because it was in the pressroom. I sent it to corps and divisions for distribution to whomever they wished, and that's how it got down in the hands of some of the troops, because it didn't come back to the states. I sent copies to all the other G2's who were investigating other concentration camps, so they could see what the Seventh Army found at Dachau.

35

RUSSIANS CAN'T WRASSLE

According to the roster I have saved, in the prisoner of war camp the 7th Army operated in Augsberg, Germany, on the 2nd of June 1945 we had, besides 100,000 or more ordinary prisoners of the Wehrmacht and SS, 618 special prisoners. There were 200 generals and admirals, to include the SS. We had a special prisoner named Heinz Gundermann; we had Reinhardt Galen who recently wrote a book, *The Service*; we had Heusinger who was the Chief of Operations of OKW (the German Army HQ); and among the few marshals besides Goering, we had von Rundstedt, Kesselring from Italy, and von Weicht of the Balkans. We had another man named Schoerner.

Field Marshal Schoerner was in command of a German Army Group made up of armies facing the Russians. On the very day of the surrender to the Allied Forces by Admiral Doenitz, Schoerner ordered all of the German Armies under his command to attack the Soviet forces on the eastern front. The unnecessary attack was launched with great losses to both German and Russian forces. After issuing his order, Schoerner got in a light airplane and flew to a small field in Bavaria, south of Munich. He discarded his uniform and dressed himself as an Alpine farmer with lederhosen, socks, an Alpine cap, a walking stick and a knapsack. He apparently was on his way to Switzerland as a refugee.

The reason we had all of these high ranking prisoners was due to Switzerland. The Nazis had developed an outline plan of what they called the "Redoubt," where they were going to make their final stand in the Bavarian Alps, against any contingency or serious military setback. Then, should they not be able to hold there, they would eventually pass over into Switzerland and make their way as best they could. They never had an opportunity to put their plan into effect. Consequently, this concentration of senior government and military personnel were found there.

But back to Schoerner. He was walking down the highway on the way to Switzerland presumably, when, believe it or not, an American agent of the OSS, who was behind the lines as a truck driver, spotted him and recognized him even though he wasn't in uniform. He'd remembered Schoerner's description at some intelligence training school. He pulled up and offered Marshal Schoerner a lift. Then by a circuitous route he doubled back and brought the Marshal into our lines, turned him over to the MP's and said, "Take him up to the 7th Army G-2," which they did. That was me.

At that time we did not know what he had done. Later SCAEF (Supreme Headquarters Allied Expeditionary Forces) alerted us to look out for him. When I notified General Patch that he was our prisoner, he immediately called General Eisenhower and said, "We've got Schoerner. How we got him, I don't know yet, but he's here in our PW camp."

Ike said, "Let me call you back." In about ten minutes he called Patch back and said, "Sandy, the Russians are about to have a fit. They've *got* to have him. They want him real bad! I'll leave it to you to get him to the Russians as soon as possible."

So General Patch called me in and said, "Have you ever been to Moscow?"

"No, General, I haven't."

"Well, you're on your way, son."

"What do you mean, sir?"

"You're going to take Field Marshal Schoerner to Joe Stalin or as far as you can get. It has to be someone in responsible authority."

As a matter of fact, I kept the order that he wrote to American forces everywhere in the 7th Army to give me escort, help, logistics, and everything else I'd need. We planned to take off in a sedan for the Enns River bridge, which was the closest point to Russian forces from our location. On the east side of the river at the bridge, there was a Russian division, and on our side there was an American infantry regiment commanded by a friend of mine, Colonel Bill Carraway.

The next day the Marshal, a Counter Intelligence Corps (CIC) Lieutenant named George Perper from New York (he was the son-in-law of Sol Hurok, the New York theatrical producer) and I took off for Moscow. George had been born in Leningrad and spoke fluent Russian and German. We found a driver who was also a Russian-speaking CIC agent. Both he and George were armed, but I was not. I handcuffed myself to Schoerner, and off we went.

By nightfall we had arrived at Bill Carraway's regimental area and had placed Schoerner in the custody of MP's. Bill had agreed to help me through the first barrier.

So after supper, at about 9 o'clock, we started across the bridge. In the party was Bill, Lt. George Perper, and myself. We were met at the Soviet end by a Russian lieutenant to whom Bill explained my mission. The lieutenant told us we would have to speak to his commanding officer, as he was not authorized to permit anyone to pass. He said his commander was in his quarters and would we be kind enough to accompany him there and, incidentally, to partake of some refreshment while awaiting the results of his commander's inquiry? This turned out to be a big mistake.

We proceeded about 50 yards down a little path to a very small Austrian cottage on the bank of the river. We were ushered through a back door which entered into the pantry area, led past the rustic kitchen and into the bedroom. It was a small room but had two single beds, one in each of the two far corners. Near the entrance to the room was a small square table and three or four straight chairs around it.

We took our seats at the table and shortly thereafter the commanding officer, a major, had his orderly bring in a big jug of vodka and small thick glasses. No time was lost in filling them. Together with the lieutenant, the major snapped to attention, raised his glass, clicked his heels and issued a short but prepared statement, to wit: "Stalin goot, Roosevelt goot, da, da, da, _ _ _." and drained the glass. Following his cue, we recited: "Roosevelt is good, Stalin is good, yes, yes, yes _ _ _." And we were off to the races.

The major asked to be excused while he went to see about supper. We told him we had eaten but he indicated that such good fortune entailed no excuse for a refusal to break black bread with him. He said that he would get one of his men to get some fish from the river and that his wife would bake a pie. When he mentioned his wife I asked him, through my interpreter, if he had just married an Austrian. He said he had not, that his wife had followed him from Russia. They had no children, she worked in supply dumps, hospitals, etc., and that the Soviet women in some units could campfollow provided they created no burden on the army. He brought her in and introduced her. She could best be described as a bouncer in a speakeasy or a cycledrome rider—a rough and tough looking woman. After the introductions she left the room to bake a blackberry pie. We saw her only once again.

Shortly after this introduction a heavy explosion shook the house. We automatically ducked and grabbed our guns. The major nonchalantly came strolling back in, noticed our expressions and announced that we would soon have fish. His orderly's method of fishing, which explained the blast, consisted of throwing out into the river a couple of sticks of dynamite tied to an armed hand grenade. This unique sportsman, taking full advantage of his noisy but effective bait, harvested a good catch.

The major then gave a talk on Austrian trout, which he ended by filling the glasses with vodka again. Everyone to his feet, with clicking heels: "Stalin goot, Roosevelt goot, da, da, da," and down the hatch.

After this second toast I began to worry about the reputation of my native land. Was this to go on (which it did)—and if so, would I falter and let down the red, white and blue? As neither of us was used to this violent form of social activity, our party decided to use the "potted plant" technique. Thereafter by one ruse or another we limited our vodka drinking to token amounts.

In an amazingly short time the major announced the impending service of the fish. I marveled at the speed at which the meal had been prepared even though there had been quite a shortcut in the procurement of the entree. However, I was soon to understand more fully the reason for its rapid preparation. The major's wife had made soup, which consisted of dumping the fish in a big pot of boiling water which included diced potatoes and onions. After the fish were boiled each person was served a large piece of dark brown bread and a bowl which contained a whole fish lazily floating in thin broth. And when I say whole, that's what I mean—uncleaned, head, et al. I remember looking down into the bowl, and with this up-turned, sad and slightly bloodshot eye, my fish was staring me down. That eye haunts me to this day.

As I couldn't quite go the first course, I had to do some fast thinking; so I grabbed the vodka jug, filled the glasses, handed the major one—stood up, and with the "same song, same verse" gave the, "Roosevelt goot, Stalin goot, da, da, da _ _ _." Following this I picked up my bowl and poured its contents into the major's bowl, explaining that that was my way of showing my appreciation for his generosity; that such a delectable dish must necessarily not be consumed by one who had recently partaken of food in the presence of those with hunger; that I must adhere to the custom of my country, no matter how tempted by the food. The major seemed impressed by this strange form of protocol, but apparently for fear of offending me made no protest as a result of this peculiar act.

Although the lieutenant, who had been with us from the beginning, physically participated in the toasts and the conversations, he was much unlike the major.

We got the drift later on when he got "plastered" and began to beat his chest about what a big shot he was. It seems he was the local battalion kommissar, the Communist Party man who constantly watches the troops for signs of disaffection or attitudes not sanctioned by the party. He wields the power of life and death over the members of his unit, in that an adverse report by him on one of the officers or men in his outfit, to include the commander, means liquidation or Siberia.

In came the blackberry pie. It was tart, for it lacked sugar, but it was good.

Just as we finished this hurried supper, in walked a captain from the Soviet division headquarters. He conferred by whispers with the host. It was obvious that we were the subject of conversation. The division officer then asked to see my orders. After my interpreter had read them he rather abruptly informed me that I should bring Schoerner to the Soviet end of the bridge the next morning and I would be relieved of same. I informed him with equal abruptness that such action on my part would not be fulfilling the instructions received by Gen. Eisenhower, nor for that matter, those of the Russian Liaison Group at SHAEF, who had recommended this procedure. I told him that on the following day, therefore, I would return Schoerner to my headquarters and report to the Supreme Commander the lack of cooperation I had received at the hands of this division (the 20th Elite Guards).

He seemed a little shaken by this and asked me to please withhold my decision until he had conferred with his superiors at the division. He left the room to make his call. When he returned he informed me that division was calling the 20th Elite Guards Corps for guidance and that more likely Corps would call the Fourth Guards Army, and it might take a little time. Would I be kind enough to please wait—and in the meantime could we not have a slight libation?

While the recent conversations were ensuing, our host kept giving me encouraging looks and it became apparent that the division officer was not too popular with him and that he was definitely sympathetic with my purpose and general attitude. Just to put all the Russians on an even keel, I suggested to our host that the visitor catch up with us on the vodka. The visitor was thereupon challenged by the host as to his capacity for vodka. The challenge was accepted and within a few minutes our new friend from division had caught up—but good.

It seems that the division captain was quite an athlete. In fact, before the war he had been a member of the All-Red Army soccer team. He was about six feet two, all muscle and built like Bronko Nagurski, but slightly smaller.

As it became apparent that we would have a long wait and the vodka began to take effect, the conference rapidly developed into an impromptu party and vodka toasts became more frequent.

It was during this semi-bedlam that my erstwhile guide, Bill Carraway, pulled the rug out from under me. He had gotten the three Russians to one side out of earshot, and had quietly informed them that I was one of the world's greatest athletes. He explained that I was an All-American football player, U.S. weight-lifting champion, and the American amateur wrestling champion.

I asked Bill later why he did this to me. He said that it appeared to him to be a good idea at the time, and that he was tired of their bragging.

After this fabrication, a sudden silence prevailed. I was then suddenly besieged by questions concerning wrestling and weight lifting. How does one play football and is it as rough as soccer? Feeling very flattered and obviously the center of attention, I began to do a little chest raising myself. These Russians weren't going to out-brag anybody from the good old USA. Anything for my country.

I was becoming completely mystified by the developments, and I looked once again to Carraway for guidance. He was doubled up with laughter and having the time of his life. George Perper knew what was going on but he too was enjoying the situation.

Before I describe the next series of events; I must state that the Russians at this point were far from sober and the only wrestling I had ever done was at West Point.

Still no word from the Russian higher headquarters. It was then about 1:00 A.M. when the bleary-eyed lieutenant, the Party boy, got to his feet and proposed another toast. After he drank his vodka, part of which poured down his tunic, he staggered back to his box and flopped down.

The host suddenly approached me, saluted and requested that I do him a great honor. I agreed. He then made the disturbing request that I wrestle with him. I was stalling for an out when the lieutenant came lurching off his box and told the major that if anybody was going to wrestle the American champion, he was the one that would have the honor. He cited his Communist Party authority. The major gave way.

With my fingers crossed, I told the lieutenant that I was extremely flattered by his request but that I had not come to wrestle but to perform a military duty. It didn't work.

After he downed another drink the lieutenant squared off, took a crouching stance and came toward me. He meant business. I had no alternative but to grab his right wrist and twist him around with his back towards me. As he was light, I picked him off the floor and threw him out in the middle of the room. He landed flat on his back, his head hit the floor and he was out. I rolled him under one of the beds and went back to the table.

The host then made noises I didn't like. He reminded me that it was his turn. The major started marching towards me in a crouch.

This guy was no pushover. He was as hard as nails. I didn't know what to do. I suddenly remembered something I'd seen in a wrestling match in Providence. I locked my hands together and dropped them ape-like near the floor, stepped towards him and swung my hands up and hit him in the throat. He let out a gurgle and put both his hands to his neck. In short order he was on his back for a fall. I then rolled him under the other bed.

On my way back to the table I was accosted by the soccer player, who had been watching the whole procedure through bloodshot and glassy eyes.

Well, here he came. I decided to use the thing I know best, a shoulder block I learned in football. I dived at him, my right shoulder catching him in the pit of the stomach, and down we crashed on the side of one of the beds and then to the floor, and I managed to get his shoulders pinned to the floor. At that moment we were interrupted by the host's wife, who shouted to the reclining wrestler that his headquarters wanted him on the phone. He seemed to sober up immediately and left the room.

The Captain returned in a few minutes, and announced that my request to proceed had been approved. He further announced in a more friendly vein that as a result of the evening's activities he felt compelled to confer upon me the Guards Army Medal, presented only to the defenders of Stalingrad and to those individuals demonstrating like courage and fortitude. Whereupon he took a medal out of his pocket, punched a hole in my Ike jacket and pinned it on. Following this, he wrote a citation and presented it to me.

Facsimile of Russian citation

Although I eventually turned the Field Marshal over to the 20th Guards Corps, it was with some degree of disappointment. I returned to Seventh Army headquarters and proceeded immediately to report to Gen. Patch. When I limped into his office, torn and battered like a torpedo ship listing into port, I was forced to salute him with my left hand. When I related my experiences, he practically had convulsions. After he had quieted down he asked me seriously, "What about these Russians? What did you learn about them?" I gave him my findings in one sentence:

"Russians can't wrassle, General, and I got a medal to prove it!"

36

VENGEANCE IS MARIE'S

As a result of the German offensive NORTHWIND (see Chapter Twenty-Five), conducted against the 7th U.S. Army, during the period January 1–27, 1945, their forces made several penetrations in Alsace-Lorraine. A significant percentage of the German troops were quite ruthless, particularly as it related to the rape of French women.

The story that follows, and written by me after World War II, is based on an operational report from a Division G-2 (intelligence), whose attached O.S.S. Detachment recruited the girl in question, and conducted her line crossing activities.

Although I have taken an editorial license with the dialogue, the basic elements of the story are true. As a matter of fact, one of her handlers lost a leg on a German land mine during this period.

The German sentry never had a chance. As his arms went about her, Marie plunged her knife into his heart.

But for the snapping of a few small twigs, his falling made no sound in the dark shadows of the Alsatian woods.

Marie removed the contents of his pockets, carefully hid his rifle in a small clump of bushes and walked back to the road. Her bicycle was leaning against the outpost bunker where she had left it only a few minutes before.

There was a satisfied gleam in her cold blue eyes as she studied the papers of the dead soldier. Whether or not he had been in the group which had pillaged her home and killed her parents that horrible day, she could not tell. She did know that he was not the one who had raped her. *His was the unit*, however.

She must go on to the village, she thought. Lt. Black, the intelligence officer, would want a report on the enemy dispositions there. As she pedaled along the road, littered with overturned and abandoned German equipment, she saw ahead of her the small village. It nestled on the west bank of Moselle, and served as part of the German main line of resistance in the Vosges mountains.

As she rode into the town, she was halted by a short stocky sergeant, who stepped from the doorway of a small cottage, which bordered on the street. He pointed a sub-machine gun at Marie's trim waist and asked, "How did you get here, *Fräulein?*"

Although French by heritage and blood, Marie, like the majority of Alsatians, spoke German perfectly. "I cycled down this road, Sergeant."

"Did not the sentry at the outpost stop you?" he asked.

"I saw no sentry on the road, Sergeant," Marie replied.

The sergeant began barking commands which resulted in the rapid dispatch of two soldiers down the road towards the uncovered position. He then moved closer to

Marie and studied her carefully. Any suspicion that might have linked her with the missing sentry was soon dispelled in his mind, as his eyes moved from her beautiful face to her youthful and sensuous body.

"What brings you here, *Fräulein?*" the Sergeant asked as he gained control of his thoughts.

"A am here to see your captain, Sergeant."

"We have no captain, *Fräulein*. Our company here is commanded by a lieutenant, and he is not present. He has gone to the rear for supplies and reinforcements and will not return until tomorrow. You must tell me your business. I am in command."

Not the slightest indication of the hatred and thirst for revenge which surged through her was apparent as her eyes returned his gaze. "I must have food, Sergeant. The American artillery has destroyed everything we have. The beasts have killed my sister, and my mother lies sick and hungry two kilometers from here. I would—"

"We have no food for civilians, *Fräulein*. And this is war," interrupted the sergeant. There was a note of sympathy in his voice as he tried to rationalize the situation.

"Surely you can give me some bread and canned meats. although I can't pay anything there may be some service I can render the Lieutenant," Marie continued. As she spoke she looked deep into the sergeant's beady eyes. What she saw pleased her.

The sergeant lowered the muzzle of his gun toward the ground, and turned to look down the main street of the town. Seeing that he was not observed by other members of the garrison, he turned back to Marie and spoke softly, *"Fräulein*, it is a serious offense to give away the Army rations. We have hardly enough to feed our own company." He paused as he studied her supple figure, then asked, "Can you return tonight?" Without waiting for an answer, he warned, "You chance being hit by American artillery."

Marie answered immediately, "I will come when you say."

The sergeant leaned his gun against the front wheel of the bicycle and reached in his tunic for paper and pencil. He wrote something, folded the paper and handed it to Marie.

"All right, listen closely and follow my instructions. Come to this cottage at nine o'clock tonight. I will be waiting here with food. The note I have given you will permit you to pass the outpost line. You must move silently even though you may hear noises at the inn down the street."

"What happens at the inn?" asked Marie.

"The men who are not on guard gather in the cellar there tonight to drink wine and beer. There will probably be much noise as the Lieutenant is away."

A shadow of a smile moved across Marie's face as she scolded the sergeant, "That is very dangerous. Suppose the Americans should attack."

The sergeant laughed, "Americans never attack at night, *Fräulein*. They are afraid of the dark. I hope you aren't," he added.

"I will be here, Sergeant. Is that all?" asked Marie. She motioned to the sergeant to pick up his gun as she prepared to mount her bicycle. He moved close to her. He picked up his gun and put his arm around her waist and gave her a squeeze. "That is all at the moment, my desirable *Fräulein* . . . but tonight you will be on my mattress instead of the Lieutenant's . . . if you return. You understand I do not risk my neck for nothing."

The filthy swine, she thought as she replied, "I will come for the food, but—"

They were interrupted by the approach of one of the soldiers returning from the outpost position. The sergeant quickly reverted to the role of the interrogator and loudly spoke to Marie, "That is too indefinite. If there are American pilots behind our lines we must know exactly where they are, how many, and whether or not they are armed. When you get that information come back and you will be rewarded. You will return home the way you came."

Without so much as a knowing glance from either of them, Marie turned her bicycle around, mounted and left the sergeant and the soldier in the middle of the road watching her disappear in the distance.

When Marie had crossed through the mine fields and had reported to Lt. Black in the American lines, the last light was fading from the sky. During her crossing of this "no man's land," she had reviewed the events of the afternoon. She had decided not to tell the intelligence officer about the situation in the village, as he might ruin her plans by instigating a surprise night attack or some other useless action. This was going to be her party. It was a perfect situation for her purposes. She would ask the lieutenant for only four men; Sergeant Ryan and three others.

"That was fine work, Marie, and good information," said Lt. Black, after she had partially briefed him. "But what I don't understand is this. What do you expect to accomplish by returning right away . . . and with a patrol? Together, you will be unable to observe as much as you have this afternoon alone. Now, if we could get a prisoner . . ."

"Lieutenant," interrupted Marie, "You know why I am serving the American forces as an agent. You know what happened to my parents. You know how you found me the day you entered . . ."

Lt. Black could not refrain from dropping his eyes from her embarrassed face as he recalled her prostrated body on the cellar floor of her battered home. "I remember, Marie," he answered softly.

As Marie continued he marveled at her fearlessness and determination. She didn't have a nerve in her body. God, how she hated those Krauts, he thought. He was glad she was on his side.

"I promise you, Lieutenant," Marie went on, "that if Sergeant Ryan and his men follow my instructions, we will return with much more information and a live prisoner too. You must have confidence in me."

"All right, but it still doesn't make any sense. I've got a feeling I'm going to catch the devil from the Army Intelligence Officer when he finds out I've sent a patrol into the German lines under the command of a French girl. Hell, he won't believe it."

It was seven o'clock and pitch black when they started through the mine fields. The patrol was armed with pistols and each man carried two grenades. There would be no friendly artillery falling in their area of movement, as Lt. Black had coordinated that. Marie had never crossed in darkness before. She knew every step of the way by daylight. Every day for the past ten days she had moved down the gentle slope towards the river taking advantage of every fir tree and evergreen bush, avoiding the open areas, yet following the openings in the minefield pattern. The night was different; it was hard to recognize the landmarks and the quietness was unearthly.

It was slow going, but they were getting close to the river. They moved silently; each man placing his foot carefully on the spot where Marie had stepped. Once across, only a short distance remained to the village road which paralleled the river. The river was narrow at the point of crossing. Marie had always crossed on a big fir tree which had been felled at its base by an explosion of some sort. It had fallen squarely across to the German side and because of its bushy top, the trunk could not be seen from the road. They crossed the river without incident.

When they had arrived at a large culvert which ran under the road, Marie removed some branches from the near end and pulled out her bicycle. She whispered to Sergeant Ryan to assemble the patrol around her. With their faces close together in a tight circle, Marie outlined her plans.

"The first German outpost is two hundred and fifty yards down the road. The village lies two hundred yards beyond. We will walk single file on the left of the road up against the cliff wall. I will halt you fifty or sixty yards from the outpost. I will then ride my bicycle to the outpost. You will await my return. Make no sound."

"But Marie," said Sergeant Ryan anxiously, "what are you going to do?"

He felt a slight shiver run down his spine when she answered after a moments silence, "First, I am going to kill the sentry."

"I don't like this, Marie," argued the sergeant. "I know how you feel, but this is no time to lose your head. Look, if these Germans have any sense they'll have at least two men on the outpost. You can't kill two men. You're going to alert the whole works. Lt. Black was right when he—"

"Lower your voice, Sergeant," Marie commanded, putting her hand over his mouth.

For a minute no one spoke. An occasional artillery shell could be heard detonating in the distance, somewhere along the front. Only the rustling of the trees made sound near them.

"Sergeant Ryan," continued Marie, "I know what I'm doing and I will not fail. Should, however, you hear me scream at any time or hear a shot fired, you must return immediately to your lines. Please, please do as I say."

The sergeant was not happy with the situation, but realized he had little choice at this point; he asked, "What happens if we get past the outpost?"

"We will proceed in the same manner to the village," she answered, "and there we will make our final plans. Now, let's move out one by one to our positions on the road."

It was eight thirty when Marie halted the patrol at a bend in the road about sixty yards from the outpost. From a little drawstring purse attached to her belt, she removed a small bottle of perfume which she applied sparingly to the backs of her ears, her neckline and her hair. After combing her hair, she straightened her bodice and skirt, mounted her bicycle, and rode slowly towards the outpost bunker.

The two sentries had been posted just before dark. They had no knowledge of the afternoon's events and were unprepared for the girl's return. One was asleep in his blankets while the other stood guard. At the first sound of Marie's approach the guard froze, then quickly nudged his sleeping companion with his foot. At the same time, he leaned over and whispered, "Corporal, get up."

Corporal Schmidt grabbed his gun, rubbed the sleep out of his eyes, and rose beside his companion. "What is it, Mueller?"

"Some one comes," he answered, leering into the darkness. "Listen."

"I hear it. It is not a person walking. Do not fire yet," cautioned the corporal.

Slowly the sound became more discernible as Marie grew closer to their position. Her heart was pounding hard against the steel blade of the knife she had hidden in her blouse. They must not shoot, she prayed.

They both saw her outline at the same instant, as she loomed out of the darkness not twenty yards away. Mueller raised his rifle and took aim. The corporal said quickly, "No, Mueller, no." He was just in time. She rode on to a point abreast the position. The corporal, in a low crisp voice, commanded, "Halt!"

Marie, feigning surprise, nearly fell from her bicycle as she dismounted and uttered a quiet but feminine screech. "You have frightened me out of my wits." The corporal grabbed her by the arm and yanked her into the bunker, letting her bicycle fall to the road.

"Shut up, you fool," he said, "you must be crazy to be on this road. Mueller, look sharp, she may not be alone." The corporal felt around for his flashlight and when he found it he turned the light full in Marie's face. Her perfume reached its target at the same moment. *"Himmel!"* he exclaimed, and then was silent.

Mueller leaned over and whispered, "I cannot hear anything. She must have come alone."

The corporal didn't seem to hear him. He leaned towards Marie in the darkness. His brain went sailing back to Hamburg, to a summer night before the war . . . a lifetime ago. He returned to the present. He had a duty to perform.

"Fräulein," he said, "do you have any plausible reason for being on this road, especially at night?"

"Yes, I have," she replied, "I have a rendezvous with your sergeant at nine o' clock."

The corporal shook his head and turned to the private, "Mueller, she *is* mad."

"Fräulein," he continued, "you are insane or you lie. I will soon find out."

"Tell me where you live," he went on, "how you got here, my sergeant's name, and when you made this rendezvous."

Marie forced a little shudder, moved closer to the corporal and said in a childlike tone, "The night air is cold."

As he leaned forward to throw his blanket around her shoulders his face was brushed slightly by a wave of her perfumed hair. He had the sensation of being touched by the petals of a hyacinth.

Marie broke his short reverie. "It is not a long story, Corporal. This afternoon I left my sick mother who lives two or three kilometers from here in the hills off the river road, and cycled to the village. Your sergeant, who is named Heusinger, offered to give me food and medicine if I would return tonight. I am on my way to meet him now. If you do not believe me, read this note."

"And Sergeant Heusinger," leered the corporal, after he had studied the pass by the glow of his flashlight, "where is he going to get you food and medicine?"

"I did not inquire, Corporal," answered Marie.

"What is to be the Sergeant's reward for this noble gesture, may I ask?"

Marie did not answer.

The corporal continued, "Answer my question."

Marie said softly, "I would rather not."

"Oh ho!" exclaimed Corporal Schmidt, as he turned toward Mueller, "Sergeant Heusinger is up to his old tricks."

Mueller replied, "You have to give him credit, Corporal. He's always been ahead of anybody else in the company."

Corporal Schmidt didn't answer Mueller. His thoughts pictured Sergeant Heusinger and this young thing together. Not this time, he decided, would the sergeant be the clever one. He leaned over to Marie and whispered, "Come with me." He led her out of the rear of the bunker to the edge of the road.

"Fräulein," confided the corporal, "Sergeant Heusinger is a man without conscience of sympathy. He will take what he wants and then laugh at you, and send you home empty-handed. Now as for myself, if you will come with me into the woods ... afterwards I will go into the village and get you what you ask. You will not run the risk of getting shot ... or being abused by that crude Heusinger. What do you say?"

As it was pitch black the corporal could not see the wide smile that crossed Marie's face. This was easier that she had hoped for, she thought. She whimpered, "You are all alike, merciless and cruel; but I have no choice. I will do as you say."

Without so much as a signal to Mueller, Schmidt took her left arm and half lifted her across the shallow ditch that separated the road from the thick fir trees. They moved up on a small knoll about twenty yards from the road. As she walked, she removed from her blouse the knife with her free hand. She held it close to her right side so that he would not see its gleam. The corporal stopped. "Here," he said. Marie turned towards him. She saw him unbutton his tunic. As he moved his arms back to remove them from the sleeves, Marie struck. Even though the blade was in his heart, he remained upright for a moment before he fell. On the way to the soft needle covered ground he cried, "You little—"

Marie moved fast. She retrieved her knife, cleaned it on his tunic and started back to the bunker. When she entered, Mueller turned to her and asked, "Where is Corporal Schmidt?" If Marie had answered him, he would not have heard her words, because he was gasping his last breath of life.

It was five minutes to nine when Marie rejoined Sergeant Ryan and the patrol. She merely reported that the road was clear and that they were to advance as planned. When they arrived at a point near the cottage Marie rode on ahead.

The German sergeant was not to be seen. She heard muted noises coming from the inn down the street; men singing and laughing. She moved quietly to the cottage door and rapped.

"Come in, *Fräulein,*" said a low voice. She entered and closed the door behind her. The small head and thick neck of the man was silhouetted against the window through which he had watched her arrival. He said, "I did not believe you would come."

"I had to," she replied. "Are you alone?"

"Not now, my pigeon," chuckled the sergeant, moving towards her. "I have a beautiful guest." Marie slowly reached for her knife. As she drew it from her blouse, he saw it flash and tried to evade her lunge. His movement, although slight, was enough to throw the blade off its mark; it entered his lung. As he fell back against the wall he fought at Marie's hand which was pulling at the blade handle. She summoned all her strength, pulled, and broke free of his grip. She had the knife. He slid to the floor as she assailed him with the fury of a tigress.

Sergeant Ryan whistled under his breath when Marie recited her activities of the half hour just passed. In the blackness of the cottage, where the patrol had assembled, he could feel the determination and cold courage of this girl in her unexcited voice.

"The inn is only a few buildings away. I believe there is only one outside entrance to the cellar where they are assembled. However, I cannot think of any way to kill them all." She paused for a moment, then continued. "Maybe if I opened the cellar door quickly and you threw your grenades at the same time . . ."

"Marie, this is where I take over," announced Sergeant Ryan. "I've got a definite plan. Now all of you listen." Marie and the men of the patrol moved a little closer in order not to miss any of his instructions.

"From here on out we move together," he said. "We know from intelligence reports that the other outpost positions are on the river and around the village. I do not believe we will encounter anyone between here and the inn, except by chance. If we are successful, Lt. Black will throw a fit," he said, almost chuckling, "because I intend to march the whole works back as prisoners." He was serious as he continued. "When we get to the inn, Marie, you will open the door and walk in with your hands raised up in the air. In your right hand you will have a grenade. Do you know how to arm the grenade by pulling the ring?"

"Yes," Marie whispered.

"They, of course, will stop what they are doing and inquire into your actions. When it is quiet so that all can hear, you will explain, 'I have a gun aimed at my back. I must throw this grenade at the first man who moves toward his weapon. The Americans have captured the village. The inn is surrounded and you are prisoners.' If there is no movement, we will move in beside you and take charge. We will then form them in a column and march them out and down the road. You will leave last and follow, as I don't want them to see you with us for obvious reasons."

"Sergeant," spoke up one of the patrol, "suppose they go for their rifles? What then?"

"If they do, Marie," the sergeant answered but addressing the girl, "throw the grenade. We will open fire and cover your exit. Everyone will have to get back to the outpost bunker as best he can. We will assemble there before crossing the lines. Are you ready, Marie?"

"You have *real* courage, Sergeant, you and your men. All I have is hate."

No sound could be heard in the village except their footfalls and the muffled noise at the inn. They moved cautiously and quietly toward their objective. No one was in sight. The sounds became louder as they approached the wide cellar door of the inn. As they moved down the stone steps, they knew the party was in full swing. The sergeant removed a grenade from his pocket and handed it to Marie. She clutched it in her right hand and raised both her arms over her head.

"Everybody ready?" whispered the sergeant. No one answered. He checked them all and after a moment said, "Well, here goes!" As he spoke he kicked open the cellar door.

As the last of the captured Germans were filing out of the tavern Marie saw *the man*. He had recognized her as she entered and had pulled his cap down to partially hide his face. As she moved towards him he instinctively moved back against the wall. Her expression seemed to hypnotize him. They were alone as her knife came out. She pulled the ring-pin of the grenade and shifted it to her left hand. The fact that he was a big man did not seem to concern her now as she pointed her knife and moved slowly towards him. She was smiling now.

Lt. Black entered the village at daybreak with the first attacking troops. Except for a few scattered shots from surprised outposts there was no resistance. The village was empty. Sergeant Ryan led him to the inn.

The candles on the tables had burnt out hours before. There remained only the solid buds of tallow which had dripped down the bottles when the flame was alive. The room was dark and cold.

Cold, too, was the body of Marie, as was the body of the man beside her. The knife lay on the floor. He had been too strong, so she had released the grenade. Her desire to live had not been as strong as her desire to kill this man.

Lt. Black studied her face; beautiful even in death. Although her lips would not move to say them, her expression spoke the words with eloquence, "Vengeance is mine at last."

"Goodbye, Marie," whispered Lt. Black.

He took a step back, saluted, and walked out of the tavern into the Alsatian dawn.

PART VI

STRATEGIC SERVICES UNIT

37

THE BACKGROUND

My first association with the Office of Strategic Services (OSS) was in North Africa in 1944. The Seventh U.S. Army had been reactivated with Lt. General Alexander M. Patch as its Commander, and I was selected by him to be his Intelligence Officer. The Army staff was assembled at *L'École Normale* at Bousaria outside Algiers for the planning and preparation of the invasion of southern France.

In the early phases of the planning, I met several members of OSS, including Henry Hyde and Ed Gamble, with whom I would work closely later on. They were to join me in southern France to support the Seventh Army throughout the war. This OSS team was extremely capable and was composed of some of the finest minds our country had to offer.

Both before and after the invasion, I had occasion to work closely with Henry Hyde, who was operating a chain of French agents by radio in the target area. On my initial briefing by him, I was so impressed with his intelligence collection capability that I decided to break the standard rules established by Allied Forces Headquarters (AFHQ), that no major unit under that headquarters could accept raw intelligence. My counterpart there was British General Kenneth Strong, who had the responsibility of evaluating the intelligence collected from all sources including OSS, and of issuing finished intelligence to the combatant forces in that command.

I decided, however, that I would work surreptitiously with OSS, as I did not know whether or not the British oriented AFHQ was utilizing their product, and I felt that I had a responsibility to General Patch and the Seventh Army troops to insure a minimum number of casualties on the landing.

I set up a small cell in my G-2 Section to handle the OSS product. Our problem was to insure we were receiving current information and that OSS agents weren't doubled. We started out by having the agents go to a certain point and report back what was there. For a month or so we would only do this where we could confirm that intelligence by Signal Intelligence or photography or by another agent's report on the same item. Consequently, we were able to confirm the veracity of an agent, and when we got reports which we knew to be false, we assumed the agent had been captured and doubled by the Germans. Over a two month period, from May to July, we identified one or two double agents. OSS then reported this to AFHQ, as we (OSS) couldn't get into the deception business by providing the double agent with requests for information which would give them a mis-cue as to where the invasion was coming. So, as indicated, OSS reported to the handling of double agents as subjects for deceptive measures in connection with the operation.

AFHQ finally found out about what we were doing, and I got a call from General Strong, who told me he wanted to talk to me immediately. I went to his office at AFHQ in Algiers. He told me he was aware of my rela-

tions with OSS. He lectured me that his office was the re-
cipient of all sources of information not available to me
initially, and that they all had to be examined and col-
lated, produced, and checked out, that AFHQ's intelligence was absolutely correct, and so disseminated to all
elements of all French, British, and American services
under General Alexander's command. He said to me,
"You are not playing the game."

I replied, "General, I understand your position per
fectly. However, I am responsible for the intelligence for
an army of Americans, and I will play any game that will
insure that they get over the beaches on D-Day with a
minimum of casualties."

He said, "We'll see about that."

A day or so later, walking into my office without any
announcement was an American colonel, a British
brigadier, and a British lieutenant colonel, all from General Strong's office. They sat down, and the American an-
glophile said in a belligerent and demanding tone,
"Quinn, we have instructions to tell you to cease and de-
sist in going directly to, speaking to, or communicating in
any way with the OSS detachment in North Africa."

I asked, "Who said so?"

The brigadier said, "By orders of General Alexander."

Their attitude was so belligerent and their walking in
without notification was so demeaning that I told them to
get the hell out of my office. They departed, I sensed, in
disarray.

Realizing that my own belligerence and breach of the
rules might well get me fired, I went immediately in to see
General Patch. I told him I was going to leave because he
was going to have to fire me.

He asked, "Have you raped a native?" Whereupon I
told him the whole story, what I'd been doing with OSS,

what dividends we'd been getting, and the threat by the AFHQ visitation. He then said, "They can fire me, too."

I never learned what action Ken Strong took, but in any event, I didn't get fired.

About this time I got my first message from General Donovan. I had never met him. As a matter of fact, I didn't meet him until we had arrived in southern France. However, while I was in Algiers, he sent me a message congratulating me for my effort in securing intelligence for the forthcoming "exercises," and indicated his appreciation for my dealing with his people and for my stand in doing so.

At this point let me state that the OSS team assigned to the Seventh Army apparently outperformed any other comparable team during the war. This was due in part to the fact that I had a great deal of confidence in them and because of the intimacy we had developed during the planning phase of the operation. Had they been thrust on me cold, as was the case in many of the other armies, such might not have been the case. Needless to say, the later operations involving line crossing, air drops of agents, documentation, interrogation, etc., provided a tremendous amount of combat intelligence to the Seventh Army.

But back to southern France. When we invaded at St. Tropez, San Maxime, St. Raphael, etc., we hit very little resistance and moved rapidly and consequently were not able to utilize the OSS team to a degree which had been planned. Our rapid advancement precluded any static efforts by OSS. Only through the efforts of people like my friend Jeff Jones, and others, who had been dropped behind German lines, and some of his contacts who were up in the hills and mountains to the northeast did we get a feel for the threat on our right flank. This was of vital importance.

Because we were going up the Rhine River lickety-split, we had great concern as to what German forces might pose a threat to the Seventh Army from the East. Hence, the underground groups, FFI, and ordinary French citizens were very helpful in providing us with valuable information.

Hyde and company were taking risks by dropping ex-prisoners over the border. They were mostly Austrians—German Army conscripts, but they were Austrians—and once dropped behind the lines, they worked their way back, and, of course, gave us "order of battle" and other significant items of intelligence. Henry had them dropping one night, and they'd be back through our lines two or three days later.

After war ended, I was ordered to Fort Sam Houston, Texas. About the 19th or 20th of September, 1945, General Jacob "Jakie" Devers called me to Washington to receive a Distinguished Service Medal as a result of my intelligence work in North Africa, France, and Germany. One reason I was awarded the DSM was that by luck, I guess, I predicted the German operation NORTHWIND.

General Devers presented me with the medal and had invited a large number of staff officers to witness the event. After the award ceremony, a messenger told me to go to General Bissell, the G-2 of the Army. I reported to General Bissell not knowing why. He said "Quinn, you are being ordered to SSU (Strategic Services Unit), a unit that is yet to be born. The President has directed that you report to what was OSS and will be SSU. Effective October 1st, OSS will be changed from an executive agency, under the President, directed by the Joint Chiefs of Staff, to a military unit under the Secretary of War."

I said, "Sir, I can't do that; I have orders for the Pacific."

General Bissell said, "You can tear those up, because you're going to SSU by direction of the President."

"The President?" It never occurred to me that the President of the United States had ever heard of me.

Bissell continued, "Now you report to G-1 (personnel officer) General Booth, and he will give you a set of orders."

So I went up to G-1, and he confirmed the fact that the White House had called and instructed the Army to order me, unless I had some serious personal reason which would preclude my compliance, to report on the first of October to Brigadier General John Magruder at OSS, now SSU, Headquarters.

I was somewhat in a state of shock; I didn't know what to do, but I had my orders, and I was going to comply with them. Later I learned that General Donovan and President Truman had agreed that the Office of Strategic Service, created for wartime purposes, could no longer be defended as an executive agency under the President. However, its assets were to be held in escrow and placed under the Secretary of War. The reasons for this were twofold. One, its status quo and continuation would have been highly controversial vis-à-vis a central intelligence concept, and the President didn't want to be bothered with monitoring the agency. Two, they did not want to put it under the Army G-2 because they felt that some animosity might exist between the two agencies which in turn might be a reason for G-2 to disband and/or eliminate some of the assets, i.e., intelligence operations that had been conducted by OSS during the war. The authorities didn't want to put it under ONI (Office of Naval Intelligence), either; and no way was Donovan going to let the FBI get their hands on it.

Donovan additionally recommended, and the President approved, that Brigadier General John Magruder, who had been in OSS on duty throughout the war, be named the Director or commanding officer of SSU and that I be designated as General Magruder's executive officer.

So on October 1, 1945, I reported to General Magruder as executive officer of an organization activated that very morning. I knew about OSS in the field, of course, but I didn't know the people, the Washington headquarters personnel, and I didn't know of the complications involved—I soon became aware of them.

The orders that General Magruder received from the Secretary of War were very simple. He was charged with preserving the intelligence assets created and held by OSS during its existence and the disbandment of paramilitary units, which included the 101 detachment in Burma and Southeast Asia, and other forms of intelligence units, like the Jedburgh teams, and morale operations, et cetera. My initial business was primarily liquidation. The main problem was the discharge of literally thousands of people. Consequently, the intelligence collection effort more-or-less came to a standstill, as very little headquarters attention would be given to intelligence operations at that particular time because of the overriding requirement to get people back home. This situation changed later on as we began to level off.

After the first of the year in 1946, General Magruder suffered a series of attacks of arthritis and progressively became more crippled as the days wore on. Consequently, he spent less time at the office. This then, of course, increased my workload, because I was now making a great number of decisions on my own and by then had gotten a kind of a grip on the operations of the unit. This meant that I put in a lot of hours, including the weekends.

It got to a point where General Magruder could not effectively operate, and he asked the Secretary of War to accept his retirement. General Magruder retired in February 1946.

Without anyone saying anything to me, I received a call from Colonel Charles McCarthy, the military assistant to Assistant Secretary of the Army Howard C. Peterson, who had been given the responsibility of overseeing SSU. He said, "Can you come up and see the Secretary?"

Although I'd never met the Secretary, I reported to him along with Colonel McCarthy. I didn't really know what it was about until he said, "Well, Quinn, I'm appointing you Director of SSU following General Magruder's retirement."

So I became the Director. Later I asked Colonel McCarthy, "Don't I get some orders or somebody to tell me what the hell to do?"

He said, "Okay, just do what General Magruder was doing. After a moment of reflection he added, "All right, I'll tell you what your orders are. You are ordered to preserve the assets of OSS and eliminate its liabilities."

Now I'd been in the Army for a long time and was to be in the service for several years after that, but I'd never before and have never since received such broad instructions, which left the conduct of an entire operation and careers of hundreds of people in my hands.

A few days after I took over I received this note from General Donovan:

New York City

My dear Colonel Quinn,

I have just heard of the very gratifying news that you've been designated to head SSU. I want you to know that if at any time you feel that I could help you, I would be glad to do so. Best of luck in your work. You also know that I am continuing to attack the inadequate provisions that are made for intelligence in the United States.

Sincerely, Bill Donovan.

38

THE PROBLEM

My responsibilities were to prepare SSU for a transition to a new agency, formed according to a central or national intelligence concept. I was in the initial transition phase, to preserve the assets created by OSS. Now the enigma: *what* should be preserved and *what* should be eliminated? My simple orders were not so simple after all. I was constantly worried that I might save a paddle but lose the canoe.

My first problem therefore was to determine what the assets were. Here is where I became initially confused. The organization of the OSS looked something like the old Japanese flag. There was Donovan in the middle, and the rays were all the agencies that he commanded. He had Ollie Doering and Ned Putzell and others with oil cans to grease the rails, and to oil the engines to keep traffic moving.

During this assessment period the mad exodus was continuing. Fortunately, I was able to get hold of Colonel Knox Pruden. I got him from the Adjutant General of the Army to help me with this tremendous personal effort. He was great.

I was also having some problems with personnel. I

fired a homosexual that Security had surfaced. It so happened that his uncle was a United States Senator, who worked me over and threatened to have me fired, etc. I told him what my orders were, i.e., to preserve the assets and eliminate the liabilities of OSS, and I referred him to Secretary Peterson with the promise to take his nephew back if the Secretary indicated that a homosexual was an *asset*. Well, that stopped that.

Those who are aware of the Walter Trohan exposé of OSS activities and the Park Report will be able to understand the pressures exerted by the Army, Navy and the FBI to kill the concept of a central intelligence system, and the entailed obstacles I confronted in preserving the assets of OSS.

Another problem had to do with real estate. I gave the Congressional Country Club back to the membership. I sent them a bundle of money to repair their golf course and their club house. OSS had used the club site for a training area during the war and had really torn up the course.

There were apartments and safe houses and cover businesses. There was a section of Catalina Island used as an OSS training area that had to be returned to its owners. We were very busy dissolving companies and institutions and closing offices. It seemed never to end, but finally, we got most of it settled.

While the assessment was going on, another major problem was reorganization. All the major capitals of the world of intelligence interest had several functions that were reporting directly to their Washington counterparts or to Donovan. During this period of studying the organization of OSS, I could never come to grips with it, because it was contrary to any principles of organization, command and control that I had ever experienced. I say this not in criticism of General Donovan, but in commendation of his unbelievable capacity to command. He commanded tremendous numbers of operations and people, almost on a one-on-one basis.

For instance, we'll just take a capital overseas. It might be Stockholm or London, it doesn't matter. The format was the same. Each agency, according to General Donovan, had its own headquarters, and its own facilities in this country, or wherever they were. The two prime operating functions were X-2, which was counterintelligence and counterespionage, and S-I, which was secret intelligence and espionage.

Now in addition to Morale Operations, Documentation, Communications, and several other services, all of these functions had separate facilities which entailed tremendous amounts of duplication. Hence I decided that if it was going to be a military unit, it ought to look like a military unit and be organized as such. So amid a highly critical environment, I reorganized the OSS or SSU as closely as I could along military lines. In other words, I had myself as commander, I had a chief of staff, special assistants, and deputy chiefs of staff. I then had a personnel office, a G-1, which I didn't call a G-1, I called it personnel management.

The organization was intelligence, so there was no requirement to have an intelligence officer, per se. And there was no reason to have an operation office, because two main branches in themselves were operational. I did, however, create a central supply or logistics office, which was responsible for support to all offices, functions, and operations at home and abroad.

These abrupt changes caused a furor for several months because people didn't know where to hang their hats or what they were supposed to do. At one point in time, I wondered if I'd really made a serious error in trying to form something based on my own experience.

As I indicated before, there was no one person in command of London or Paris or anyplace else. I changed that situation and established the policy that there would be one commander in each operational area outside the United States. It didn't matter whether he was S-I or X-2, whether he was an officer in espionage or counterespionage, but there would be one man who would report to me rather than two or three. I think this change was more agonizing and difficult to alter than the personnel and logistic functions, because this tore into the heart of past *modus operandi*. Who were these people going to be? I examined each outpost and tried to determine who had the greatest assets in each of these capitals. In so doing, I would select an S-I or X-2 officer to be the station chief. This station chief concept exists today in the CIA.

The change did, however, stop a condition involving particularly X-2 and S-I. In many capitals they had run afoul of themselves in duplication efforts and actually had been subjected to double agentry, or dual agents, when each didn't know what the other was doing. As a matter of fact, they spent quite a bit of time trying to penetrate each other. This happened in several instances.

I learned later that from its inception in 1943, X-2 had argued that it should see all S-I source lists since it had exclusive access to British security information and could therefore "vet" S-I for Donovan. Apparently, by the summer of 1944 the security war had been won by X-2, meaning that it was receiving on a regular basis complete lists of S-I agents.

X-2 had been a tightly knit cloak-and-dagger group. They were the dirty trick boys; not that the dirty tricks aren't good tricks, it's just the people who had developed a high degree of professionalism in counterespionage operations were extremely reluctant to expose their particular *modus operandi* to anybody who was not an X-2 type, and resented the fact that in several capitals I selected an S-I man to be the boss. Now, this created a problem which I eventually had to solve. It had to do with the leader, the director of X-2, James Murphy, a very knowledgeable operator and probably one of the best counterintelligence men that the nation has ever produced.

Murphy was a lawyer by profession and had a great gift for the selection of people and for the organization and conduct of counterespionage operation.

Jimmy was reluctant to go along with the new command structure and fought the concept. On certain issues he was either countermanding some of my orders or not obeying them. The whole outfit was watching this conflict with eagle eyes, and I had to do something about it. So it came to a showdown, and I had no other alternative but to ask him to resign. When he left SSU he took an awful lot of good talent with him, and this was a tribute showing their loyalty to him. Jimmy Murphy was a good man and a patriot. His only problem was that he didn't have a military mind and couldn't understand the machinations of a groundpounding infantry officer from West Point.

At this point in time in early 1946, a new requirement vis-à-vis the reorganization surfaced. This had to do with intelligence on the Soviet Union.

Now, the war was over, and although we were dealing with the Soviets on an "old buddy" basis, I got the feeling that somewhere along the line we ought to get all the information we could on them. I found that SSU had no depository, no bank of military or economic intelligence inherited from OSS, and for that matter a void existed in the U.S. Government.

As the Soviets had been our companions, or otherwise partners in the conflict, we hadn't gone through the drill of collecting information on them. This bothered me, because no other agency in the government had anything on the Soviet military or on their installations of strategic interest. The FBI, of course, from the standpoint of internal security, had some information on the Soviet intelligence services, but nothing or very little on the military. The State Department had only lists of their diplomats, etc.

Consequently, I began to look around to see who we could get to organize and run what I might call the Soviet or Russian Section in SSU, a division which would collate—not only collect, but collate—to a degree, intelligence collected on the Soviet Union. The Section would, however, issue requirements to the collection agencies regarding the Soviet military, the KGB, and collaterally, political information and economic intelligence.

I called in Bill Tharp and explained the problem. Bill Tharp was my Executive Officer at that time, a former FBI agent and then a major in the Army. I outlined my concern about the Soviets.

He said, "Let me get together with Doyle and Thurston and see what we can come up with."

Later they came in and said, "We've got a candidate, his name is Harry Rositske. He is in Europe on an assignment at the moment. He's a very able intelligence officer. He might be the person you're looking for."

I said, "Well, let's see if he will accept a transfer and set up an office here in Washington." Harry agreed, so he was returned to SSU headquarters and started the Russian Section.

When he reported in, we sat down and had a long chat about what we were going to do and what was the purpose of the exercise, i.e., to build up a bank of information on the Soviet Union, particularly on the military establishment, the KGB and the GRU, and related threat capabilities. So he set off to work and did an outstanding job. Most everyone in the business applauded his work.

Another major problem was, of course, money. We were running out. We'd been funded by OSS funds, but for 1947 we had to go to Capitol Hill. Now I expected, being under the Army, that the Army budget officer would take me under his wing and provide the necessary assistance. He didn't, for some reason, and I never knew why. I've always thought the Army G-2 was behind this, in the hopes that we would be put out of business. I could be wrong.

I went to Colonel McCarthy in the Assistant Secretary's office and informed him that I was going to have to have an appropriation for the forthcoming year. The President had provided money to maintain OSS-SSU for the current year, but our second year was approaching, and as far as I knew, there were no authorizations and no appropriations for SSU.

McCarthy said, "Well, Bill, I can't help you on this; you've got to fend for yourself."

I said, "Yeah, but I don't know anything about budgets or Capitol Hill. I know how to spend money, but I've never had to ask for it."

He told me to go see General Moore, who was the Army Budget Officer at that time, a Major General who knew everybody on the Hill. I went to see him and told him my problem.

He said, "Quinn, you don't fall under any category of the Army budget system. You're an adjunct to the Army attached to the Secretary of War. It's up to the Secretary's Office to provide whatever your requirements are."

"But Colonel McCarthy says that I should see you."

"Well, I can't really help you. What I'll do, though, is set up an appointment for you to see the appropriate committee. Everything you do apparently is highly classified; so I can't even justify your existence in a request for funds, because I don't know what your contribution is to national security or to the country as a whole."

"Well, if that's all you can do, please arrange for me to testify before an appropriate group so that I can get some money to maintain this unit. I have directions to maintain it, but I have to have some wherewithal."

Well, we began to work up a budget. Previously, Donovan had his various divisions and offices state their fiscal requirements. It was not a very scientific system that OSS had, because they got anything they wanted any time. But the war was over now, and this was a little different proposition.

Eventually, I was notified that I was to appear before a sub-committee of the House Appropriations Committee. I was informed by General Moore and the counsel of the committee that I should appear, along with G-2, FBI, ONI, and the Secret Service, i.e. those within the intelligence family grouping. I had never appeared before a congressional committee, and I didn't know what the protocol was. I called in Larry Houston, who was the counsel for the SSU, and I said, "Larry, we've got to go to the Hill and try to get some money for this outfit, and I would like to find out who's on the committee, i.e., see if you can get me a biographical sketch of each of the members, their districts, etc., because I'd like to know to whom I'm talking."

Larry replied, "No problem."

The day came when Larry and I went over to the Hill and went into this committee room. I was the last one on the intelligence roster, as all of the other agencies had testified. When I entered, General Moore was there and announced, "Mr. Chairman, this is Colonel Quinn of the Strategic Service Unit, and he will present his case."

The Chairman said, "Colonel, what do you do?"

"Well, sir, I direct the operations of the Strategic Service Unit, which was OSS."

"I thought the OSS had been done away with."

"Not exactly, sir. OSS has had its name changed, it's no longer an executive agency, and has been greatly reduced, but I am charged with the responsibility of preserving the assets created during the war by that organization."

"That's a pretty broad scope. But I don't know what you could tell us, Colonel, because we've heard practically all the secrets that the nation has. We've listened to the FBI, the Army Intelligence, the Naval Intelligence, and Secret Service, and I can't imagine what else you could add to our intelligence picture."

Well, I knew this was coming. I just knew that these people didn't know what we did. Donovan didn't have to tell the Congress anything, because the President took care of his funding, and so, the Congress knew very little about OSS operations. So I said, "Mr. Chairman, what I have to say is very highly classified, and it involves the security of agents who are now undercover in various countries and working in environments which are hostile to us. Therefore, I'd appreciate very much if you'd just give me five minutes in an executive session in which I will reveal to you, you and the members of the committee and General Moore, several very sensitive operations."

"This is rather unorthodox, Colonel. The Army didn't ask us to clear the room."

"Sir, I'm only asking for five minutes, and if in that

five minutes I can't convince you that what I am going to tell you should not be held very tightly, then we'll open it up, and I'll give you the rest of my testimony without restriction other than the fact that it's classified."

The Chairman looked around at the other members, and several of them nodded affirmatively as if to say, "Yeah, give him a chance." The room was cleared.

So I opened up. I had selected two or three very hairy operations. One involved an East Berlin cleaning woman who had been hired by the Soviets in their Interior Department, the section which controlled their section of Berlin. This cleaning woman was not really a cleaning woman; she was an agent whom we recruited, that is, our people in Germany recruited. She was a photographer, also a very intelligent girl. Of course, she looked like a housefrau and wore old, ugly clothes. In any event, I told the story of how this woman one night with her camera was photographing documents in one of the Soviet executive's offices. She had passed the guards who were all over the place. But while she was going through the files, she heard footsteps coming down the hall. Thinking it might be a guard checking the offices, she crawled under the large desk with her equipment. She heard the door open. It was not a guard; it was a Soviet officer who had returned for some reason and sat down. Although it was a big desk, he kicked her a couple of times, apparently thinking she was the wastebasket.

In any event, it was a real cliff hanger. Eventually the officer left, and she got out with her photos which found their way to Washington.

Then I told another story that happened in another country in which we had a penetration in a code room of a certain country's foreign office. This was another very close call. After I got through with that one, I had been talking 15 or 20 minutes, and nobody had thought to watch the clock. They were absolutely entranced, as far as I could tell. When I finished the second story, I said, "Mr. Chairman, I could go on; there's an awful lot of things that we are doing, and if you'd like to hear some..."

"No, that's plenty. That's unbelievable, what you are doing. I didn't hear anything like that from the Army or the Navy. What do you need?"

"Well, I need 15 million dollars for vouchered funds, for salaries, operations, supplies, travel, and so forth. I have a list here. And I need eight million dollars of un-vouchered funds."

"You know, eight million dollars is a lot to give a person on his own signature."

"Yes, sir, I understand that. And of course, you have to trust me, and I think you can, because there's nowhere I can go with eight million dollars that belongs to the government."

So while they were discussing the pros and cons of my request, one of the Congressmen turned to me and asked, "Colonel, in these kinds of operations, who do you look for to do this kind of work? What kind of a person do you need to handle agents and double agents and all of the razzamatazz and cloak-and-dagger stuff?"

As Larry Houston had provided me with their biographical sketches, I noted that all of the committee members were lawyers. So I answered, "What we would like to have, but we can't always find them, would be people with legal backgrounds, because it seems that the legal mind has a greater capacity for conducting operations of this nature, particularly where a high degree of thought flexibility is necessary in complicated situations, and so forth." I said this in a very matter-of fact manner, and I could see them all smile.

That did it. I got the eight million dollars un-
vouchered, and fifteen million appropriated. I thanked
the committee Chairman and departed, and General
Moore went out with me. General Moore was in the
meeting and his sum contribution was to introduce me to
the Chairman. After that he sat in a corner and had yet to
say anything for or against me or what I was doing. And
no one asked him. When we parted, he did say, "You did
a good job."

Although this episode had some humorous elements,
it was a very serious and historic moment when I walked
out of there with that money. If I had been refused, one
of two things, or both, would have happened. Either the
Army G-2 would have come in and carved up SSU and
taken over some of the operations (it *was* an Army unit),
or the whole unit would have been disbanded. The talents
of Richard Helms, Harry Rositzke, William Harvey,
Alfred Ulmer, Jr., Frank Wisner and William Colby, and
some of the other great leaders and minds in the intelligence field, would have been thrown to the winds. Their
talents would have been lost, as well as the background
and mass of experience and bulk of intelligence that had
been collected.

As there were no computers to record this material, it
also might have gone down the drain. As it was, the Reg-
istry, with most of the wartime materials, I ordered sealed.
Because I was not a historian, I was not going to go
through the files to find out what had been done. Besides,
I was too busy, my job was towards the future. But I did
take the necessary steps to store everything vis-à-vis
worldwide operations. As I am writing this, the Archives
are now open to historians and students of intelligence
operations.

In connection with the survival of SSU, I repeat that

the impact of that budget meeting was to maintain the Strategic Service Unit as a nucleus for a central intelligence system, which ultimately became the Central Intelligence Agency.

39

THE SOLUTION AND
J. EDGAR HOOVER

Meanwhile, back at the ranch.

During the summer and fall of 1946 and early 1947, certain elements of the press, particularly the Alsop brothers and Mr. Harold Ickes began to cast shadows on SSU as being a harbor for communists and fellow travelers. They stated that I was okay, I was just a dumb flatfoot soldier and wouldn't know a communist if I saw one. Consequently, I had no way of knowing that I had been penetrated, and it was just too bad that the Russians were picking our brains through incompetence, or words to that effect.

At first these articles didn't bother me, but as they continued, I was afraid other intelligence agencies would avoid us, which is exactly what happened. Besides enjoying the articles, most, if not all of the members of the intelligence community began a political effort to defeat the central intelligence concept, both on Capitol Hill and with the media.

One day I received a call from Dave Bruce, who had

been in charge of OSS in Europe during the war. He said he had been talking to General Donovan, who thought I could use a little help; could I come to dinner at his house in Georgetown on this particular evening?

On arrival that night, I found a group of former OSS leaders, all of them close friends of Donovan and quite influential. Besides David Bruce, there was Charlie Cheston of Philadelphia, Lestor Armour of Chicago, Russ Forgan of New York and a couple of others. We discussed my problem. As a result, they assigned tasks to themselves, to contact selected congressional leaders and the media to insure passage of the Reorganization Act of 1947 and to quell criticism of SSU.

Even though this was a morale builder and a great help to me, I was concerned that if these rumors and articles persisted, my people would experience a lowering of morale and I might lose them because of it. There were two incidents that forced me to some form of action.

The first one was the Soviet Baltic Fleet intelligence package. I received word that one of my operatives in Denmark had procured the plans, diagrams, and sketches having to do with the design, armament, characteristics, etc., of the Soviet Baltic Fleet. When this material arrived, I hastened to take it to the Office of Naval Intelligence. I made an appointment with the Admiral and went to call on him at his office.

When I waltzed in, he asked, "What can I do for you?"

"The shoe's on the other foot, Admiral; I think I can do something for you."

"What is it?"

"Well, I have here everything you would like to know about the Soviet Baltic Fleet, that is, the major ships."

"Quinn, first I'd like to tell you that, well, I've looked

you up. You have a very fine combat record, and I would be the last one to accuse you of being a fellow traveler. However, the 'community' knows that your organization is infiltrated with communists, and as such, I couldn't possibly accept anything that you might want to give me; first because I don't want to have any association with your organization, and number two, I would suspect, off the top of my head, that this might well be deceptive material."

Well, I didn't know how to respond. I said, "I'm sorry, Admiral; I think it's good material, and I'm sorry the Navy doesn't want to use it." Whereupon, I left.

That really hurt.

Not very long after that the second incident occurred. Again, one of my station chiefs came, in person, from Europe. He had brought me the diplomatic code of one of the European countries. He explained to me how he got it. He had recruited an agent who robbed the home of one of the government ministers and had found a code book used by that country's foreign office. I could hardly wait to get this to the Army cryptography people. This type of intelligence is just about the zenith of intelligence collection, because you're reading the messages that come to and go from this country, whether it's friendly or not, and you're also reading the observations from that country's representatives all over the world and any possible relationship it has with potential adversaries.

In any event, I made a date with Colonel Carter Clark, who was then the head of the Cryptographic Division of the Army Security Agency. Carter Clark was Mr. Crypto. I made a date with him for eleven o'clock one morning. I arrived at 11:00 and was told to be seated by his secretary. I waited. I knew there was no one in his office, because an officer had left as I came in. And so, for 20 minutes I cooled my heels. The buzzer rang, the secretary went into Clark's office and came out and said, "Colonel Clark will see you now."

I went in with my briefcase in my hand, and I stood in front of his desk. I was going to salute, because I knew he was waiting for me, but he was reading a paper, and he didn't look up. I guess for a full minute he kept reading. It may not have been a minute, but it was an embarrassing length of time. Finally, he looked up and said, "Quinn, what kind of a son-of-a-bitch are you?"

This kind of threw me for a short loss, but after I thought about it, I said, "Well, Colonel, I guess I've got you at a disadvantage."

He mulled that over for a little while, and he laughed like hell. "You know, that's pretty good. Come on, sit down," he added in a very friendly way, "Why are you here?"

"I can be very brief, because you probably will throw me out of the office, as I've been thrown out all over town, but I have here the codes, the diplomatic codes of X country."

"You've got to be kidding."

"No, I'm not kidding. If you don't believe it, just take these and try them in the next intercepted message you get."

"Hell, yes."

"You know what everybody in town thinks about SSU."

"Yes, I do. But I don't give a shit. If you can deliver this kind of stuff, I'll take it, because in ten minutes I can find out whether it's crap or not."

I left the material in his hands. From then on, Carter Clark was a friend of ours, even if no one else was. He would call me from time to time and say, "Hey, get your boys moving. I'd like to get something else like you sent me the other day." So be it.

But again these columns and denial of my products began to prey on my mind to the point where I decided I had to do something. I knew it couldn't be the media, because to raise a furor would bring more attention to the unit, and it was not my idea to get our operations kicked around in the press.

One night lying sleeplessly in bed, I thought, "Well, I guess the only solution is to seek the help of the FBI." So the next morning one of the first things I did when I got to the office was to call Mr. J. Edgar Hoover. I said, "Mr. Hoover, my name is Quinn, Colonel Quinn. I'm the Director of the Strategic Service Unit."

I'm sure he was smiling, because he said, "Yes, I know. What can I do for you?"

"You can help me, Mr. Hoover."

"In what way?"

"Sir, I'd like to come over and talk to you."

"Well, come on. How about tomorrow?"

"Yes, sir, tomorrow's fine."

"Ten-thirty."

"Yes sir, I'll be there."

At ten-thirty, I was escorted to his office, and Mr. Hoover graciously asked me to sit down. "Now," he said, "Colonel, what's on your mind?"

And I told him my story. I told him about the articles, and its impact on the morale of my people. I told him about my visit with ONI and the Army. I told him I was depressed in that our contributions to the national security seemed to be lying fallow or going down the drain. I said that not only was my operation being hurt, so was the country, and that I was there to seek his help.

It was very interesting to see Mr. Hoover kind of lean

back in his chair, put has hands in back of his head, and say, "You know, this is quite a relief. Colonel, I fought that Bill Donovan tooth-and-nail, particularly regarding operations in South and Central America." He described his differences with Donovan and finally said, "I admired Donovan, but I was certainly not fond of him. So here we are at the end of that road. What do you want me to do?"

"Mr. Hoover, the simple answer to your question is to find out if I have any commies in my organization."

"How do you propose we do this?"

I answered, "I started out with about ten, between ten and eleven thousand people, principals, and I am now down to roughly seventeen hundred, and they're all over the world and here in Washington. I would like to give you whatever biographical data you need under these people, who are the overt operators of the agency, but are under State Department business or other cover. They are overt and are not agents. I would not want to give you the name of their operators, but these are my principals, and these are the people who are being accused of being fellow travelers or out-and-out communists."

"Well, we can do that. We can run a national check."

"While you're doing it subversively, would you please check them criminally as well?"

"All right."

"Before we decide on how we are going to do it, for posterity, and for ultimate cooperation, I would like to ask that you send me a representative to be your liaison with my organization."

He looked very surprised and said, "Do you mean that?"

"Yes, I do." I knew what was going on in his mind, he was probably thinking, my God, this guy is asking for a direct penetration in his agency. I didn't mind that, because I had enough security to realize that I wasn't going to be penetrated.

In any event, I provided the FBI with finger prints, basic data, and in some cases photos from a form I sent all over the world. Some didn't come back. Some came back screwed up, but enough basic information was provided by the Washington office vis-à-vis our personnel files.

I was still taking a beating three months later when Mr. Hoover called me and said, "I'm sending Agent so-and-so over, who is your liaison officer. I've given him his instructions, and he's going to brief you on our findings. Actually, the news is good, with only one minor questionable item."

It turned out that there was a girl in the logistics division, a clerk in supply, who had been seen with a fellow traveler, who in turn had been seen with a member of the Soviet Embassy. So we were not really penetrated. It was a very innocuous position, and whatever security breaches there were, they were of a very minor nature. She was, of course, fired.

Well, I then breathed a great sigh of relief, and within the next two or three days, I got my satchel, filled it again with the Soviet Baltic Fleet, and went back to ONI—same admiral, same song and dance, "You're loaded with commies."

"You know, Admiral, there are people who have a different opinion on that subject."

"Who, for instance?"

"Mr. Hoover."

"You mean J. Edgar Hoover?"

"Yes. The FBI has checked all of my people, and they came up with a single girl whom I let go."

"Is that correct?"

"Call Mr. Hoover."

"No, I'm not going to call the Director of the FBI."

"I'll call him for you."

"No, you don't have to do that. What have you got?"

I spread the material out on the table, and he looked at it and called several captains in. They just devoured it. So off I went.

Now we were looking up; we were looking pretty good. The word got around. I saw to it. We were back in business. We were acceptable. Even the people up in higher headquarters of the Central Intelligence Group no longer were afraid of us. They were all looking, watching from a distance for fear of infection, but not intruding. They read the papers, too.

Now after Admiral Sours came General Vanderberg as Director of CIA, Pinky Wright as his chief of Staff, and Don Galloway, who became Director of Operations and my immediate boss. However, nothing was interfering with what I was doing and General Vanderberg saw to it that I was appointed to the National War College. I deactivated the SSU as a military unit and departed.

In retrospect, I note three features of unusual interest to me. One of them was the lack of interest in the operation and function of SSU during that two-year period. Up until 1987, only two people ever came to me or called me to ask what happened. One of them didn't really address what had been done, but was inquisitive regarding the personalities involved. The other was a Princeton man who was on the staff of the Senate Select Committee on Intelligence who was working on a book on counterespionage and counterintelligence.

Upon announcement of my appointment to the National War College, I sent the following note to General Donovan:

My dear General,

    As you are fully aware, when General Magruder re-
tired last March, Mr. Peterson, the Assistant Secretary, appointed me as Director of SSU and charged me with the
liquidation of that body and with the settling of the affairs
of OSS. During the past year I have attempted to accomplish that mission, and with the exception of a few agent
claims and minor administrative matters, we have attained
a very well-balanced ledger. Therefore, this week I am
publishing the final general order for the liquidation of SSU
and am submitting to the assistant Secretary my final report.

    However, I believe that for several years to come there
will be occasional problems relating to OSS cropping up. In
the event that such matters are of interest to you, I would
recommend that you contact Colonel Knox Pruden, who
will probably remain in his present capacity as adjutant for
some time and who is familiar with the general problems.

    Two weeks ago I received orders to attend the Na-
tional War College, starting in September. I hope to take
leave this summer and, if fortunate to find a cottage, will
spend this time on the beach.

    Incident to the past year and a half, I would like to tell
you that I have certainly appreciated your attitude regarding the liquidation of OSS. Although you naturally had
an intense interest in the welfare of your former people and
in the business as a whole, I can say that you have to my
knowledge in no way attempted to influence the conduct of
affairs in this organization. This certainly made the job here
a lot easier and certainly less vulnerable to criticisms.

    Although leaving the business, I will continue to have a
deep interest in its future and certainly hope that we can
evolve nationally a top-flight central intelligence organization.

    Please give my best to Ollie and all, and I hope you
continue to enjoy the best of health. . . .

In response, I received the following:

My dear Bill,

I'm sorry to hear that you're leaving. I am glad, how-ever, that you are going over to the National War College. You'll be able to do good work there. I know very well how competently you have dealt with the problems of liquida-tion of the situation there. Everyone agrees that you've done a remarkable job.

There is one thing that you are to do for me, please. Send me a list of the citations that the men have won and also the list of those who have been recommended but have not obtained their awards.

I hope that when you come this way, you'll give me a chance of seeing you.

Sincerely, Bill Donovan

In sum, I guess the effort was worthwhile.[1] I thought it had been forgotten until I received the Legion of Merit later while at the National War College. The recommen-dation appears on the following pages.

---

[1]See Appendix F.

CENTRAL INTELLIGENCE GROUP
NEW WAR DEPARTMENT BUILDING
21st and VIRGINIA AVENUE, N. W.
WASHINGTON, D. C.

JAN 1 7 1947

SUBJECT: Army Commendation Ribbon,
           (2nd Oak Leaf Cluster).

TO   :   The Adjutant General,
           War Department,
           ATTN: Brigadier General H. B. Lewis,
           Room 2D 600, The Pentagon,
           Washington, D. C.

1.   It is requested that reconsideration be given to the
recommendation that Colonel William W. Quinn, 019283, Infantry, be
awarded the Oak Leaf Cluster to the Legion of Merit.

2.   In preparing the original recommendation it was impossible
to include therein a vast amount of highly classified facts and
material involving the clandestine operations of the Strategic Services Unit which, during the liquidation of the Unit, have been
safeguarded and successfully preserved for the use of current intelligence activities. Colonel Quinn's complete and comprehensive
grasp of the entire situation enabled him to render inestimable aid
in this delicate transition period.

3.   Operationally, the Strategic Services Unit, under the outstanding guidance and direction of Colonel Quinn, was called upon to
produce, through unique and secret means, espionage and counterespionage of a strategic nature for dissemination to the highest staff
levels in the United States, including the President and the Secretaries of State, War, and Navy, as well as MIS, ONI, etc. Staff
intelligence officers and their operatives under his direction were
called upon in the foreign field to procure such intelligence under
most trying circumstances. Coincident with the maintenance of this
operation, he also effected an orderly liquidation of the personnel
and facilities which were not suitable for maintenance as a nucleus
for further development in the peacetime intelligence. During this
interim period when the future of peacetime intelligence was in an
extremely undecided status and the morale, as a result thereof throughout various intelligence agencies, was at its lowest ebb, he personally
encouraged, through his dynamic personality and farseeing vision,
representatives in the Eastern Hemisphere to maintain their high
standard of production.

4.   His outstanding success in the field of civilian personnel administration is evidenced by the fact that a liquidation program, which is generally conceded to be the most difficult to carry out because of the many rights and interests of various employees, such as veterans' status, Civil Service status, etc., was carried out without any major appeals or complaints to either the Civil Service Commission or the Office of the Assistant Secretary of War. During this period the civilian strength of the organization was reduced from 2,012 to 915 in a period of twelve months. The effectiveness of this program has been evidenced on innumerable occasions, even when people terminated complemented the organization on the fairness in which the personnel program was administered.

5.   The explicit trust in his general administrative practices throughout the SSU was evidenced by the attitude and the fine spirit of cooperation which developed with the Office of the Assistant Secretary of War, Civil Service Commission, Bureau of the Budget, and other major operating agencies in the Federal Government. Incident to the general liquidation program, Colonel Quinn was called upon to work closely with the Navy, Marine Corps, and Coast Guard.

6.   Colonel Quinn was further called upon to counsel with those officials formulating the peacetime intelligence program. As a result of his vision, enthusiasm, and comprehensive grasp of intelligence requirements, he contributed greatly to the planning therefor. His careful screening of assets of SSU and the conservation of the essential elements thereof enabled him to turn over to CIG an established and implemented nucleus in the field of clandestine intelligence for peacetime operations.

7.   It is felt that the exceptionally meritorious service of Colonel Quinn fully justifies the higher award.

Col. EDWIN K. WRIGHT
Executive to Director

PART VII

JAPAN AND THE KOREAN WAR

Col. William W. "Buffalo Bill" Quinn
Commanding Officer, 17th Infantry Regiment
Korea, 1951

40

TOKYO PARADE

Each year during his "reign" in Japan, General McArthur had a parade in a stadium in Tokyo on the Fourth of July. Each division normally sent its band and a battalion of infantry to participate in the parade. There were other elements in the parade as well, but mostly they were small units with bands. This particular year, 1949, General Anthony "Nuts" McAuliffe, the Division Commander of the 24th Division, called me to his headquarters and told me that he had selected me to command his battalion, the 24th Division Battalion. He would put the Division band at my disposal, and issue us all the essential equipment that was necessary to field a battalion of infantry, that is, with scabbards, rifles, bayonets, uniforms, canteens, ammunition belts, equipment for the belts, and so forth. He told me that everything had to be perfect and that I had my pick of the men I thought I needed. The Division had issued orders to all of the regiments to send the very tallest and best-looking men they had to report to me with some non-commissioned officers in control.

At that time I was assigned to the 34th Infantry as Executive Officer in Sasebo in southern Kyushu, Japan. The general also said, "I'd like to suggest that you take over and use old Camp Hale." Now, Camp Hale was at the southern end of Honshu. It had been a Japanese air station, but was then abandoned. Although it was not in use, it had a runway and barracks and consequently, turned out to be an ideal training ground for a group like mine.

Around the second week in June, we began to assemble our people. We had cooks, bakers, mechanics, armorers and everybody we needed. The troops were accompanied by top-flight non-commissioned officers. And a fine-looking bunch of men they were! Many of the privates were raw recruits, which I'll comment on a little later.

I knew what was expected of us, but I didn't know what the problems were in Tokyo, if any. As I had some West Point classmates and friends in Tokyo, and they had been up there for a couple of years and had seen these parades, I asked them, "Tell me, what are the problems associated with the parade itself? What is the problem that the participants face?"

"The problem is music," they told me. "You have your own band out in front of your battalion; i.e., the division unit. In back of your battalion is another band, followed by another battalion. So no one knows which music to march to, because it's a band, a battalion, a band and a battalion, a band and a battalion, all through the whole course. So there are somewhere between eight to twelve bands playing all at the same time in a stadium—and," they all agreed, "it's usually murder."

That gave me all I needed to know. I then decided I would have the troops take their step or marching gait from me, and to hell with the music. It didn't matter what march was played by our band, because bands would be heard all over the place. I decided that I would be out in front of the battalion and I would set the cadence. I would march in a cadence not set to music, but following the pace of the band in front of us.

Now, one of the other instructions given to me by General McAuliffe was, "We don't want any venereal disease. You've got a band, and you've got a whole battalion, a lot of new kids here, and we don't want any V.D. reported when they get home that they've contracted in Tokyo."

To attempt to solve this problem, I had every sergeant who had a group from his own unit to instruct the new soldiers how to put on a condom. This would seem idiotic or unnecessary, but believe me, it was not. We had some young soldiers there from *Anywhere, USA*, who had never had a sexual experience and didn't know what a condom was.

I therefore ordered the non-coms to use the following instructional technique. A platoon sergeant would hold a class of his own troops. He would take a broomstick, put a condom on its end, and explain its function in detail.

He was to tell his men the equivalent of the following: "You don't have to get laid in Tokyo, but if you're in a situation where you feel that you're going to, here is a package of rubbers for each of you, three to a pack. You take these, and don't you dare fail to use them. If you get a dose of clap, besides six months in the guard house, I will beat the living shit out of you."

But back to my major objective. Day in and day out, for hours at a time, I was out there in front of this battalion, marching on the runway. The supply people were making our equipment look new.

I instructed the Division Band, which was billeted with us and under my orders, to play discordant music and also to change tempo and tune, *but to maintain their own marching gait*. The battalion took its step from me and not from the music.

So off we went to Tokyo for the parade and what we anticipated happened. The stadium was full of battalions of infantry with their own bands. It was bedlam. As planned, our troops took the step and cadence from me, and I had both ears stopped up. It didn't matter what the hell our band was playing, my troops were right on the ball in step with me. The other battalions were pathetic—the front elements following their own band, and the rear elements following the music of the band in back of them.

The bottom line was that as we went past the reviewing stand, General MacArthur turned to General McAuliffe and said, "Tony, I think you've got the best battalion here."

In addition to that performance, we learned later that our outfit was the only battalion in the parade that didn't come up with a single case of venereal disease from the visit to Tokyo.

As a result of this exercise, I received the letter of commendation on page 272.

Two years later, General McAuliffe and I were both assigned at the Pentagon. He was the Assistant Chief of Staff for Personnel, and I was in a staff position.

One day I received a call to report to his office. When I went in to see him, he simply said, "Bill, you're going to be promoted to a Brigadier General." He told me when and where, but not why. He didn't have to tell me, because I knew.

Lesson learned:

Question: How do you get to be a general?
Answer: You march against the music, and you don't let your troops get V.D.

TWENTY-FOURTH INFANTRY DIVISION
OFFICE OF THE COMMANDING GENERAL

APO   24
8 July 1949

SUBJECT: Letter of Commendation

TO: Lt. Col. W. W. Quinn
           Executive Officer
           34th Infantry Regiment
           APO 24, Unit 3

     1. I desire to commend you for your part in the
4th of July parade in Tokyo as Troop Commander of our
provisional battalion.

     2. Many senior officers who viewed the parade
from the reviewing stand commented to me most favorably
on the smart appearance and soldierly bearing of the
personnel in our provisional battalion. The lines were
good and execution of commands was, in my opinion, all
that could be desired.

     3. Such comments were a source of great satisfac-
tion to me and I am happy to pass them on to you.

     4. The personal conduct of the members of the
provisional battalion both at Ozuki and in Tokyo was
beyond reproach and reflected the highest credit on
the division, the regiments from which the personnel
was drawn and on you as Troop Commander.

                          A. C. McAULIFFE
                          Maj. Gen., USA
                          Commanding

41

THE INCHON
LANDING

On August 23, 1950, General MacArthur called for a now historic meeting in the Dai Ichi Building, his general headquarters in Tokyo. He wished to discuss Operation Chromite, which entailed a major amphibious landing at Inchon in Korea, only 22 days later.

In attendance besides MacArthur was Lt. General Edward M. Almond, MacArthur's Chief of Staff, General J. Lawton Collins and Admiral Forrest P. Sherman from the Pentagon, Admiral Arthur W. Radford from CINC-PAC in Hawaii, Rear Admiral James H. Doyle, Commander of Naval Far East Forces, Major General Edwin K. Wright, Operations Officer (G-3) for General Mac-Arthur, Major General George E. Stratenmeyer, Commander of Far East Air Force, Marine General Lemuel Shephard, several other generals, admirals, staffers, and Lt. Col. Quinn.

Almost everyone, certainly the principals, knew what the conference was all about, as the operation had been the subject of debate in Japan and Washington for some time. The main issues related to the current situation in the Pusan Perimeter in Korea, troop availability, the hazardous tides at Inchon Harbor, and the confining nature of the Yellow Sea for naval operations.

The meeting was conducted by the G-3, General "Pinky" Wright, who directed a briefing of the plan for the operation. Several staff officers outlined the scope, participation, and contribution of the various services. From time to time, questions were asked by various attenders, which either General Wright or General Almond (who was to command the GHQ Reserve Force, later renamed the X Corps) would answer. Adm. Doyle had serious reservations vis-à-vis North Korean Air, confined area for naval maneuvers, and split second timing regarding the landing of Marines with the tide. The briefing lasted approximately an hour, and all that time General MacArthur said nothing, quietly puffing on his corn cob pipe as he sat in a chair over to one side.

When the briefing was over and no more questions or observations had been put forth, General Wright turned to General MacArthur and said, "The briefing is concluded, sir."

Then came the dramatic ending of the meeting. For an incredible length of time General MacArthur just sat there, apparently in deep thought. After what seemed an eternity, he finally rose to his feet and strode majestically to the map of Korea in front of the group. He launched into a soliloquy that was serious, dynamic, emotional, loaded with pride, historical—the works. I thought at the time that he would have been equally as famous as a Shakespearean actor. As I recall, he emphasized the need to relieve the surrounded troops in the Pusan Perimeter, his high regard for the Navy, and the advantage of surprise, citing in some detail Wolfe's surprise attack at

Quebec, i.e., that the North Koreans would not anticipate an attack at Inchon. At one point he addressed Admiral Doyle and said, "Admiral, you know I fought with the United States Navy from Australia to the approaches of Japan, and I am of the fixed opinion that the Navy can do anything it sets its mind to do." He stressed the impact on the severance of the jugular vein of the North Korean Forces at the enemy's logistic support at Seoul; he talked of the Communist threat to Asia, its importance to the Western world; and finally, he staked his reputation on the plan in that it would succeed.

It was an incredible performance. The audience was spellbound. When he finished speaking there was complete silence. I felt a cold chill run up and down my spine. Then in a more casual way, he said, in effect, "Now, I leave it to you and General Almond to get your forces together and be prepared to make the assault on September 15th as planned. Of course, this has to be one of the most classified meetings ever held in this building; so consequently, I exhort all of you to maintain complete silence with your families and associates. Surprise will be the great factor."

When this was over I was informed that I was to be the Intelligence Officer for the operation. I went immediately to see "Pinky" Wright's deputy, Colonel John Dabney. He and I had served in sister infantry regiments in Kyushu, Japan, a year or so earlier. He had known all about this, but hadn't told me a thing. I said, "John, what the hell?"

He just said, "You better start cracking instead of just standing there complaining."

I had been told to go to the meeting without knowing what had been going on. I later learned that a planning group (JSPOG) had been working on the problem when I was in "Pinky" Wright's G-3 Section working for Colonel Carl "Tiny" Jark in Operations. The next day I really started cracking and flapping. Now one can fully visualize the scratching you have to do when you start to build a staff, develop procedures, analyze intelligence, plan for its dissemination, and procure equipment for its processing. This is particularly difficult when you have only twenty days before hitting a foreign shore. When your people are assigned to you, how do you tell them anything, in view of the security aspects? What do you do about a mundane problem like reproduction? We were, for instance, issued a reproduction kit that had been in storage since World War II. It utilized a so-called gelatin process on a flat rubber bed. The rubber was brittle, and the jelly ran all over the rubber bed, and our product was terrible. These were to be intelligence documents identifying enemy position, order of battle, boundaries, etc. Initially, they were primarily for the Marine Division, as they did not have comparable resources or capability.

Such trivia gave Major General Charles A. Willoughby a lever to get me fired. He had nominated five or six full colonels in his section for my job. However, the enmity between Almond and Willoughby being so intense, Almond wanted anybody except Willoughby's "boys," and though Willoughby didn't know me from Adam, he worked like hell to get me replaced. Only Major General "Nick" Ruffner, Almond's Chief of Staff, and Almond stayed by me through those two or three critical weeks, and once I boarded the flagship, the *Mount McKinley*, at Sasebo, Japan, along with General MacArthur, Admiral Doyle, et al., to go to Inchon, I was in like Flynn.

The landing at Inchon on the morning of September 15, 1950, was incredibly successful and will take its place in history alongside of Wolfe's comparable Plains of Abraham victory, almost two hundred years earlier.

As I have indicated in other areas, the war in Korea, including the Inchon Landing, is so well documented that I shall not attempt to upstage real historians.

42

HAUCHON RESERVOIR

Early one afternoon the 17th Infantry Regiment was on its way to take the west end of the Hauchon Reservoir. It was necessary for us to make a critical river crossing en route to our objective. Normally, one should take a day to make sure that the logistics are over the river by dark and that the command is not split in half. However, I had flown the area in an L-5 and had seen some retrograde movement on the part of some of the North Koreans, and I decided to take a gamble. Consequently, I ordered all three battalions to cross the shallow river to assault the large hill mass in front of us. The hill was about a thousand feet above the river line. I had artillery give it a good lacing before we attempted the attack. The three battalions of infantry moved forward in echelon.

My command post was in a gravel pit on the side of a road bordering the river, which made a turn north at that particular point. For some reason it was unusually hot that afternoon, and particularly hot in the gravel pit, which received no breeze at all. In any event, I had to stay in the pit for the simple reason that I was under small arms fire from the hill mass. I did have an observation point where I could see the movement of these three battalions, and I must say that they moved with classical precision. As a matter of fact, it looked like a parade ground formation. Things were going along fine, and we were just about to get to the base of the hill mass when who drives up in a jeep but General James Van Fleet, the Commander of the 8th Army and the Allied Forces in Korea!

After I had briefed him on the situation, he said, "Quinn, let's get out of this gravel pit. It's hot in here. Let's go to the river bank where there's some breeze."

I said, "Sir, it may be hot in here, but it's hotter out there, because we'll be under small arms fire."

"Oh," he replied, "they can't hit anything."

So we stepped out on the river bank, and I pulled out a map. Almost immediately we were taken under fire. After you've been in combat a while, you know when you're being shot at. As the bullets go by, you hear *pssst, pssst*, and you realize that if you don't take cover, you're going to get hit.

I said, "General Van Fleet, do you mind if we stand in back of this tree, in the lee of it, so if any strays come they'll hit the tree and not us?"

"All right," he said, "if that's the way you want it, we'll do it, but I want to see this operation."

"Sir, I've committed all three battalions. They're moving in echelon." I explained my rationale for crossing at the time I did, knowing full well that I was almost sure I could get to the top of the mountain and dig in before darkness. I was not concerned about my logistics because I had enough over the river to carry us for the rest of the night.

Well, General Van Fleet looked at those three battalions, and from where we were he could see a perfect operation. He said, "That looks like a demonstration at Fort Benning. I've never seen anything like this since I came to Korea." Then he turned to me and asked, "Bill, why aren't you a general officer?"

"Sir, that's a sixty-four dollar question. When you get back to your headquarters, would you mind calling the Pentagon and asking them that?"

And I have reason to believe that he did just that.

43

KING FOR
A DAY

At one period during the fighting in Korea in March 1951, the 7th Division was fighting its way toward the Hauchon Reservoir. Our Division Commander was Major General Claude Ferenbaugh, better known as Buddy. He was a tremendous man physically, with a great heart to match. He was a sincere, warm, and friendly guy. He was the kind of man for whom I would have fought and died if it were necessary for victory.

On this particular day, General Ferenbaugh decided to make a reconnaissance. I don't recall whether it was to get an observation point or to visit one of the regiments. In any event, the route he took unknowingly was in North Korean hands. As his escort jeep, leading the tank in which he was riding, rounded a bend, it was taken under fire by the North Koreans. All in the jeep were killed or wounded.

It was evident to the tank driver that his tank, with the General, would soon be under fire and/or surrounded. In an attempt to turn around, he drove into a gully or ravine

281

and became mired down. The circumstances were such
that Buddy and the tank crew had to make their escape
through a floor hatch of the tank.

Well, old Buddy had one hell of a time getting his behind through that hatch. He finally made it, and he and
his crew deserted the immobilized tank and started
crawling back through the weeds and vines in the ravine.

In the meantime, Brigadier General Bob Sink, the Assistant Division Commander, had left for Okinawa on
business for the Division. Remaining in command in
Sink's and Ferenbaugh's absence was the other Division
general officer, Homer W. Kiefer, a Brigadier General of
Artillery, and Commander of the 7th Division Artillery.
When darkness came, there was no word from Ferenbaugh. Communications with him were out because the
jeep with the Command radio had been knocked out, and
of course, the tank crew had left their communications
when they abandoned the tank. So Buddy was presumed
to be dead, captured, or wounded—in any event, missing
in action.

About eight-thirty or nine o'clock when the Artillery
Commander realized that Buddy was probably lost, that
we had an attack scheduled for the next morning, and
that the attack order had not been issued, he called me.
He said, "Bill, I want you to come up to the Division and
issue an attack order."

"Why don't you do it?" I asked.

"This is basically an infantry operation. I'm not an Infantryman, and I don't know just exactly how to go about
doing it. I'd rather you do it."

"What you're telling me is to come up and take command of the Division."

"If that's it, then that's it."

"I'll be right up."

So I went back to Division Headquarters. After arriving, I called in the Division staff and issued an attack order. For several reasons, I put my own regiment in the forefront, to make sure I wasn't playing any favorites, with the other two regiments in echelon to the right and to the left of my 17th Infantry. I designated my executive officer, Bob Pridgen, to take command of the regiment.

The next morning we took off at daybreak, and I stayed at Division Headquarters till the attack had been launched. Then I got in a small L-5 airplane and flew most of the morning up and down the lines, both on the enemy side and our side, to watch what the hell was going on and to direct the operation by radio from the air. As a matter of fact, I even informed some of my battalion commanders of what their own units were doing and where they were having problems and what kind of weapons might be used to unlodge them and get them shaken free. When we had taken our objective, I returned to the Division Headquarters.[1]

In the meantime, Buddy and his tank crew had worked themselves back up to our lines during the night. They were picked up the next morning by a friendly 7th Division unit and brought back to the Division Headquarters.

Well, Buddy came in very much dishevelled. He was dirty and needed a shave. The ass of his pants was torn out, and he looked like he'd gone through hell, which in fact he had.

Bob Sink had been notified of the circumstances and was on his way back from Okinawa to issue an order for the next day. When I arrived back at Division Headquarters, I was told that the General was safe and wanted to

---

[1]For my aerial observations that day I was awarded one of the several air medals I received during the Korean War.

see me in his trailer. I went over. He greeted me and said, "What a helluvan experience." He opened a bottle of bourbon, and the two of us sat there and damned near finished it. He thanked me very much for what I'd done.[2]

Then I thanked the Lord that I had a jeep driver, because I couldn't have made it back to my regiment that night without someone other than myself at the wheel.

In any event, although as a colonel I had never commanded anything larger than a regiment, for one day I had been a Division Commander, a King for a Day. I enjoyed the experience of being one.

Maj. Gen. C. D. Ferenbaugh, Lt. Col. W. W. Quinn and Brig. Gen. Thomas Cross in front of Command Headquarters, Hauchon, Korea.

[2]See Appendix H.

44

TRUTH AND COURAGE: LT. THOMAS A. KELLY

At about six o'clock one evening in early 1951 in Passaic, New Jersey, a rap came on the door of the apartment occupied by Thomas Aloysius Kelly. Kelly was a bachelor manager of a department or hardware store of some kind, and was in his early thirties. He answered the door, and there stood a military policeman.

The military policeman said, "Are you Lieutenant Thomas A. Kelly, U.S. Army Reserve?"

"I am Thomas A. Kelly, but I'm not a lieutenant, and I am not in the Army Reserve."

"Sir, did you get a notice to report to Fort Dix, New Jersey, for active duty?"

"Yes, I did, but it was addressed to Lieutenant Kelly, and I am not a lieutenant."

"Well, sir, you're AWOL."[1]

"I can't understand why I'm AWOL when I'm not a lieutenant or in the Reserves."

---

[1] Absent without leave.

"Sir, you are absent without leave, and you are supposed to do what that order said, to report to the commanding general of Fort Dix, New Jersey, and you should do so, tomorrow."

Kelly said, "Soldier, I am not a lieutenant. I never was. During the war I was a parachute packer in the Army Air Corps. I was only a private, and the only thing I know about the military is how to pack a parachute."

"Sir, I'm not here to argue with you. I'm here to tell you that you'd better report to the Commanding General at Fort Dix no later than tomorrow night; otherwise, you'll be placed under arrest."

Kelly replied, "Soldier, this is a big mistake. I'm not going to Fort Dix, New Jersey, because I'm not a lieutenant, or in the Army Reserve."

"Okay, sir, I've told you. I've repeated what I was supposed to tell you, and consequently, you'll have to abide by the results."

So that was that.

Two nights later Kelly was home fixing his dinner about six-thirty. A rap on the door. He went to the door, and there was a major of infantry and two military policemen. The major said, "Are you Lieutenant Kelly?"

"No, sir, I am not Lieutenant Kelly. I am Thomas A. Kelly, Private, *ex*-Private, United States Army Air Corps."

"You are under arrest. You have five minutes to make any telephone calls you wish and to get whatever you want to take with you. You're going to Fort Dix, and you're going to the guardhouse."

"You can't do this!"

The military policemen reached in and took him, one by each arm, and said, "We can. We will. And you're going with us. So don't give us a hard time."

Well, Kelly knew that he was going; so he decided to

do what he had to do. He called some people he knew, as well as his landlord. He picked up a toothbrush, a razor, and some changes of underwear; he put them in a little satchel, locked the door, and was led off to Fort Dix.

At Fort Dix the next morning he was ordered to go with escort to the post exchange to buy uniforms and outfit himself. He was issued combat clothing and was flown to Korea the next day as an infantry officer replacement.

Thomas Aloysius Kelly, First Lieutenant —USAR?— reported to me for duty with the 17th Infantry as a replacement officer. It was my habit that any time an officer was assigned to my regiment I had a long talk with him. My purpose was to find out what I could about the officer within a short time, figure out where I needed a replacement most, and above all of that, to tell him what I expected of him. The speech went something like this:

"Kelly, you're going to be in control of men, and you'll also be, if you will, besides a commander, an intelligence officer. That is, you will always have an assessment in your mind of what is out in front of you, whether somebody tells you or not, you're going to have a gut feeling about what's there. Now, when you report to your captain about what you think is in front of you, I want you to tell the captain the *truth*. Do not use scare tactics. Do not tell the captain there are five battalions when there's only a squad, because the captain is going to tell the battalion commander, and the battalion commander is going to tell me, and I'm going to have to act on what you have told the captain. Now, if it's fallacious, if it's overdone or underdone, this could mean that we could lose the regiment. So I want the *truth*, the honest to God truth as you believe it, to come from you whenever you report anything.

"The next thing I expect of you is to demonstrate an element of *courage*, and when I say demonstrate, I do not mean that you should stand on the parapets with a flag in your hand as you see some pictures, or with a saber with which you say, 'Charge.' I do not expect that. What I do expect of you is that you present yourself to your troops and be with them when they are under fire. You can't do this all the time. You can't be a rifleman. You are a leader, and you must be to the rear for leadership as you have reins on a horse; you can't lead the horse, you must steer it by the reins. But again, I repeat, place yourself at risk at various times so that your men may see you experience the same physical risks that they do on daily basis."

I finished my lecture and said, "Now you're going to Company L."

He said, "Colonel, can I tell you something before I leave?"

"Yes," I replied.

"Sir, I don't know whether or not I have *courage*. But I will always tell you the *truth*, as I will do now. I am not an infantryman." *Then he told me his story.*

Well, here was a problem. I couldn't send this man up to Company L anticipating that he'd take over the Second Platoon and lead it into combat, because he didn't know how to fight a platoon. So I said, "Kelly, I can't send you home because the Army just sent you here. So, here's what you do: report to Company L; I'll tell the captain to assign you to the 2nd Platoon. Right now, Sergeant O'Brian is commanding it. When you take over, call Sergeant O'Brian aside and tell him your story, and then ask him to teach you how to be a platoon leader."

The next time I saw Kelly, it was three weeks later. He was on a litter in the regimental aid station after a very bitter fight. His right arm was almost shattered. He'd been shot with an automatic rifle. Otherwise, he was okay. He wasn't going to die.

I said, "What happened?"

"Well, you know, I'm a fast learner, Colonel. Early this morning I took the platoon out. We went around a hill and came up in back of a group of North Koreans who were asleep. We butchered 'em. We really clobbered 'em. We cleaned off that hill. But two or three of them let go, and of course, I was out there kind of in the front, and I got it in the arm."

"You know, Kelly, that's a short stay—three weeks."

"Yes, Colonel; however, I'm very happy that I did what I did. I feel very proud about going home. I understand I am going to Tokyo General Hospital. The thing that's hurting me, though, is that I'll never get an infantry combat badge, because you have to serve in the infantry in combat for one month."

I said, "You've got one, soldier. I removed my combat infantry badge and pinned it on him. I said, "I'm going to back date the order assigning you to Company L. I'm proud of you, Kelly. Wear this the rest of your life."

About four or five months later I was replaced and ordered back to the Pentagon from Korea, as I had been there in combat for a year. I was flown to Taegu and later to Tokyo for another plane home. As I got off the plane in Taegu, I went towards the headquarters building restroom to get a cup of coffee before I got on another plane. Who should walk out and bump into me but Captain Thomas Aloysius Kelly, now a captain not only in the Reserve, but in the Regular Army. We embraced. I said, "Kelly, what in the hell are you doing here?"

"Sir," he said, "I decided to stay in this man's Army; I'm making a career of it. After I left Tokyo, I had a choice of going home or not, and I decided I would prefer to come back to Korea." And he added, "I've still got it up here," and pointed to the Blue Badge, the combat infantryman's badge that I had given him. Underneath it I could see a Silver Star Ribbon, a medal for heroism.

Because of him, and many others like him, the 17th Infantry Regiment adopted as its motto—*Truth and Courage*.

17th INFANTRY REGIMENT

45

I SAW BUFFALO BILL

From *Pacific Patrol Magazine*, July, 1951

I Saw

Buffalo

Bill

*THE PIONEER RUGGEDNESS OF
BUFFALO BILL APPEARS AGAIN
ON THE KOREAN
BATTLEGROUND*

By Craig Scott

Dust erupted from the wheels of the machine-gun jeep as it braked to a stop at the junction of spiraling Korean mountain roads. A helmeted man leaped out, firmly planted a sign at the road's edge. A black buffalo was emblazoned on the sign; the legend read, "Danger—Buffaloes Crossing."

A man in battle dress came to his feet, remained standing in the jeep. A hint of grey peeked from beneath his steel helmet. Intelligence burned from his eyes and his bearing was an etching of pride. As he surveyed the line of steel-toting infantrymen approaching the junction, his chin jutted with confidence. . . .

Curiosity pushed me over to the soldier who had planted the sign and I asked, "Who's the colonel?" the man pierced me with a look that had all the cold steeliness of a thrust bayonet. It was if that single question had branded me an idiot. Finally, "That's Buffalo Bill Quinn," he snorted, "the best damn regimental commander you'll ever see!"

And I took a good look at Buffalo Bill, for this was not the first time I'd heard that name in Korea. During a recent visit to the replacement company, I had been told, "There's one regiment we don't have to worry about replacements for.... Men are begging to join the Seventeenth Infantry Regiment. They've all heard about Buffalo Bill."

The command post of the Seventeenth Infantry was not far from my present location. I remembered that the unit was one of the oldest (activated in 1812) United States regiments. A half hour of jeeping along the Pyongchang river, then into the mountains, and I reached a tent city— Korean headquarters of a legendary regimental commander. In a few minutes, I was standing before a staff officer. "What foundation," I asked, "is there to the story that men are going Absent Without Leave to join your regiment?"

The major smiled. He picked up a sizable stack of letters from a nearby field desk and thrust them into my hands. "There is your answer."

One hour and fifty pages later, I had mulled over such urgent messages as—"Sir, I hope that you can make room for me in your regiment as I am willing to go all the way even if it means my life, and that is giving all I got, Sir, so please give me a chance."

Word had spread, with the rapidity of a medieval plague, throughout the Korean peninsula and the Japanese isles. Men with fighting fever were "taking off" from all types of units to join Buffalo Bill and his "hot outfit." Colonel Bill Quinn was the warlock and the Bison his talisman. Together, they spun a web of glamour that is paying off in enemy dead and high troop morale.

Earnest men were requesting permission of their commanding officers to be transferred to the Seventeenth Infantry Regiment. One man in his eagerness had skipped channels. His letter urged, "Like three other men who went Absent Without Leave to join your Regiment so did I but before I could see anyone the Military Police sent me back to Pusan. I am now awaiting Court Martial. Sir, I've heard so much about your outfit that I want in. I just have the urge to fight and I am stuck back here. I would be deeply indebted to you if you would please take me with you."

Colonel Quinn answers all the letters personally but cautions these volunteers to apply for a transfer through their present commanding officers.

To men bogged down in such terminology as GI, doughfoot, mud-churner and fox-hole artist, the words Buffalo, musketeer and infantryman strikes a concordant note. No infantryman likes to think of himself as a mudslogger . . . like the pikemen in the armies of history, they're proud of their title and will stand shoulder to shoulder to uphold it. Words that paint a drab likeness of the bayonet-wielding, line-charging infantryman are avoided in the Seventeenth.

Pride and self-respect are essential elements in the make-up of a sound fighting man. This was reflected in one of the letters which said, "I have applied for a transfer to your unit three times. I am writing you hoping you will be able to do something for me. I have heard a lot about your outfit and I know that if I can join you I would respect myself and my unit much more than I do now." Another soldier wrote, "It would bring me unbounded joy and pride if I could become a soldier in your regiment."

The urgent requests I was reading came from men in the artillery, quartermaster, engineers, signal corps, many service organizations and other infantry units. A letter from an Army baker requested, "I hope so earnestly to enter the field of combat as a soldier in your Seventeenth Regiment and, should this request be granted, I will serve you to the best of my ability and in such a manner as to bring

credit to you, your regiment, and to the United States Army. I fully realize that my qualifications as an infantryman are few, Sir, but I am a native Texan and an expert rifleman. I have two stripes which I am willing to give up, if necessary, should this request be granted."

Motives for wanting to join the Buffaloes differed but the underlying urgency of the requests never wavered. A letter from a corporal on Okinawa expressed, "I would give anything to get assigned to your outfit. I would like very much to replace my brother who is listed as missing in action. I have six brothers who were all in the service and all have seen some combat. I want to show my brothers that I can take anything that they did. Please, Colonel, help me to reach Korea. I will be more than grateful to you the rest of my life."

Three artillerymen asked Buffalo Bill for an advance letter of acceptance so that they could initiate a transfer. Their letter said, "We are members of your outfit. We would consider it an honor to serve under your command."

I noted that many of the men requesting transfer to the Buffaloes were proud of the units in which they were currently serving. An engineer explained, "Sir, this is one of the best engineer outfits there is. But I would like to be transferred to your regiment. It doesn't matter what kind of work I do at first . . . truck driver, rifleman, ammunition bearer, anything so long as I'm helping."

To me, these letters were an indication that the fighting spirit—which has won the American soldier fame and respect in many countries—was receiving a spark of new life and being fanned into a conflagration of fighting power in this old infantry regiment.

I returned the letters to the major. "They mean every word of it," he assured me. "Those men are serious."

• • •

In every war soldiers have rushed to join a leader, the Korean campaign is no exception. The military science of tactics is built around incidents in which leadership has turned the tide of battle. Every fighting man sees his own introverted qualities mirrored in a spirited and colorful commander. These fighting men are not easily fooled. They watch their man carefully. They've seen "eyewash" before and can measure sincerity. When a man is imbued with the magnetic current of chieftaincy, men in his command cloak themselves in the mannerisms he radiates. The pattern is set. Each individual prides himself upon achieving the standard. Fears are conquered. Heroes rise.

Volunteer replacements continue to "crop up" in the regiment—sometimes where least expected. A

sergeant of the Seventeenth was counting the men in a pack train carrying heavy loads of ammunition to guns firing in the mountains—three too many. He counted again. The result was the same. After a quick investigation, he ordered three heavily-laden soldiers to step out of the line. The men reluctantly admitted that they were members of a rear area unit but had "taken off" to join the Buffaloes.

The will to fight is the most significant thing about the Seventeenth Infantry Regiment. *Esprit de Corps* is a somewhat "dog-eared" expression that takes on new meaning as the observer moves into an area occupied by the Buffaloes. The impression is dynamic—and it's catching.

UN War Correspondent William Burson, watching the Buffaloes storm Hill 1242, wrote, "It was spectacular in the determination with which the assault was mounted." After the action, the colonel admitted, "Taking that hill was the toughest assignment of my Army career—tough because of the hardships and sacrifices I had to ask my men to suffer." His eyes sparkled as he added, "We proved the American soldier is not the roadbound sissy our enemies took him to be." Hill 1242 is six air miles from the nearest road.

Bayonets often flash in the Seventeenth Regiment and their flash instills the spirit of close combat in the charging infantrymen. No man in the Seventeenth will ever forget the lesson that aggressiveness taught on the high ground west of Amidong. Bayonet-thrusting riflemen broke up an enemy attack and chased terrified Reds from the strategic high ground. Buffalo Bill had made it known throughout the command that bayonets were for active use—charging Buffaloes had used them well.

I had heard many stories of the powerful punches this proud unit delivered in combat action. Now I determined to see for myself how they reacted under fire. An intelligence officer told me that Company "I" would lead the attack the following morning. I jeeped to the company location and arrived at dusk to witness preparations for the jump-off. Operations were deliberate, thorough. Information was specific and was passed down through the ranks in a well organized manner. Orders were unquestioned. There was no lost motion. It was a thrill to watch a seasoned outfit prepare for combat action.

At dawn the company, draped with bandoleers and grenades, left the road and moved to the foot of a mountain mass—their first objective for the day. As I looked upward at the hazy mountain heights, I wondered how these infantrymen, each man carrying an extra round of ammunition (for supporting heavy weapons) and a bed roll, could even hope to scale those rugged slopes. We started the climb. Mines were located in the vicinity—another test of infantry courage. Men were cautioned to step in the footprints of those who were leading the way. Officers and noncommissioned officers continually reminded the men to stay at least five yards apart ("think five yards ahead" is the company motto) so that incoming mortar rounds would take as light a casualty toll as possible.

I saw the "Buffaloes" of Company "I" storm the heights of Hill 504 that day. I watched riflemen with fixed bayonets drop packs when they were under fire and unhesitatingly assault enemy positions. . . . And when I caught the expressions of wound-scarred young officers during the attack—eagerness was there; excitement was there—fear was absent.

Fighting men of the Seventeenth Regiment lived up to their much vaunted reputation that day and, from latest reports of frontline action, they are continuing to do so. Moving among the troops constantly, lending encouragement, setting the pattern, is the strong figure of the chiseled-chinned regimental commander. The man was using "unit pride" as the key to victory and he had sprung the lock.

Yes, I saw Buffalo Bill. There's no mistaking the undying spirit of that great pioneer. I recalled that during my trip to the West Coast, prior to embarkation for the Far East, I had climbed the heights above Denver and

observed from the spot where the man
in buckskin had once stood. Now, as I
watched a dusty column of infantrymen spiraling northward, I knew that
the statue on Lookout mountain had
come to life and was campaigning in
the mountains of Korea.

46

TALKS WITH NEW BUFFALOES

At the graduation ceremony of the new 4th Battalion of the 17th Infantry Regiment (Buffaloes) at Fort Benning, Georgia, in May 1984, the Secretary of the Army, John O. Marsh, Jr., appointed me as Honorary Colonel of the 17th Infantry Regiment. This was the regiment I had commanded in Korea in 1951 during the period of some of the heaviest fighting.

As Honorary Colonel it became my duty to visit with the various elements of the regiment and to evidence a paternal interest in their training, well being, and morale, on call.

Shortly thereafter, in anticipation of the reactivation of the Headquarters of the 17th Infantry at Fort Ord, California, the Chief of Staff of the U.S. Army, General John Worsham, dedicated a building at that installation as "Quinn Hall."

Upon invitation by the Commanding General of the 6th Infantry Division at Fort Richardson, Alaska (who commanded the 1st and 2nd Battalions), and the Commanding General of the 7th Infantry Division at Fort Ord, California (who commanded the 3rd and 4th Battalions), I proceeded to those two Army posts during the summer of 1988 to speak to the men of those four battalions.

At each post the officers and men of the two battalions assembled in the post theater. I spoke to them as their Honorary Colonel, about their heritage and exemplary conduct in action during the period that I commanded their regiment in Korea.

Although my remarks to these young soldiers were delivered some thirty-seven years after that conflict, I felt obligated to recite to them the lessons to be learned through combat and to try to inoculate them with the element of pride in the accomplishments of their predecessors.

Here follow my remarks to these new members of the "Buffaloes":

I'm delighted to be here and meet with you soldiers. I would like to tell you the three main reasons why, as your Honorary Colonel, I am here today. The first one is to be back again with Buffaloes. This regiment has for me something that is very hard to describe, in affection and pride and appreciation. Secondly, I'm here to congratulate you. You know, everybody can't be a Buffalo. Everybody can't be in the 17th Infantry. But you are. And I want you to appreciate this, because actually what I'm going to say today, I hope will engender in you a better understanding and a better feeling for being what you are. I'm not going to take too much time in describing your heritage; but it's great. Your forebears have done one helluva job for their country and yours, and they've helped preserve the rights and privileges and freedom that you enjoy today. In World War I, they did a great job in Europe. In World War II, in the Aleutians, and other places in the Pacific, they performed well. But in Korea, they starred!

I recall the day that I received the honor of being designated as the Honorary Colonel. It was at Fort Benning, Georgia, on the day of the graduation of the 4th Battalion, which was a *COHORT* Battalion.[1] I'm sure they felt very happy to get out of basic and advanced infantry training, especially one named Private Johnson. He had this drill sergeant who really worked him over, day in and day out. And one day, this drill sergeant took old Johnson apart. I mean, he tore him down and built him over again, practically. After this was over, the sergeant stopped short, and he said, "Johnson, you know, I bet you, that when I die you're going to come and do something on my grave, to desecrate it."

Johnson said, "No, Sarge, once I get out of this man's Army, I'll never stand in line again!"

Well, the story starts, as far as I'm concerned, with the 17th Infantry, on the day that a new Division Commander arrived on the scene. His name was Major General Claude Ferenbaugh. His nickname was "Buddy." A great big guy, a wonderful commander, a wonderful man. At that time I was in the X Corps Headquarters as the Intelligence Officer working for Lt. Gen. Edward "Ned" Almond. The first evening he's with us, Buddy calls me out to his trailer and says, "Bill, would you like the 17th Infantry? I'm bringing Herb Powell up to be my Chief of Staff when I take over."

You know, I nearly dropped my teeth. I said, "My Lord. Yes sir! I'm ready to go right now!"

He said, "Wait a minute. You've got to go in and tell General Almond that you're going to do this."

---

[1]COHORT—Cohesive Operational Readiness Training

"Well, you're supposed to get your colonels, why don't you . . . ?"

He replied, "No way. If you want the Regiment, you go get it."

Well, this was a tough one. However, I went immediately in to see General Almond, whom I'd gotten to know pretty well. It was after dinner, so I walked into his office in a Korean school house. He greeted me and said, "What do you want?"

"Sir, I just came to say goodbye."

"Where in the hell do you think you're going?"

"Well, I'm going to take a regiment."

"Which one?"

"The Seventeenth."

"No, you're not. You're not leaving this staff. I just can't break up a staff because . . ." he went on and on.

"General, you're the Chief of Staff for General McArthur. You're serving one of the great men of all time, and you're serving in a great capacity as the Chief of Staff, and yet, what have you done, to leave an exalted position, but to get a Corps. And why?" I continued. "That's to command."

He answered, "Yeah, that's right, but you shouldn't use that excuse."

I kept on. "I am. Because that's what I want. And you wanted it, and you have it, and you understand my feelings."

After a thoughtful minute he said, "Well, Bill, I don't want you to go, but I'll tell you what I'll do. If you can find me a replacement, satisfactory to me, I'll let you go."

Well, I had already done that. Just in that hour, I'd called a friend of mine in Tokyo who was dying to get to Korea. His name was Colonel James H. "Jimmy" Polk, a classmate at West Point (who later turned out to be a four-star general). Jimmy agreed to take the job, and General Almond said okay. I got the Regiment.

Now, I'd had a battalion, and I'd had a regiment before, but not like this one. They had not been in combat, but this outfit had been to the Yalu River! It wasn't something that I'd picked up in the dump. I thought, I've got a good start. Now how can I improve on its performance? What can be done to create pride and higher morale?

The first thing I did, I went by the Corps Quartermaster and picked up 15 American flags, small storm flags. When I took over the regiment, I called all the company commanders in for a meeting, and I gave each one of them an American flag, and said, "This is the flag that you're fighting for. I want this to be a rallying point. You're not going to carry it up on the front lines, but wherever the company command post is, that flag should fly. I'll fly one in front of my headquarters tent here."

Well, that sort of turned Korea upside down. Nobody at that time had ever seen an American flag outside of some post, camp, or station, certainly not in combat. There, the same day, this incredible coincidence occurred. Our call sign for communications was changed because somehow the old call sign book had been lost or compromised. The Signal Officer of the 7th Division changed all call signs and issued the 17th Infantry the call sign of "Buffalo."

It just so happened that a group of press people were up front when I joined the regiment. I took command in the middle of a fight. We took the hill, and when it was all over, these correspondents began to show interest in the new commander, etc. I introduced myself as Bill Quinn, but by that time the word had gotten around about the change in the name of the call sign to "Buffalo." One newspaper guy said, "What do you know? Look, we've

got 'Buffalo Bill' here." And to me, "Where's your beard?"

In any event, the Division Commander called me up that night and said, "Nice job up there, Buffalo Bill." And that's how I got the nickname. It isn't something that I gave myself.

Now, a flag issue surfaced. Initially there were no flag poles, however, the first thing you know, we had a regimental company competition as to which one could get the tallest flagpole. That created a hell of a problem, because I had a lot of AWOL's going to Pusan, three hundred miles south of our position, to find thirty-foot bamboo flagpoles for their companies. Of course, the cry of "Foul" reverberated through the Regiment. I had to issue an order that no flagpole would exceed twelve feet in height.

The flying of the flag was a real morale builder. It and our call sign "Buffalo" gave us a tremendous lift. As a result we began to see buffaloes painted everywhere. All our tanks had a buffalo painted on them. Also trucks, jeeps, tents, you name it.

Now we got in the sign business. Besides several wags in the Regiment, the battalions were putting up signs about their role. For instance, you might be moving along a road, in the middle of nowhere, and pass a sign which read, DANGER, BUFFALOES CROSSING. Let's take the sign at Hauchon, a town that had been battered to a pulp. There wasn't anything standing over three feet high. It had really been pulverized by tank and artillery fire. At the entrance to the town, the company which took it erected a sign which read, WELCOME TO HAUCHON, A PEACE LOVIN' TOWN, AND WE AIM TO KEEP IT THAT-AWAY. THE BUFFALOES.

Speaking of signs, I must interject here, although it happened later in the Korean War, the story of the Second Division sign. On their arrival in Korea they erected, at the entrance to their area, a sign which read:

WELCOME
SECOND U.S. INFANTRY DIVISION
SECOND TO NONE

About a mile down this main road was billeted an Australian Battalion, which erected an equally large sign which read:

NONE

Our signs evidenced a boost to our spirit, pride, and sense of humor. The press intensified their coverage to see what we were up to and to find out just how and why we were kicking the living hell out of the North Koreans.

We also had some other gimmicks to keep things moving. Some one suggested that we grow "Buffalo staches." So I initiated a program whereby every two weeks, I gave the soldier with the longest handlebar mustache a case of beer. You wouldn't believe some of the specimens that showed up. I know I had a beaut when I left the Regiment.

About this time I brought a Battalion executive officer who had previous public relations experience to Regimental Headquarters. He was instructed to put out thirty hometown news releases a day. These were stories about the activities of the GI's. They were all laudatory. It was interesting to note that within three or four months most of my casualties had a clipping in their pocket from their hometown newspaper indicating that they were serving well, doing a fine job for their country in the 17th Infantry.

It was also about this time that I sent an officer to Tokyo to purchase several thousands of buffalo nickels, which were undersized and made of aluminum. On one side was the buffalo and date of 1812, the year the regiment was first activated. On the reverse the Regimental crest and Korea 1951. When their tour of duty was completed, and on their departure from the Regiment, the men were given one of the nickels for a keepsake. They were told that if ever challenged by another Buffalo and couldn't produce his, he bought the drinks.

Now, the tactics we employed increased our capability. I must say to you soldiers, that in training, I believe that troops should be nearly exhausted on a daily basis, and I say that because it prepares you for the rigors of combat. It has to do with condition and the mind. However, in combat I concluded that in rugged terrain, that men should not be completely exhausted every day for the simple reason that a tired man is not alert in combat. He's more careless. He'd rather sit down than look behind each bush. We had a concept in our American military schools that you have to do everything starting at dawn. You had to get up before daylight to get breakfast, to move to the line of departure, and to attack at dawn. The concept was supposed to entail the element of surprise. Manure.

My concept of the North Koreans was that they were surprised when we didn't attack early in the morning. They were waiting for us because that was the American tactic. Sometimes you're thinking about your troops and you don't really play the game as it's supposed to be played.

Here's what we did. We waited until daybreak to get out of the sack. Now, the orders, of course, indicated that at dawn the unit was supposed to cross the line of departure. The objective was named, and so fourth. But I felt that troops should get as much sleep as they could. They should get up and have a hot breakfast and take a leisurely crap, and believe it or not, do so with a current *Stars and Stripes* to read, and then go to work. They worked eight hours, and roughly at four o'clock, were still fresh. However, the Koreans were pooped by noon, because they had been waiting for us since before daybreak. We fought, and we kicked the living hell out of them. At four o'clock, we stopped where we were and dug in for a counterattack. We developed avenues of fire, or fire lanes, and we were ready for the counterattack, which quite often came very early in the morning. We were never driven off of our position at night, because even though we didn't see what we were shooting at, we'd already outlined the fields of fire, and we clobbered them night after night.

Now this thing about tired troops is that if every soldier, except those in security on outposts for one reason or another, was completely fresh in the morning he should have an eight hour day, I felt. It was not only a feeling, but a fact—the war was not going to be won the next day or the day after. Consequently, I wanted all of my men to be there at the finish, and not be carried home some other way.

Now then, here we were, really clobbering the enemy, getting great press, and what's the result? Letters start coming in literally from all over the world, to me, asking if I can get them transferred to the 17th Infantry. I had over a hundred and fifty letters of requests for transfer. One day, around 5:00 P.M., we had just completed our operation. A truckload of soldiers from Pusan came barrelling into my command post. They were all fully equipped, with rifles and so on. They had commandeered a truck and came to join the 17th Infantry. I told them, "There's no way this can be done. You're all AWOL."

"Yes," they responded, "you can take care of that."

"No, I can't. As I said, no way. You're all headed for a court martial. However, come on in, and I'll give you something to eat. I'll take each of your names, your company commander's name, and I'll write him a personal letter, because if you're so hot to get into this regiment, I'd like to have you. But tonight you're going back to Pusan."

Actually, three of them finally made it into the Regiment.

Now when your outfit establishes this kind of reputation and when the press is pouring all over you, and you get world recognition, you begin to have problems with your sister regimental commanders. They're not very happy about this. For instance, one night I was ordered to come up to 7th Division Headquarters for a briefing in connection with a forthcoming operation. The other two regimental commanders, the artillery commander, and some staff of the Division were in the Division Commander's trailer. I was the furthest away, because we were further out front that the rest of them. So I was a little bit late getting there, and when I walked into the trailer, these characters stood up and sang, "Be careful of where you walk, or be careful where you sit, because the first thing you know you'll be in buffalo shit." Well, I told them if they'd just get their noses out of our behinds and get out in front every now and then they wouldn't have to step in it.

Now, all of this sounds like it was a junket, but fighting is never that. There were problems. These problems, of course, were not morale, they were physical, and it had to do with the weather. In some instances it was 30 below. We had troops in the hills trying to sleep through this incredible cold with inadequate clothing. Consequently, we had an awful lot of frostbite, primarily of feet. It got to a point where I had to develop, and build to carry along, a laundry for socks. Each night when we delivered a hot dinner to each individual soldier, no matter where he was, we also issued him a pair of dry socks to put on to sleep through the night. We took his wet or used socks back to the laundry.

There is another story I want to tell you, and it may not be directly related to morale, but has something to do with it. One day I conducted an inspection when we finally had a break. We were on a river, it was spring, and it was warm enough for everybody to get cleaned up.

Lt. Col. Quinn helps launder socks.

I decided to talk to all the men in three battalions, in three successive days. I wouldn't talk to everybody, naturally, but I went down each line and looked at every soldier and from time-to-time, I stopped in front of one of them, and would ask, "Why are you so good?"

And he would think for a minute, and then respond, "Well, sir, you know, I appreciate that, but I fight, really, because of my buddy." You see, I had a buddy system, and there were always two guys together. One would pull the other one out if he got hit or otherwise watch out for him. "I also fight because I am in the best regiment in the American Army. And I guess I'm fighting communism."

The ideological standpoint seemed to be the least of the motivation. But then I asked, "What bugs you? Chow or R & R or something else?"

"No, sir. I'm okay. No problems here. But what bugs me is that the leadership and politicians in Washington don't have as much guts as I do."

You know, I couldn't fight that one, because I was of the same opinion. They stopped us, whoever "they" were in Washington. They stopped the Buffaloes when they were roaring. We were on our way to North Korea, clobbering the Chinese Communists on the way, and the North Koreans knew it; so they said, "Let's talk." Now there's Panmunjong. That's how the Buffaloes and other winning units were stopped, not by the enemy, but by Washington D.C.

There's hardly anything in the world in the military except pride and morale and a way of doing things right. And as your Colonel, I charge you with maintaining the pride that you should have in being a Buffalo and the pride that you're going to have the rest of your life for having served your country.

So long and good luck.

47

THE BUFFALO THAT DIDN'T GO TO WAR

The following article was published in *This Week* magazine, Sunday supplement to the *New York Times*, in 1953.

T he fascinating story of William the Buffalo as of this moment still has no ending. Its beginning goes back to one cold and raw afternoon in February 1951, while the 17th Infantry was tenaciously fighting its way up a Korean mountainside. I received a field telephone call from Major General Claude D. "Buddy" Ferenbaugh, my division commander.

"How are those buffaloes doin' up there, Buffalo Bill?" he asked. I told him we were stampeding the North Koreans back to the Yalu River and that before nightfall we would be on our objective.

That was the day that the Regiment was definitely

"pegged" with its nickname, as was its commander.

As a result of the enthusiasm shown by the troops for their nickname, I made up my mind to try to get us a live buffalo. I had noticed an article in the *Buick Magazine* describing the Clark Buffalo Ranch in Independence, Kansas. Gene Clark, the owner, had the largest private herd of buffalo in the country.

I wrote Gene Clark, told him about the Regiment, and asked him if he would be kind enough to sell the outfit a young calf. He cabled immediately, "Mascot available with my compliments. So am I, if you can use me."

There and then began the unexpected and prodigious effort of drafting William, as Gene had named him. I never guessed how many obstacles would stand in the way.

I made a quick trip to Seoul to the 5th Air Force Headquarters and asked the officers there to send a message to General Vandenberg, Chief of Staff of the Air Force in Washington. I briefly described to him the "William Case," and asked him if he would please fly our mascot to us. Unfortunately, General Vandenberg was in Europe on an inspection trip and through some mix-up between the Air Force and the Army on the departmental level, the request was turned down.

This was a big disappointment to the Regiment, as by that time the project, previously kept secret to preclude disappointment, had leaked out. Actually, the men would have given up their beer, candy and magazines in exchange for William. It's hard to realize the morale aspects connected with such a simple thing; and fighting men oddly enough do not demand much.

During July, Gene Clark tried everything he could think of to ship William. He approached the governor of Kansas, who was sympathetic, but in view of the necessity of taking care of flood victims, felt that it would be inappropriate to spend $2,500 to transport a buffalo to Korea.

Senators and representatives from Kansas queried the Department of Defense about William, but no satisfactory answers were forthcoming. Being referred to the State Department, one congressman received a staggering blow when told that William's shipment was impossible because he might carry hoof-and-mouth disease to Korea.

This caused a loss in yardage on the part of the home team and a nasty disposition on the part of William, who began receiving shots for everything.

In August my tour of duty in Korea ended. While I was in Tokyo en route to the United States, I enlisted the services of members of the Pacific *Stars and Stripes* on William.

They attempted to work out the problem through Northwest Airlines. That didn't work either.

In Washington I propositioned Pan American Airways. They were very enthusiastic, but had to turn it down as it required Air Force Military Air Transport Service, and the Air Force had previously disapproved the project.

In September Gene Clark finally worked out a plan to ship William to Tokyo. Everything was set. Officers were dispatched from the Korean front to Tokyo by Lieutenant Colonel Hal McCown, my successor in command of the 17th. Just as William was being loaded in a plush crate, lined in buffalo hide, and had received all his shots, word was received that a "military permit" was required in order to ship him into Korea.

This permit had to come from Eighth Army headquarters, which had little or no information concerning this case. The request was turned down because the Eighth Army Quartermaster had no feed for animals in his inventory. Once again William hit the pasture.

Meantime, Gene Clark reported periodically to the Regiment on William, who, apparently by this time conscious of his situation, was turning into something of a spoiled brat.

"We have a pen for him so that hundreds of tourists can see him and feed him. And we are having a sign made which will show his name and the fact that his owners are the men in the Buffalo Regiment. He will make the trip okay, since he is too cockeyed ornery to do anything else."

Again: "William now weighs over 400 pounds, making him the largest calf in the herd. He's found that by jumping at the fence, he can scare the hell out of people. And that is precisely the way he wants it."

Another report: "Last week he got out and went down to the big pasture where the herd was grazing. There was a tall fence between him and the herd. He shadowboxed against the fence looking for an opponent all day, arriving home late in the evening weary and hungry."

One more: "We have a bunch of baby chicks which have made their home in William's pen. He likes to lie down and let them walk all over him searching for any flies or bugs he might have acquired."

In February, Gene Clark took William and the calf's father and mother on an exhibition tour of the state fairs in Florida. At Tampa, the Fair Association awarded William the Grand Champion Buffalo Bull Ribbon.

I was invited to receive the ribbon in behalf of the 17th Infantry which, of course, was still fighting in Korea. This was the first instance in stock history wherein a buffalo had received such an award. I sent the ribbon on to the Regiment.

William is still growing and is still stamping at the

ground in his impatience to get to Korea. Does any reader have any ideas? If not, I guess that we will have to look to the Navy, because if many more days go by, it will take a battleship to move him to his new pasture on the Korean hillsides.

Lt. Col. William W. Quinn
in front of huge white buffalo.

48

THE BLUE
BADGE

When I returned from Korea I was assigned to the Office of the Chief of Staff of the United States Army. I was ordered into the Planning Coordination Section which was run by Brigadier General Marcus Stokes, and we all worked for General Charles Bolte, who was Deputy Chief of Staff for Plans and Operations in the Army. After a few months in the Pentagon and in reading the local newspapers and magazines, I suddenly realized what the G.I. or the infantryman was up against. The Pentagon and the public were not aware of the tensions involved in combat conditions. They were not really aware of the family problems at home: divorces, deaths of members of the family where troops were unable to attend, etc. There did not seem to be an awareness of these difficulties. And yet the men were still fighting with a high degree of morale. This attitude on their part, I thought, was not fully appreciated.

One day at lunch I met a young man named Rusty Moore, who was in the Audio-Visual Section of the Chief

of Information/Public Affairs, and he was quite knowledgeable about television and radio. I expressed to him
my great concern. As a result of this conversation, he said,
"Well, run a TV show on one of the stations here in
Washington and bring these points out which you think
are not necessarily appreciated by the public."

I said, "You know I don't know anything about television."

"Well, I don't know too much either, but I'll tell you
what I think we could do."

So we talked and talked and finally came to the conclusion that we could go downtown and talk to a network
and see if they had a spot, on any day of the week,
preferably on a weekend, when we could do a half-hour
show. We outlined a program for three or four shows.
The general theme/proposition was to open the show live
with some witnesses or equipment or a discussion having
to do with a military subject and then cut that and put in a
documentary film for about 15 to 18 minutes on various
aspects of the war, i.e., the war in the Pacific, the war in
Europe, documentaries on McArthur, Eisenhower, Bradley, Patton, and then come back live and end the show
with the live portion.

Well, we took these projected shows, that is, the programs for them, and had them roughly timed out. We
went first to the head man of CBS in Washington, and he
said, "Well, beginning January first, we have a 2:00 to 2:30
spot on Sundays and we are debating on how to fill it.
Would you fellows like to try that?"

We said we would.

So we decided to name the show "The Blue Badge."
We got the name from the blue combat infantry badge
and of course, the infantry color is blue.

Consequently, we began to get down to the minutiae

from the standpoint of timing, although we had no re-
hearsals. We just went on TV cold, but live. And I must
say, on the first program, I was a little jittery because I
didn't know how it was going to work, or whether or not it
was going to flop. But it turned out to be a very interesting program, and as we went along we got a little more
savvy and a little more professional, and finally we came
out with banners flying. As a matter of fact, of all the four
TV networks in Washington, our rating was number two
for the 2:00 to 2:30 time slot on Sundays. We were out-
voted only by "Hopalong Cassidy" with William Boyd,
which was a movie serial starting at two o'clock.

In any event, we progressed very well. We had received no particular comment from the public one way or
the other until one show. I had recruited an American
soldier of Chinese descent who agreed to dress up in a
Chinese Communist soldier's uniform and appear on our
program. He was rehearsed, in that we told him what we
would do, and so forth. He was brought on the stage by
MP's, or one MP, who was part of the act, and he sat
down. I began to interrogate him. He was very rude,
which was part of the act. He challenged me and the
United States for being capitalistic—quite a tirade—and
finally, I had him taken off by the MP, again part of the
act. That following week we got floods of letters saying,
"How come you let a Commie prisoner talk to you like
that? You should have slapped him in the face!" It was
really humorous, the reaction we got. However, what
made us happy was that we were good enough to make
the public think the action was real, hence the reaction.

In any event, the program eventually ended after the
thirteenth show. We signed off with the hope that the
public had enjoyed the program; we explained what we
had been trying to do and how we thought we'd accom-

plished our goal, and hopefully, they would look forward to more military programs.

I got a nice letter from the Secretary of the Army, the Chief of Staff, complimenting me on the show. (I should have noted that the Army did not support me at all in this, nor had I asked for help; I just did it myself with Rusty). Later on the Chief of Information apparently was greatly impressed with this effort of ours, just off the top of our heads—strictly amateurish—but it gave him the idea which he pursued as a follow-up to "The Blue Badge," that is, a show that ran for years and years afterwards called "The Big Picture."

I guess the moral of this story is that if you really have something on your mind, and you really want to have people hear you, then sound off.

PART VIII

GREECE

49

THE VITTRUP
AFFAIR

One day at Fort Rucker, Alabama, in September of 1953, I received a call from the Office of the Assistant Chief of Staff of the Army for Personnel in the Pentagon. The officer who called told me that my services were urgently needed in the Joint U.S. Military Advisory Group (JUSMAGG) in Athens, Greece, and could I be there in 48 hours? I told him I wasn't sure, that he should call a travel agency for the answer. He replied that if it were logistically possible, could I make it? I told him I didn't think so, as I would have some problems in extracting myself from certain duties in my division and that I would have to make plans for my family, etc.

Besides Bette, Sally, Donna, and Bill, Jr., my mother was living with us at the time in Enterprise, Alabama. As my mother would be unable to go to Greece, I had to see that she was properly taken care of. The officer continued to inform me that orders were being cut which authorized "concurrent travel," which meant that my family could travel with me to Greece. I asked him about inoculation requirements. He said cholera and tetanus were required. I informed him that my children needed these shots or boosters and it would take three weeks to get all they needed. He said he understood that, but my orders would authorize "concurrent travel" anyway. Shades of *Catch 22*.

After the dialogue, I asked him what the rush was all about. He said he didn't know much about the situation, but he had been told that a Brigadier General Vittrup, head of the Army Section of the JUSMAGG, had been declared *persona non grata* by the Greek government and had been ordered to leave, and that I had been designated as his replacement.

Well, the scrambling started. I sent my mother to stay with her sister in Crisfield, Maryland. Bette was left to pack and ship the furniture, evaluate our house in Enterprise, drive herself and the children to Statesboro, Georgia, for a three week stay for the shots, and make arrangements for the shipment of our car to Greece and for their passage to Piraeus.

While awaiting at the New York Port of Embarkation to board a ship for Greece, the children all acquired food poisoning from chicken salad sandwiches and were hospitalized for three days. Having missed the sailing, they were transported to McGuire Air Force Base at Fort Dix, New Jersey, and then, on a space available basis, flown to Tripoli, where I met them. I will not attempt to relate here all of Bette's trials and tribulations caused by that exercise, but I know that if she ever writes a book, she could fill half of it with those experiences alone.

It was not until I started this book that I tried to recall the Vittrup story. I remembered the reason he left and why I was sent to Greece, but not the details. I decided to call him, as he was the best source.

Lieutenant General Russell L. "Slim" Vittrup, U.S. Army (Retired) was a Brigadier General when he was in Greece. He is a West Pointer with whom I served in southern France and Germany during World War II and was a classmate of mine at the National War College. As Slim had received superior ratings throughout his career, I was at a loss as to why he could have been the only American officer serving in Military Advisory Groups, in all of the NATO nations, to have been declared *persona non grata*.

So one day in April 1988, I called General Vittrup and said, "Slim, once upon a time you told me the story of how and why Panayotis Canellopoulos threw you out of Greece. The reason I'm asking again is that I'm writing a book and in my chapter on Greece, I'd like to give the reader, if any, enlightenment on why I was sent to Athens."

"No problem, Bill. Actually, I've been doing about the same for my kids and grandchildren, and only a short time ago, I recorded the Greek episode. You're welcome to listen to it."

We made a date, and I recorded his story. Here follow excerpts of Slim Vittrup's verbatim version of the affair (the words in parentheses are mine):

One of my responsibilities (as Chief of the Army Section of JUSMAGG), which was included in the terms of the Bilateral Agreement, was meeting with the High Military Council of the Greek Army. They would meet periodically to decide on various and sundry affairs. Not only did they have their Chief of Staff of the Army and other senior representatives there, but also the Minister of Defense, Mr. Canellopoulos, who always sat in with the Chiefs at those meetings. In order to know what was going on, I had Pete Cannelos (Captain, U.S. Army) as an interpreter, and he could hand me a note so I could know generally what was going on. I would tell the Greeks what our reactions were. In other words, we were supposed to insure that the resources we were furnishing them were used for intended purposes, properly maintained, etc.

Colonel Howard John, who was the (U.S. Military) Attaché, had told Eddie Hart (Major General Charles E. Hart) and me that there was a coup beginning to boil in the Greek Army and the leader of the coup was Major General Christeas. In the Greek Army there were various factions, and some of them would leak things to our Attaché and keep him informed as to what was allegedly going on in the Greek Army. So we were kept pretty well abreast of this impending coup and zeroing in on who was involved with Christeas.

(I later learned) that Christeas had been appointed Commandant of the Greek War College, a very sensitive position in which he could operate much more effectively in accomplishing his mission of getting along with the coup. . . .

Well, we decided we couldn't let the Greeks get away with this without at least saying we were aware of it, and we questioned the wisdom of placing a man who was suspected of generating a coup in such a sensitive position. So at the next High Military Council meeting at a propitious time, I thought, I told Pete Cannelos to tell them what I thought about it.

Canellopoulos blew a fuse. He, the Minister of Defense, said, "This is a sovereign nation; we shall do as we see fit. We shall make such assignments as we desire. This is an insult, and this meeting is closed." I didn't think they'd blow up quite that high, but I had expected some sort of fireworks. I went back and told Eddie Hart what had happened. He wasn't too surprised.

Within five minutes we got a call from Jack (John E.) Peurifoy, the U.S. Ambassador. He said, "What in the hell is going on? Come on over here."

So General Hart and I brought Pete over. Fortunately, I had written out in English precisely what I wanted to say to those people, and Pete had translated that into Greek, presumably precisely as I had written it. When I followed in after Eddie Hart to see the Ambassador, he wanted to know what was going on. I told him, and fortunately, I said, "Here's exactly what I said on this piece of paper." Pete said, "Yes, I said that in Greek."

The next thing, word came down from (Prime Minister) Papagos that that guy Vittrup would be out of the country before dark, or words to that effect—*persona non grata*. I didn't think he'd go quite that far, but that's all right. I'm the guy that did it.

As to the meeting, Canellopoulos took the position he considered appropriate, that we'd gotten our nose too far into his business. Well, that's debatable, depends on how you look at it, whether or not we were willing to disregard an individual who is bordering on the edge of mutiny. . . . That's what I said in nickel words in this piece of paper which was read, that we could not condone mutiny. . . .

There's a little bit more to the story . . . because later on there are some other things that may be worth noting. There I was being told by the Prime Minister in Greece, through the Ambassador, that I should be sent home. Well, they sort of left it at that, but they didn't send me home that night. Actually, I went to a big reception that General Harkins was given that night. I didn't say anything to Muriel (his wife) at that time; so we went ahead to the reception, and it turned out that Canellopoulos was there. I saw him talking to General Hart (and I knew that) they were talking about me and what to do about me. In a few minutes Eddie Hart came to me and said, "I've just been talking to Canellopoulos, and he said, 'Let's just forget this whole affair. We're really good friends and don't want any unnecessary trouble.' What do you think about it?"

"Well," I said, "These people have taken a pretty tough position about our making comments which we considered appropriate in the Military Council, and they've accused the United States Government, with me as their representative, of sticking their noses too far in Greek business and insulting them. Now this is either serious or not serious. My feeling at this point is if we let them get away with this by coming back and saying, 'Oh, let's kiss and make up,' we're going to have trouble every time we state a position, give a suggestion, or make comments in accordance with the terms and conditions of the Bilateral Agreement. Then we're going to get more and more static. So I recommend you send me home and I take the rap."

He said, "Okay, that's what we'll do." Apparently, he went back and told Canellopoulos, "No soap. We're not receptive to your suggestion that we 'kiss and make up.'"

When we left Athens, quite a number of high ranking officers including the Chief of Staff of the Army, General Tsigounis, General Vassilopoulos, Chief Engineer Pallis, and many of the senior members of the Greek Army came out and waved us off. We went by air to Naples to catch a ship.... Meanwhile, Eddie Hart had flashed (Lt. Gen. Anthony) Tony MacAuliffe, Deputy Chief of Staff of Personnel (of the Army), and Hart wrote the finest letter I've ever had written about me, in which he said that I was carrying out my instructions and representing the United States as it should be.

Some time later when I was stationed in Washington, the Greek Ambassador gave a reception for Canellopoulos, and I was invited. When I came in, we put our arms around each other and fell on each other. Incidents like these are like a Gilbert and Sullivan comic opera.

And so I took over from Slim. I too left by ship approximately two years later. Without going into detail, as to my conduct and association with the Greek military, Slim Vittrup gave me a big fat clue as to the sensitivity of the Greek government. His experience was basically responsible for the farewell letters I received from the Greeks on my departure,[1] along with comparable editorials in the Athens papers.

KATHIMERINI

Wednesday, 8 June 1955

EDITORIAL

BON VOYAGE

ΚΑΤΕΥΟΔΙΟΝ

Ἡ ἀναγγελία τῆς προσεχοῦς ἀναχωρήσεως ἐξ Ἑλλάδος τοῦ στρατηγοῦ Οὐΐλλιαμ Κουΐν, ἀρχηγοῦ τοῦ στρατιωτικοῦ τμήματος τῆς Κοινῆς Στρατιωτικῆς διαδος τῶν Ἡνωμένων Πολιτειῶν, δὲν εἶναι δυνατὸν παρὰ νὰ προκαλέσῃ αἰσθήματα λύπης μεταξὺ τῶν πολυαρίθμων ἐνταῦθα φίλων του καὶ ἰδιαιτέρως εἰς τὰς ἑλληνικὰς ἐνόπλους δυνάμεις. Κατὰ τὴν διάρκειαν τῆς διετοῦς παραμονῆς του εἰς τὴν χώραν μας, ὁ στρατηγὸς Κουΐν εἰργάσθη δραστηρίως καὶ ἐπιτυχῶς διὰ τὴν ἀνάπτυξιν καὶ τεχνικὴν βελτίωσιν τοῦ ἑλληνικοῦ στρατοῦ καὶ συνέβαλε τὰ μέγιστα εἰς τὴν προώθησιν τῶν φιλικῶν δεσμῶν, ποὺ συνδέουν τὰς ἑλληνικὰς καὶ ἀμερικανικὰς ἐνόπλους δυνάμεις.

ΤΥΠΟΣ ΤΗΣ ΚΥΠΡΟΥ

The news of the forthcoming departure from Greece of Brigadier General William W. Quinn, Chief, U. S. Army Section, JUSMAGG, is not possible but to create feelings of sorrow among his numerous friends over here, particularly among the Greek Armed Forces.

During his two years of assignment in our Country, General Quinn has worked hard and successfully for the development and technical improvement of the Greek Army and has contributed greatly to the promotion of the friendly ties which bind the Greek and the United States Armed Forces.

[1]See Appendices K and L.

50

A Keg of Nails

When I was chief of the Army section of the Joint United States Military Advisory Group in Athens, Greece, I had occasion to visit many installations—the various schools and colleges of the Greek Army and many of the military units. One day I received an invitation to visit the regiment that was on the Bulgarian frontier. I accepted, and had my staff research this unit's history, location, mission, commander, and also something about living conditions of the troops actually facing the Bulgarians on the top of the mountains.

Well, I got all of the information that I needed, and one of the things that was rather unusual was the fact that the Greek Army supply system, besides lacking small spare parts for equipment, was short of nails. At this particular regiment, the troops were pitifully exposed and were living in stalls which were covered but open. This was their barracks, sheds unsuitable for the sheltering of animals.

The town nearest this regimental command post was

Alexandroupolis in Thrace, just a few miles from the Turkish border on the European side of the Bosporus. So on my way, in my light L-5 Army plane, I stopped in Salonika, found a hardware store, bought a keg of large ten-penny nails, and put them on my plane. I flew to Alexandroupolis, where I was met by the regimental commander. We drove in a jeep up to his headquarters in a small village about halfway up the mountain. We arrived at lunch time and sat down to a very Spartan meal—some soup, bread, and a piece of lamb, washed down with *retsina*, the resin-tasting Greek wine.

When I presented the regimental commander with this keg of nails, he was absolutely flabbergasted that anybody would think to bring a gift so menial, yet so vital, as nails. He immediately called in his adjutant, gave him some instructions in Greek, and then escorted me to the jeep. We started up the mountain to inspect the front line troops which were on the line of demarcation or boundary between Bulgaria and Greece.

I was appalled at the rugged existence that these soldiers were experiencing. Besides manning bunkers, earth fortifications and outposts in all kinds of weather, their sleeping and recreation quarters were open to the elements on one side. The nails would be used in closing in that side. Later on, when we came down the mountain, and before I departed, the Colonel assembled his small staff to read a proclamation, which made me an honorary member of the regiment, and also gave me a letter of thanks and appreciation for the generosity of the American people. As a matter of fact, I had presented the gift of nails in the name of the American people.

He said, "This proclamation will be read to every soldier in the regiment, and you must know that we've never had a more welcome or generous visitor."

That was fine, but before I left, I said, "Incidentally, I know what your war plans are. I know that in the event of hostilities, that is, in the event of a major thrust by the Bulgarians, you are to evacuate, to proceed to Alexandroupolis, to commandeer all small boats in the harbor and sail to Turkey, which is only a few miles away; and there you will become refugees or expatriates."

He said, "You know, General, that's what Athens says, and that's what they have written, and that's what they have told me to do. But General, we are not going to do that. This regiment is not going to run anywhere. We may be destroyed, and probably so, but we will stay here to the last man. And you may or may not divulge this—I hope you don't, but if it's necessary, you may. I just want you to now that my last act will be one of disobedience to any order to retreat."

Well, so far, he has not had to disobey the order, as peace has reigned, from that day to this, in Greece.

51

ADMIRAL JOE
IN ATHENS

Joe (whose full name is immaterial) was the British advisor to the Greek Navy in the Military Advisory Group from Great Britain. As such, he was, as were all general and flag officers, part of the diplomatic colony and so accredited. As a result, Joe and I were together socially quite a bit at various cocktail parties, receptions, and dinners.

One night Joe and his very delightful lady invited us to dinner. We went to their house, and after cocktails, took our place at the table, which seated ten people. We were served a typical British dinner of roast beef and Yorkshire pudding, a wonderful meal. The conversation was great, and we were having a fine time. After I finished my entree, the roast beef and salad, etc., I lit a cigarette. Joe said, "I say, old boy, you know in Great Britain we don't smoke at the table until after the sweet."

I asked, "What do you mean, after the sweet?"

"Well, you might call it dessert, but in any event, it is our tradition not to smoke until then."

"Well, fine. You can certainly do that if you wish, but we're in Athens right now, and consequently, I choose to smoke a cigarette, which is my custom after the entree."

Joe answered, "Really, you know, old boy, you're in a British home, and in British homes, we don't smoke until after the sweet. You'll notice that there are no ash trays on the table. And there will not be any ash trays put on the table by the servants until after the sweet."

"Well, Joe," I said, "that's no problem, I'll get an ash tray myself." So I got up, found an ash tray in the living room, brought it back, put it down in front of me, sat down, and smoked my cigarette.

Joe was furious. There was nothing more he could say, however. He'd warned me about the delicacy of the matter, but there was nothing he could do about it. The evening ended rather jovially, but not as warm as it might have been because of this irresponsible breach of protocol of a British custom which I had committed.

Two or three weeks went by, and Bette and I decided to have a dinner party. We invited Joe and his lady to attend. At cocktails before dinner, Joe took on an unbelievable load of martinis. He drank them as if they were going out of style. Finally, when we sat down at the dinner table, Joe passed out, fell out of his chair, and landed on the floor. Well, nobody paid much attention because we were all feeling wonderful and concluded that Joe was happy. So we let him lie on the floor until we all finished our dinner, then poured him into a car. His wife and his chauffeur took him home.

A couple of days later, I ran into Joe, and he was very humble and apologetic and said, "You know, old boy, I guess I had too much to drink the other night, didn't I?"

I answered, "Yes, Joe, you did, and I must tell you that was a very serious breach of protocol."

"What do you mean?"

"Well," I said, "In America, we don't pass out until after the sweet."

52

FAREWELL TO
A KING

When I received orders in Greece to proceed to the 9th Division in Germany, I thought I should probably go and say goodbye to His Majesty, King Paul. While I'd been in Greece with the Joint U.S. Military Advisory Group, I had occasion on any number of instances to be associated with the King, and in some instances with Queen Frederika. Any time I was with Her Majesty, it was a social event, either a horse show or regatta, or something of that nature, but I was with King Paul mostly on some official military business. During the period I was there, there were a number of bridges that were opened, dedications, graduation ceremonies at colleges, Easter celebrations at Special Forces Unit Headquarters, and other like occasions which I attended. Consequently, I got to know His Majesty quite well.

I said to myself shortly before we left, "I'll just go and say goodbye to him." So I called the Grand Marshal of his court and the major aide to the King, Colonel Levides.

Bette and I had gotten to know Colonel Levides and

his wife quite well. I called and said, "This is General Quinn, and I have orders to leave Greece. I would feel very disappointed if I left Greece without saying goodbye to His Majesty."

He said, "I think His Majesty would enjoy seeing you very much. Why don't you come to the palace Thursday afternoon at two o'clock?"

I said that would be fine.

Within two hours, maybe three, I got a call from the American Embassy at my office. A member of the staff said, "The Ambassador would like to see you at your earliest convenience," which meant right now.

I knew Ambassador Cavendish Cannon well. He was a rather dour Scotsman, but a reasonably nice man and a pretty good ambassador, as I recall. So I went up to see him within the hour; I was ushered into his office, and he asked me to sit down.

He said, "General Quinn, I find this a little embarrassing. I hate to remonstrate with you, but you have called the palace directly for an appointment with the King."

"I called Colonel Levides to tell him that I hoped I'd be able to say goodbye to King Paul before I left Greece."

"Well," said the Ambassador, "I understand that, but aren't you aware that an ambassador is the only person who is permitted by law to address the head of state in the country to which he is accredited?"

"Sir, I didn't think about that. I've been associated with the King time and time again; we've gotten to be pretty good friends, so I just thought, well, he's a friend of mine, and I'd just like to say goodbye."

"I understand that, but I think maybe this is a case in which you as a military man think that you have a soldier-to-soldier relationship. But it doesn't work that way."

"Are you telling me that I should call Colonel Levides and cancel the meeting?"

"No, no, you can't do that. I just want you to know what the rules are. Now, you have made an appointment, and Levides of course notified us, for two o'clock on Thursday. You proceed to the summer palace, present yourself, stay fifteen minutes, and then gracefully depart. That would give you long enough to say goodbye."

"All right, Mr. Ambassador. I'm sorry. If an apology is necessary, you have it, because it certainly was not my intention to breach protocol. Apparently I have, so please forgive me."

"All right, Quinn, but just so we can remember this."

On Thursday I went to the Summer palace as planned. Queen Frederika was up visiting some villages near Salonika and was not there. I was ushered into the study and greeted by the King. He said, "General, have you had lunch?"

"Yes sir."

"So have I. Would you like a brandy?"

"I think I would like one."

He poured brandies, and we sat down. He was very interested in my observations about the Greek Army, about its leadership, about the defense orientation, the status of the forces, the troops, and their morale. So I told him what I thought. It was pretty good news, because they had a good army. They didn't have as much equipment as they wanted, but they had great morale. Then we started talking about sailing, about horses, about Greek economy, about travel, etc. One thing led to another until finally, I looked at my wrist watch and said, "Your Majesty, I have instructions to stay fifteen minutes, and I've been here an hour. If this becomes common knowledge, I'll be in trouble with Ambassador Cannon."

"General, you have been here fifteen minutes. I'd take an oath on it."

I said, "Well, sir, I think I'd better depart."

We said goodbye, I proceeded down the hall, and when I got almost to the end, he stuck his head out of his study and said, "Tell your lovely wife hello and that the Queen and I wish you both the very best. It has been great having you in Greece."

And so I said goodbye to a King—and a brush with diplomacy.

PART IX

BACK TO GOD'S COUNTRY

To Sally —
With Love —
Dad
Christmas 1951

53

FORT CARSON, COLORADO

While I was Assistant Division Commander of the 9th Infantry in Goepingen, Germany, we received orders to "gyroscope" with the 8th Division at Fort Carson, Colorado. I was given the mission of taking the Advance Party of the 9th Division from Germany to Fort Carson in exchange for the Advance Party from the 8th Division to Germany.

The concept of "gyroscope" was that people only would move in a complete transfer of a division, i.e., body for body, and that all arms and equipment were to be left in place at both installations. I arrived at Fort Carson, Colorado, as my counterparts were departing, and I immediately set up a Division Headquarters in the old headquarters building of the 8th Division; i.e., as they moved out, we moved in.

My purpose and plans, of course, were to prepare for the arrival of the remainder of the Division, which was somewhere around ten to twelve thousand bodies.

It so happened that the former Commanding General

of the 8th Infantry Division, a man named Watlington, had caused quite a furor in the city primarily because of a lack of cooperation with the city fathers. As a result of his general attitude and hostility towards the public, the townspeople, to include the police, began to take it out on the troops. For various minor indiscretions, even low degrees of insobriety, the police would slap the soldiers in jail or fine them. General Watlington would go downtown and raise all kinds of hell, which did not ingratiate him at all with the townspeople. Consequently, I stepped into a situation which was going to be intolerable for the 9th Division. All our men were looking forward to coming into Colorado Springs and being back in the United States again. To have them walk into an environment of hostility was something that I couldn't accept, and I felt that my commander, Major General Harry Stark, would be very upset to find this condition on his arrival with the bulk of the Division. I also knew he'd be disappointed in me.

Therefore I sat down and tried to figure out what in the world I could do to alter this set of circumstances. It so happened, fortunately, that General Watlington decided to go to Germany with the advance group of his division. Consequently, he had departed the post and had left his subalterns behind to take over the rest of the Division. I soon came to realize that this was just a matter of simple public relations, and if we were to change the entire attitude of the city, we had to go to work to do it. But how was that to be done?

I decided on several courses of action. First thing I went to see the mayor. I introduced myself and told him who and what I represented and that I had ten or twelve thousand new people coming to his city and I realized that I was in the eye of a PR hurricane. I asked him for guidance on how to change the public image of Fort Carson, and would he help me do it?

"I'm delighted to see you, and of course I'll do everything I can, because as mayor of this city, I am very unhappy about what's been happening at Fort Carson. The first thing you have to do is get the newspapers on your side, ask for an interview, and tell them what your goals are. In the meantime, I'll start working in your behalf around town with various organizations in which I have some influence. So let's go from here."

The next day I went to call on the editor of the leading daily. He was very friendly and seemed pleased to anticipate a change of attitude at Carson, because he had been writing nothing but derogatory editorials and reports on arrests, etc., about the Fort. Another element in this equation was the fact that the Air Force Academy was under construction, and so it looked like the Army reputation was going downhill from a comparative standpoint.

Next I decided I'd talk to the merchants. I visited most, if not all, of the restaurant owners. There I met Joe Reich, who owned the Swiss Chalet, a popular restaurant, and Joe and I became good friends. He told me what the problem was as he saw it, and provided me with some excellent ideas on how to deal with it. I then went to all the pool halls and bars; I talked to bartenders, owners of pool halls, and to everybody in any place where I thought a soldier would visit.

We didn't have any problem with the officers, per se, but the town was just against Fort Carson. I went to the banks; there I met a Mr. Stone who helped me a great deal. Another banker, Jasper Ackerman, became one of my best friends and advisors. He later on helped me organize the Colorado Springs Chapter of the Association of the United States Army, which eventually became the largest chapter of AUSA in the United States.

Later on, I went to see the El Pomar Foundation people who owned the Broadmoor Hotel. I called on Charley Tutt and his sons, Thayer and Russell. The Tutts were a hospitable and generous family. As a matter of fact, they invited us to come to live at the Broadmoor at a nominal cost, which we did, because there were no quarters for anyone at Fort Carson at that time.

In my efforts to turn Fort Carson's PR around, I let my staff run the Fort. I was downtown day and night, going everywhere and meeting everybody and telling them what the incoming 9th Division was trying to do.

Finally, I went to see Dad Bruce. Dad was the Chief of Police in Colorado Springs, and a nicer man I never met. He was a genial and happy-go-lucky man and popular, much loved in the city. He was torn up about the fact that he had to make so many arrests of soldiers, but, as he said, the various establishments were demanding it.

When I thought I had the town moving in the right direction, I said to myself: How about our troops? We've got one side of the problem solved, I think; but what about the attitude of the soldiers themselves?

I called a meeting of all the officers and non-commissioned officers on the post, except for those in the 8th division who were going to leave—there was no need to call them. I told the assemblage, "Here's what we're going to do until the troops get here, and we'll follow through with them also. I'm sure that General Stark will approve. You know we have a problem: everybody hates our guts here in this town, and it isn't our fault, it's somebody else's. But we won't talk about why it all happened. It did happen, and now we're going to have to rectify it." I told them what I'd done, and I added, "Now the other half of the equation is us. You know what we can do? We can act like Communists and try to take over this damn town, and I'll tell you what we can do it with—individual good will.

Now, all of us are going to have to live off of the post; there are no quarters here. When you rent a house, you're going to have neighbors. When you move into your house (and when the others move in, we'll pass this right on down as the troops keep coming in), meet your neighbors, go rap on their doors and say, 'I'm Sergeant Joe Zilch. I'm from Germany, just transferred to Fort Carson, and I'd just like to say, 'Hi' and if you think I can ever give you a hand at any time, please give me a call. In any event, I hope we can be friends.' "

They went out, and by God, with their work and mine, we took over the town. You wouldn't believe the editorials that began to roar about what a warm group of people these *Germans* were! I think an awful lot of people reading the paper thought we were Germans, but in any event, that really solved the situation.

Apparently, this word found its way back to Washington, because in short order I was promoted to Major General and ordered to take command of Fort Lewis, Washington. On my departure I received many fine compliments and going-away parties from the city fathers. So that's one problem that I think I solved to the satisfaction and to the benefit of the United States Army.

54

WILLIE
PALMER

One day in the fall of 1956 I received a call from the Headquarters of the 6th Army at Presidio, San Francisco, informing me that General Willis D. Palmer, Vice Chief of Staff of the Army, would be traveling in the area and would visit Fort Carson in Colorado Springs. I was instructed to prepare a briefing on the status of the post and of the 9th Division. I met General Palmer at the Peterson Air Force Base and escorted him to the Headquarters at Fort Carson. That afternoon, I proceeded to brief him.

When I took command of Fort Carson as head of the advance party of the 9th Division from Germany, I inherited several special post units. They consisted of a band, a quartermaster pack company, mule-drawn, which was designed to be used in the mountains, and a 75-millimeter artillery company armed with so-called French 75's, which were also packed and carried by mules for mountain operations (this was before we had the heavy lift helicopters). Another of the units was a dog training organization for police dogs, watch dogs, or security dogs. Individuals assigned to this unit trained their own dogs, and after the dogs were trained, they would go out as a team. Finally, I had a small unit of fourteen bagpipe players complete with Scottish kilts.

I had my entire staff in the briefing room to meet General Palmer, because many people had never met a Vice Chief of Staff before. I started the briefing on the layout of Fort Carson, its training facilities, and the local environment, as well as the troop status. Towards the end of my comments, General Palmer said to me, "Quinn, why do you consider the quartermaster pack unit to be essential to the United States Army?"

"Sir, I didn't make that assumption; somebody else did."

"But you were telling me what they could do."

"Yes, sir, I was explaining what their capabilities were."

"Well, don't you think we should have some other way of moving supplies than on the backs of mules?"

"Sir. . . ."

"I don't think very highly of this."

"General Palmer, these are not my troops. I'm in command of them, yes, but they're here by direction of Army Headquarters."

"Well now, about these bagpipe fiddlers or bagpipe people. What the hell is an Infantry division doing with men in skirts blowing on a damned bag?"

"Sir, these were inherited. The former commander of Fort Carson saw fit to use fourteen spaces of the post complement for this purpose, and believe it or not, they are probably the most attractive and popular thing that Fort Carson has to offer. Every civic organization, church, bazaar, fair, anything in the world that has or wants people to come, advertise the fact that the Fort Carson bag-pipers will be there. It's the biggest PR thing that the Army has out here, believe it or not."

"Quinn, you're going to be reduced by fourteen spaces when I get back to Washington. And you get rid of those bagpipes."

"Sir, I wish you'd reconsider."

"You heard what I said."

"Yes, General Palmer, I heard that."

"Now, about this 75-millimeter artillery outfit. I think that stinks. Why in the hell take a paper cap pistol up to shoot a lion?"

"Sir, again, these are not my troops."

"Well, I'm going to eliminate them. Now finally, Quinn, I want to ask you a personal question about that dog outfit."

By this time I was uptight. He had rolled me over the coals for things for which I was not responsible. Then he said, "Don't you think it's pretty goddamn bad to marry a man to a dog?"

"To do what?"

"To marry a man to a dog."

"General Palmer, you know I've taken quite a beating here today, and what you just said to me, I resent, and I wish you would apologize to me in front of my officers."

"Quinn, now wait a minute."

"Sir, that was just—you can't say things like that to me."

"I'm just trying to find out what you think about things."

I said, "Sir, that you know now. But I wish you would just say to the officers here what your purpose was and that you were . . ."

"Okay, Quinn, I am sorry you are offended."

That terminated the meeting, and I dismissed the staff. We then took off for our apartment in the Broadmoor Hotel to meet Bette, who had prepared some hors d'oeuvres. The General had planned to have cocktails with us before he went to dinner with friends in Colorado Springs. We got in the sedan, and on our way to the hotel, I didn't open my damn mouth. As we were riding along, I guess we'd gone one or two miles, he reached over, patted me on the knee, and said, "Quinn, you know, I'm awfully sorry about what happened. You know we are reviewing our force structure in the Army, and these things have been on my mind for some time, and I just wanted to get it off my chest."

I said, "I understand, sir." But I didn't open my trap any more. I was too pissed off.

We got home, Bette was waiting for us, and we poured him a drink. He was in my home now; so I became very cordial because he was my guest, and not only that, but the Vice Chief of Staff of the Army. Eventually after he had had a drink, I was telling him how great the El Bolmar Foundation was, managed by the Tutt family and how they'd graciously put us up in this apartment for just my commutation allowance, which at that time was $170 a month. The suites we occupied were usually seventy dollars a day.

Bette didn't know of the briefing but sensed something was not right. She said, "General Palmer, we have a masterpiece that you should see."

"Okay," he said, "I'd like to see it. What have you got?"

Bette led him into the kitchen, which was a little pullman type, and up on the wall we had a big drawing in color of three old ladies. It was an advertisement for a flour company, and one of the ladies has a mixing bowl in front of her. She is looking at the other two, and the caption reads, "To hell with Betty Crocker! We'll double the brandy this time!"

General Palmer flipped. He laughed and laughed and laughed. He said, "I've got to get a copy of that. If you don't mind, I'm going to send an Army photographer here to take a picture of it because this is one of the funniest things I ever saw."

Well, the day ended on a jovial tone. I learned later on that that was Willie Palmer's way of operating. Instead of resenting my demand of an apology, he gave me good marks when he returned to the Pentagon.

PART X

THE PENTAGON

Lt. Gen. Quinn, Bette Quinn,
Gen. Quinn's mother, Barry Goldwater
1965

55

MARK
WATSON

When I was Chief of Information for the Army, Mark Watson was the dean of the press corps assigned to, or otherwise identified with, the Department of Defense at the Pentagon. Those permanently assigned to DOD were known as the "Pentagon Regulars." Mark Watson was the *Baltimore Sun* military writer, a contemporary of Hanson Baldwin of the *New York Times*. Mark was venerated by all who knew him, and in my mind was one of the finest media people and one of the finest persons of any profession that I ever knew.

I first met Mark Watson when I was in the Chief of Staff's office after returning from the Korean War. I was in the Office of Army Planning Coordination, serving under Brigadier General Mark Stokes, and all of us worked for General Charles Bolte, the Vice Chief of Staff for Plans and Operations.

One day Mark Watson came into my office and introduced himself saying, "I have a favor to ask of you."

"What is it?"

"I am the chairman of the publicity committee of the Maryland Historical Society, and on Flag Day, June the 14th, we're having a celebration in Baltimore at Fort McHenry, and I would appreciate it very much if you would be the principal speaker."

"Mark, I appreciate that. Are you sure you want me? I'm just a colonel, and maybe you ought to have a general or someone well-known."

"No, what we would like to hear are your experiences in the Korean Conflict and your estimate of the young men whom you recently commanded during the fighting there. I'm sure you could give our members something more intimate about their boys than someone who hasn't been there, but might have more rank."

"Okay, Mark, I'll be there; you just tell me when and how to get there."

On his way out of the office, he turned around and said, "I want to tell you how much I appreciate this. I don't know if there will ever come a time when I could repay you, but if you think so, just give me a call, and I will be glad to repay this favor."

That was in 1951.

In 1959, I became the Chief of Information (essentially the Public Relations Officer for the Army). When I got this assignment, the first person I thought of was Mark Watson, because in my new job I would be dealing with the "Pentagon Regulars," as well as other correspondents. As a matter of interest, here follows a list of media people with whom I dealt in varying degrees of intimacy and their assignment at that period:

Elton Fay, AP; Ed Edstrom, Hearst News; Dick Fryklund, *Washington Star*; Harry Kern, *Foreign Report*; John Scott, *Time*; Denny Griswold, *P.R. News*; Orville

Crouch, MGM Studios; Gerry Green, *New York Daily News*; Sam Kauffmann, *Washington Star*; Bill Lawrence, *New York Times*; Louis Krah, *Wall Street Journal*; Fletcher Knebel, *Look*; Yates McDaniel, AP; Sara McClendon, *El Paso Times*; Tony March, *Army Times*; Hanson Baldwin, *New York Times*; John Norris, *Washington Post-Times Herald*; Mel Ryder, *Army Times*; James Reston, *New York Times*; Warren Rogers, *New York Herald Tribune*; Jack Raymond, *New York Times*; Ben Price, AP; Phillip Horton, *Reporter Magazine;* Steve Tilghman, *AN-AF Register*; Peggy Whedon, ABC; Phil Goulding, *Cleveland Plain Dealer*; Danny Henkin, *AN-AF Journal*; Ted Koop, CBS; Marvin Stone, *U.S. News & World Report*; Bill Wyant, *St. Louis Post-Dispatch*; Peter Hackes, NBC; Jerry Main, *Time*; Lloyd Norman, *Newsweek*; Wayne Parrish, *Washington Evening Star*; Dave Sentner, *Hearst Newspapers*; Bob Eastabrook, *Washington Post-Times Herald*; and Ed Prina, *Washington Evening Star.*

In any event, at this point in time I didn't know anybody in the press corps except Mark Watson, who happened to be the dean. Either on the first or second day that I was on the job, I sent a message to him which read, "Mark, could you come up and have a cup of coffee with me?" He was there in five minutes, and we were drinking our coffee when I said, "Approximately eight years ago, Mark, you came and asked me to speak for you on Flag Day at Fort McHenry."

Mark answered, "That's right, I remember."

"Mark, you also told me when I accepted that assignment that if there was anything you could ever do for me, all I had to do was to sound off. So Mark, I am now sounding off. This is a new job for me. I know little, if anything, about it. I want you to tell me how to run it, and if you can't tell me how to run the job, please tell me how not to run it. I understand public relations, and I understand an awful lot of things that have to do with relationships with the public, but I've never worked directly in this kind of an environment with the press."

"Bill," he said, "I'm going to tell you just one thing, which will affect how you run your job as well as how not to. *Don't try to deceive the press.* Play it straight, and either tell the truth or say nothing. If you begin to quibble and to play around the fringes of the truth, it will eventually emerge, which results in a loss of confidence. The confidence factor is very great with the press. So tell the truth.

Gen. L.L. Lemnitzer congratulates Maj. Gen. W.W. Quinn on his promotion to Chief of Public Information, U.S. Army, as Gen. Quinn's family looks on.

"Now," he added, "let me give you an example of how not to run the job. You recall not too long ago in Japan, a Japanese woman was shot and killed while attempting to steal some empty brass shells from an ordinance dump. She had crawled under the fence and had several of these shells in her little bag and could sell them to the black market for some food. The sentry on duty called her to stop. As she apparently didn't speak English, she didn't know what stop meant, so he shot and killed her as she was trying to get away.

"Well, this was pretty violent action; she should have been apprehended to let the local justice take care of it, but this G.I., presumably following orders to safeguard the dump, took what he considered to be the proper action. Whether he intended to kill her or not is immaterial. He did.

"The local public relations officer of that particular command attempted to hide the exact circumstances, and although the incident leaked out, it was denied. Eventually, however, the truth surfaced, and all concerned, including the senior commanders up and down the line, were scalded by the Department of Defense for not having addressed the problem in a direct and proper manner.

"I'm trying to show you that that was stupid. So, again, I think probably the only thing I can urge you to do is to tell the truth. One of the main dividends, oddly enough, is that honestly *is* the best policy. It really is, because if you are honest with the press and tell them the truth, and they know and believe that it's the truth, for some unknown reason, the story ends; the problem, if any, goes away. There's no more sex to it, no more mystery. There's no reason any more to dig and dig to find out what really is the truth. Once the truth is known, it can't be made into an untruth."

Finally, he said, "Besides being the best way to do it, it's the simplest and the fastest to end a problem—to come out and explain the whole thing, all the facts, from beginning to end. You do not have to make any reasons or justifications, just explain what happened, and it'll go away. All things pass, and the truth passes faster than a mystery or a lie."

I thanked Mark for that dissertation, which became my credo. I called in my senior staff the next day and gave them a lecture on Mark's philosophy. I must say that it certainly kept me in good stead for almost three years in that hot spot.

I survived primarily on the advice of a pro's pro, Mark Watson, a great reporter and a wonderful friend.

56

ELVIS

One day in 1958 or '59, I got a call from Colonel Tom Parker, who was Elvis Presley's manager. He said, "General, I would like to come over to the Pentagon and have a chat with you."

"I'd be delighted to talk to you."

"How about this afternoon?"

"Sure, any time."

"Two o'clock?"

"That'll be fine."

So Colonel Parker came in, sat down, and we had a cup of coffee. He said, "I might as well tell you right off why I'm here, because I've got a problem and it has to do with Presley. Now, he's made quite a name for himself, and he could get out of military service. I could see to it, either in Congress, or his own doctor could 'gin' up something that would keep him from going into the army. But, knowing that you're a public relations officer, what do you think I ought to advise him to do, either go and serve for the two years it takes out of his life or take the gamble of being called a shirker."

I said, "Colonel, I don't see any choice. Let me tell you, we've had all kinds of people in the Army, including the famous. We've had entertainers, singers, professional athletes, boxers. And we've found that once these people got into the service, wherever they go they're not only permitted, but asked to do shows and are usually placed in an entertainment division that entertains the troops.

"Now, in this case, let's assume that we could arrange for him to go to Europe. When he's in Europe he's not going to stop singing. He'll sing more than he's ever sung in his life. He'll be all over Germany, and it's quite possible that with the relationship we have with the Germans, he may be invited to sing before German audiences. If so, he'll get a world of exposure and publicity.

"So take the chance, no matter how convincing his visible crutch may be, if he's going to be an active singer, he's going to look like there's nothing wrong with him. I suggest you get him into uniform as fast as you can, and then he will be a real hero, because when he's singing in his uniform, he's singing for America."

The Colonel said, "Well, I'll be damned. You know, I'm glad I came here. I wouldn't have thought of all that. That's what the boy's gonna do. He's going in the Army."

57

THE PATTON
MOVIE

Many attempts were made by several producers in
Hollywood to do the George Patton movie. The Patton
family, Ruth Ellen Patton Totten, her sister Beatrice, who
was married to General John Watters, and her brother,
George Patton III, objected to any motion picture that
had to do with their father, primarily because of the slapping incident in Sicily in an Army hospital. This incident
had gotten national and international attention. They also
objected to the fact that a paperback book which was un-
complimentary to Patton had been written hastily and
might be used as a basis for the movie.

In 1959, before the MGM movie on Patton was made,
I was the Chief of Information of the Army, and as such,
this type of activity in the Army came under my jurisdiction, or at least in my particular area of interest.

As most military people know, some reserve officers,
in case of mobilization for war, have a specific unit or office to which they report. In this case a brigadier general
was assigned to my office in the event of an emergency.

His name was Frank McCarthy and he was a producer with MGM. In any event, he reported and spent two weeks of each year in my office when he took his active duty tour. As a result, we became quite good friends. His first year, he said, "There's absolutely no reason why we can't do a story, a movie, on George Patton."

I said, "I'll agree, but I don't think the Patton family will stand for it."

"Can we find out?"

I said yes, so we contacted the Patton family. They said no, they would not agree to it. Of course, it was possible for any movie company to make a movie about George Patton. They'd risk libel suit, however, in the event the family were so inclined, and hold up a showing through a legal action, which would not be good for the movie. In addition, it was necessary to have the cooperation of the Patton family because of the various vignettes about his life known only to the family, particularly his childhood, his West Point career, and his service in the Army.

So Frank went back to Hollywood with empty hands that first year. This bothered me, because there was a great story to be told of a very fascinating man and military leader. Consequently, I decided I would do one of Patton myself, as I had the authority to make a documentary of any Army officer.

In the Patton movie, I didn't show the slapping incident. There was no existing film which covered it. I could have dubbed it in somehow, but I didn't want to cause a furor. I showed our film to the Patton family, but they thought a Hollywood movie would not be as gentle with the family and might detract from the memory of their father.

The second year that Frank McCarthy came to report

in my office, we began serious talks with the Patton family, and he said, "Would you please tell the Pattons that I plan to do a movie on George Patton one way or another. I would prefer to have the Patton family support it. I wish you would tell them that if they will cooperate with me and the film writer, I will permit the family to review the finished film before it hits the public; if there's anything in there unacceptable to them, I will take it out or work around it. That's a promise. I am, however, going to do the slapping incident, but I have ways to soften the scene."[1]

So I called Jimmy Totten, Ruth Ellen's husband. He and I had served together in Japan. I told him, "The movie is going to be done. If I were you, I would go along with it, and if you don't like something, you will have a chance to eliminate it. Otherwise, if you don't cooperate, the film may do exactly what you are afraid of. You have a great opportunity to show your father-in-law in the best light."

They finally agreed to cooperate, and Frank McCarthy went to work on the Patton movie.

The world premiere of the movie was held in Washington in a theater on Connecticut Avenue, and we received an invitation. When we got out of our car, which had been sent for us, Frank McCarthy was on the curb in front of the theater. He said, "Bill, welcome to *your* movie."

I was kind of thunderstruck. Here was the producer of the movie meeting me at the curb like a doorman. He ushered us down the aisle and seated us beside General and Mrs. Omar Bradley.

And that's how the movie came about. It's one of the great movies about a great leader of men.

---

[1] Which he did.

PATTON ★ ★ ★ ★

A FILM PRODUCED BY FRANK McCARTHY   DIRECTED BY FRANKLIN J. SCHAFFNER
TWENTIETH CENTURY - FOX STUDIOS   BEVERLY HILLS, CALIFORNIA, 90213

                                        January 4, 1971

Dear Bill:

      Thanks so much for the calendar date book. It
is really one of the most attractive and useful I
have seen, and you may be sure that it will be employed with pleasure and profit.

      PATTON has just been selected the best film
of the year by the National Board of Review, and
George C. Soctt has been cited as best actor by
the New York Critics Circle. The film has been a
tremendous success at the box office at a time when
20th Century-Fox needs successes.

      I shall never forget the tremendous part you
played in making it possible for the film to be
realized. Your letter to the Pattons broke the
ice, and although Ruth Ellen and George opposed production to the very end, they went overboard when
they saw the picture, lavishing approval upon it
and saying they thought we treated General Patton
more fairly than his contemporaries did. They are
our best boosters.

      So, Bill, I have a great deal for which to be
thankful to you. Together with my appreciation, I
send all best wishes for 1971,

                       Sincerely,

                       Frank McC.

58

PHYDEAUX

Sally ran upstairs to her room sobbing, and I had to tell the Lieutenant that she had suddenly become ill and was unable to go out with him that evening. Whereupon, he departed.

• • •

When I was Chief of Information of the Army, my office was in the Pentagon, and we had quarters in Fort Meyer, Virginia, just outside of Washington D.C. Knowing we would be there for several years, we decided to purchase a basset hound.

The girls, Sally and Donna, named him Fido, but because of their Swiss schooling spelled his name Phydeaux. Phydeaux was quite a dog. He was a lovable hound, and his predominating feature, besides his long ears, was that he was unusually well-endowed sexually, so endowed that when he walked, his jewels literally swung from side to side and became very embarrassing to the girls, particularly if they had dates at the quarters.

Phydeaux was also an adventurous dog. He would leave the house when he got out, hotfoot it over to a bar outside the post of Fort Meyer, a soldier hangout. It was an ordinary kind of a bar, and some of the soldiers began to feed him beer and hot dogs. They also threw him a pretzel every now and then.

Phydeaux became an alcoholic, and every time he got out of the quarters, he would make a beeline for the bar to live it up, drinking beer and eating pretzels and hot dogs. When this got to be a standard practice, I went down and talked to the post provost marshall, and I said, "Listen, if Phydeaux annoys anyone on the post, please bring him home or lock him up."

Well, towards the end of Phydeaux's career, he was brought home practically every night by the MP's, and he always sat up in the front seat with the driver, hanging his head out the window to sober up. He knew exactly when he got home, because he would start to moan when he came in front of our quarters. If we weren't home, the MP's would open the screen door and put him in the porch.

Unfortunately, about that time there was a "dog-napping" epidemic. Dogs were disappearing from all over Arlington and the vicinity, and it turned out that they were being picked up on the street and taken out to farms in Virginia. They were penned up, most usually without food and water. The purpose was to sell them to laboratories in the general area and anywhere there was a need for a dog for experimentation. We assume that one day somebody opened a car door, and Phydeaux jumped in—that was the way he was. And so off he went, and we never saw or heard of him again.

The purpose of this story is to immortalize him as a great friend and companion and also to tell the story alluded to in the first paragraph. At the time Sally was a freshman at Smith College and home for the holidays. She had a date with a young army lieutenant, and he was to pick her up. Now as I mentioned before, Phydeaux wasn't really stupid, but he wasn't smart either. He never learned any tricks except one. You would say "Phydeaux, do your trick, shake hands," and occasionally he would lift his right paw to your outstretched arm. He loved the applause after going through such an ordeal.

This one night Sally said to Bette, "Mother, whatever you do, don't let Phydeaux in the living room when the Lieutenant comes. He's so embarrassing." Bette agreed. Sally continued, "Also please tell Sergeant Williams to watch him and don't open the kitchen door so he can get out and come in the living room."

So we instructed Sergeant Williams not to let Phydeaux out of the kitchen, and all was set. When the lieutenant came, he and Sally were seated on the sofa making small talk when who in the hell strolled into the middle of the living room casually, and swinging his possessions from side to side, but Phydeaux! Well, Sally was fit to be tied. As he approached Sally on the couch, she said to the Lieutenant, "This is our dog, Phydeaux."

"What a nice dog. Does he know any tricks?"

Sally replied, "Only one." She called him over to the couch, put out her hand, and said, "Phydeaux, do your trick." And Phydeaux farted.

59

WILBUR BRUCKER

When I was serving as Chief of Information, my duties included service not only to the Chief of Staff of the Army, but to the Secretary of the Army as well. At that time it was Wilbur Brucker, and the Chief of Staff was General Lyman Lemnitzer.

I thought the secretary and I were working well together until two things happened. Both had to do with articles in two publications.

One was the *Washington Post* by columnist Walter Lippman, who was writing critically about some person; he mentioned the fact that this individual took too long to make his point. As an aside he wrote, "He reminds me of Wilbur Brucker, who is also a speech addict."

Well, when the Secretary read this, he called me up to his office and said, "I want you to go see Walter Lippman and ask him what he's got against me."

I said, "Mr. Secretary, he doesn't have anything against you."

"He made that disparaging remark calling me a

'speech addict.' "

"Well, Mr. Secretary," I replied, "you are well known for your long talks. I have to say that."

The Secretary didn't like that, but he knew it was true; once he got started, he didn't know when to stop. He was a loyal Army partisan, and I do not mean to detract from that, because he fought very hard for the Army. I told him that I was not big enough to go see Walter Lippman, that he would probably throw me out of his office; he wouldn't know who I was. But if the occasion arose, I would talk to him.

The second item involved a short article in the *Armed Forces Journal*. It had to do with an action taken by the Army and was complimentary to General Lemnitzer, the Chief of Staff. I forget what the item was, but it was very favorable. When Secretary Brucker read it, he called me to his office immediately, and I reported to him and stood before his desk.

He said, "Quinn, there are two things here that have happened this past week that involve disloyalty. I question your loyalty. I certainly don't believe that you have a high degree of loyalty to me."

"I don't understand, Mr. Secretary."

"The Walter Lippman thing. You failed to have him retract his criticism of me." He pointed to the *Journal*. "And now, this particular item does not give me any credit at all. I shared in this particular decision with General Lemnitzer. He and I both decided that this was the thing to do, but you gave this story to the *Armed Forces Journal* and left me out of it."

"Mr. Secretary, I did not do that. I did not know about the article. I did not give it to anybody, and I don't know who wrote it or where it came from, except one of the 'Pentagon Regulars' from the *Armed Forces Journal* must have picked it up somewhere."

"Well, I still believe that you're disloyal."

"Sir, I guess that terminates our relationship."

I saluted and left the room. I went downstairs and began to empty my desk, because I knew I was going to be, not necessarily court-martialed, but transferred. Although I didn't think he would have the guts to demote me, I knew I was dead in the water as far as Brucker was concerned, and probably the Army. So I'd gotten some big envelopes and had begun going through my files—very depressed, of course—when the telephone rang about fifteen or twenty minutes later. The Executive Officer of Mr. Brucker called my Executive Officer and said that the Secretary would like General Quinn to report to him. I told my secretary to tell the secretary to the Exec. to inform the Secretary that I was no longer reporting to him, that I didn't know to whom to report, but that I was on my way to the Chief of Staff to ask for reassignment.

About ten minutes later, my secretary came in and said, "The Secretary of the Army, Mr. Brucker, is on the telephone and wishes to talk to you." I picked up the phone,

"Yessir."

"General Quinn, this is Secretary Brucker."

"Yes, sir."

"I would appreciate it very much if you would come to my office. I think we should have a talk."

"Mr. Secretary, we've had our talk. And I am about to go to the Chief of Staff and ask for reassignment."

"Don't do that, General Quinn. Would you please come to my office."

"Mr. Secretary, if that's an order, I'll comply."

"General Quinn, I don't wish to put it in those terms, but would you please come to my office?"

I went upstairs, walked into the Secretary's office, and saluted him. He said, "Sit down, General Quinn." Then he said, "You know how I am about things. Regarding the matters we discussed, I now find I was misinformed or misinterpreted the situation and called you disloyal. I wish to apologize, because I know you really aren't. As a matter of fact, I checked on the article and found that one of the aides to the Chief of Staff gave that item to the *Armed Forces Journal*; so you were not involved, as you indicated."

"Mr. Secretary," I said, "I've been in the Army for a long time, and no one before has ever called me disloyal either to my superiors or to my country. And I deeply resented that. You absolutely staggered me."

"I know, I was very hasty, General Quinn, but you must understand that I'm very sensitive, too, about anything that has to do with the Army. Once again, I apologize and trust that you will forget and that we can work together as we have in the past."

I said, "Yes, sir," and walked out.

60

DEFENSE
INTELLIGENCE
AGENCY

At the time that I was about to terminate my tour of duty as Chief of Information of the Army, I received a call from Mr. Gilpatrick, who was then the Deputy Secretary of Defense. He asked me if I would be interested in going into the to-be-formed Defense Intelligence Agency. I told him that I was currently serving the Secretary of the Army and the Chief of Staff, and whatever they wanted me to do, I would do.

General Lyman L. Lemnitzer at that time was Chairman of the Joint Chiefs of Staff, and had been instructed by Secretary Robert McNamara to create an intelligence agency to serve the Department of Defense. He was not happy that he had no control over the collection and collation aspects of military intelligence, and that the CIA was not always responsive to his needs.

In any event, it so happened that General Lemnitzer,

with the concurrence of General George Decker, the Army Chief of Staff, nominated me to be the first Director of the DIA. Mr. McNamara rejected that nomination in that he would prefer the services of Lieutenant General Joseph Carroll. He knew Carroll as the latter had worked for the Secretary, on loan from the Air Force, in running down leaks and other investigations. Mr. McNamara told General Lemnitzer that he didn't know me, hence his decision. However, I was to be named as Deputy Director in the rank of major general, a grade which I then held.

General Decker, thanks to his good offices, informed Defense that I was not available under those conditions; that he had plans for me to take command of a Corps in Germany; that this was where he intended to send me, which entailed a promotion to lieutenant general. Because of this set of circumstances, Mr. McNamara promised to promote me if I would accept the appointment, which I did.

Consequently, I went to work with Joe Carroll, to put together an agency which would respond to the intelligence requirements of the Secretary of Defense and the Joint Chiefs of Staff. We took turns serving on the Intelligence Board, chaired by Allen Dulles and John McCone. I was on that job for two and a half years before getting ants in my pants to move on.

Then one day I got a call from General Earl "Bus" Wheeler, Army Chief of Staff, who said, "Bill, would you like to take over the Seventh Army in Germany?"

When I said, "Yes, Sir!" although I was in the Pentagon, I'm sure that my reply could be heard at the Washington Monument.

PART XI

ON THE STREET

61

MARTIN MARIETTA CORPORATION

In June 1965, while I was still in command of the Seventh Army in Germany, I was invited to Paris in June to attend a NATO exercise. After attending the exercise and critique, I went to the Paris Air Show at Le Bourget Air Field. Having known George and Natalie Bunker, I dropped by the Martin Marietta Corporation chalet on the grounds, where I visited with George. We had a beer and discussed the pros and cons of the show, how Martin Marietta's exhibit was being accepted by the public, etc., and he asked, "What are you doing tonight?

"I'm going to a reception given by the Chief of Staff of the French Army."

"How about after that?"

"I'm free."

"Why don't you have dinner with Natalie and me after the reception? Come on over to our hotel, and we'll go out for dinner."

So, after the reception hosted by the French Army Chief of Staff, I walked to their hotel and went up to the Bunker's suite where I had a drink with George and Natalie and "Buz" Hello. Buz was then an engineer with Martin Marietta Corporation, I believe in the Baltimore Division, and later on he went with Rockwell. The four of us went to Laseur for dinner, had a fine meal, good conversation, and afterwards George said, "Well, let's go paint a small portion of the town." We all concurred and went to a nightclub George knew where there was dancing and a floor show.

We all took turns dancing with Natalie, and when Buz was dancing with her, George asked, "What are your plans?"

"What do you mean, George?"

"Well, one day you'll leave the Army, won't you?"

"Yes, but I've got a couple more years; I don't have to retire until I'm sixty."

"Bill," he said, "I would like to have you join Martin Marietta, and when you decide to retire, give me a call, and we'll work something out."

I didn't think too much about it until later on after I got caught up in a political updraft in connection with the Presidential election of 1964—a set of circumstances described in the Prologue of this book, having to do with the campaign of Barry Goldwater.

Shortly thereafter, I began to realize that, since I was not given command of USAREUR (United States Army in Europe), which was a natural step for me, the handwriting was on the wall, so I might as well turn in my suit. Recalling my conversation with George Bunker, I wrote him, and he replied, "Any time you want to retire from the Army, come on and join me here at Martin Marietta."

*Lt. Gen. William W. Quinn, Seventh Army Commander,
troops the line during farewell honors ceremony.
Stuttgart, Germany—February, 1966*

In any event, I came back to Washington in the fall of 1965 and called on my classmate General Harold K. "Johnny" Johnson, who was then Chief of Staff of the Army. I told him that I would like to volunteer for Vietnam, realizing that my tour was soon to be up in Germany. He said, "Bill, you're too damned old. As a matter of fact, these young brain trusters up in Defense think 'Westy' Westmoreland is 'over the hill,' and he's a helluva lot younger than you are; so you're not going, you're not going to Vietnam."

I replied, "If that's where the action is, and if I can't go to Vietnam, can I kind of duck out of the picture?"

"You're a free agent to do whatever you want to do."

"If that's the case, I'll retire at your convenience."

I retired on the last day of February in 1966, and on the first day of March that year, I walked in and started working for Martin Marietta.

My retirement ceremony was in Stuttgart, and afterwards there was a reception. My relief was Lt. Gen. Theodore "Ted" Conway, another classmate of mine. What was nice about that particular retirement was that Gen. Creighton "Abe" Abrams came over at the request of the Chief of Staff of the Army. Abe, who was then Vice-Chief of Staff, presented me with a Distinguished Service Medal at my retirement ceremony and then flew me and my family back to Washington in the plane that had brought him over.

I reported in the Washington office of Martin Marietta (the corporate headquarters was in New York City) and checked in with George Bunker. I said, "I'm reporting for duty, George."

"Well, let's see if we can find you a desk or a chair. You ought to have a chair, anyway, to sit down in; you can't stand up all the time."

The office manager was a young man named Gene Percell. George called him in and said, "Get Bill a chair and a desk and put it right over here by me, and get him a phone, and assign one of the girls to give him some secretarial help. His title is Assistant to the President of Martin Marietta Corporation. Get him some cards made."

I sat down with George, and we had a cup of coffee. I asked, "What do you want me to do?"

"Bill, frankly, I can't tell you what I want you to do just yet, for the simple reason that you've got to find your way around the corporation, and once you have a feel for the operation, you may be able to pick something that you're interested in and would like to pursue."

He added, "Take six months. You go everywhere we've got a plant, facility, or office, and get to know the corporation and its managers. As a matter of fact, in six months, you ought to know the corporation a helluva lot better than I do. I don't go out as much as I ought to."

So that's what I did. I started traveling. One of the first things I did was to disarm everybody about my rank and title. When my secretary made arrangements for me to visit the installations, they always started out on the formal side on my arrival, assuming that I was the President's boy. Everyone was very protocolish, apprehensive and cautious, so I had to get things straightened out early on.

"Please disregard rank and title," I would say in so many words. "My name is Bill Quinn. Period. I don't have any flags or medals or status. It's all behind me. I'm out here on my own now and trying to hack it in my own way without any particular crutch to lean on."

This approach seemed to make everybody relieved and relaxed, and as a matter of fact, it turned out to be very beneficial wherever I went after the first few visits. I was received cordially and with open arms and with "We're glad to have you, Bill," attitudes. So the "General" rank was never associated with me and Martin Marietta, at least, not to my knowledge.

Well, in going to the various plants and establishments, I began to realize that the headquarters in New York was very thinly staffed. It had its financial people, its legal people, its public relations officer, and its various heads of major elements, but it didn't have any office that seemed to have a feel for how the government operated. They knew what the laws were, but did not comprehend the machinations of the regulatory agencies and Washington bureaucracy.

The small headquarters staff consisted of George Bunker, plus a few hands. He refused to adhere to Parkinson's Law. He maintained control through his facility managers. Most technical decisions were made by the major production centers. This, of course, had many advantages.

However, there were people in the field who were not being served by this headquarters because of their inability to know the inner workings and political aspects of the nation's capital. For instance, I went to Charlotte, North Carolina, to visit the Southern Dye Company, which was a Martin Marietta subsidiary. On my departure, I asked the president, "Is there any way I can help you when I get back to Washington?"

He said, "Well, could be, Bill. We've got a helluva problem. It hasn't been solved, and we don't know when it will be. We've hired a British chemist who is one of the leading experts in the world on dyes. We're hurting for him, but he can't get over here, because he can't get a clearance from the U.S. Immigration and Naturalization Service in Washington, or somebody. He keeps going to the American Embassy in London and they say, 'I'm sorry, but we have no word on you,' and so forth. Here's the man's name, etc., and if you can help us, we'd surely appreciate it."

So I came back to Washington from that particular trip armed with their problem, and without saying anything to anybody, I started going through the government channels to find out where this action was being held up. I found the office. I found Martin Marietta's application and request lying on some guy's desk in a "hold" basket. It seemed that there was a very minor technical problem, an element of information required, which I furnished immediately, but which had been holding up this thing for months. So, I got it all straightened out, and the paperwork proceeded on its normal course. The chemist was working in Charlotte three weeks later.

Another instance. I went up to one of Martin Marietta's rock quarries in West Virginia. It was run by a great guy named Jerry Seale, a wonderful person and an avid hunter. We became good friends. We used to hunt together down at Wye Island on the Eastern Shore of Maryland. Seale was president of the Rock Products Division of Martin Marietta.

On a visit to one of his quarries in West Virginia, I asked, "Jerry, do you have any problems?"

"Boy, do I have a problem. For the last month the county police have been pulling my trucks over at weighing stations and weighing them. They are filled with gravel, and it's common knowledge that everybody overloads their trucks. I know I am violating the law when I do it. I really have no gripe about having to go back and take off maybe a ton or two of gravel or rocks from the trucks to obey the law. So I don't have any real argument. The only problem I have with this is that my main competitor

is not being pulled off the road as I am. And consequently, he's going to break my back eventually by being
able to haul illegal loads while I have to abide by the law.
It's just not fair. If he were treated as I am, then I would
have no argument. But to pick on me and let my main
competitor go unchallenged is unfair."

I said, "I couldn't agree with you more."

"Do you think you could help?"

"Have you called New York?"

"Yeah, yeah, I've called New York, and they more or
less tell me that it's my fight, it's my problem, and I'll have
to solve it, they can't do anything about it."

When I got back to Washington, I immediately called
on Senator Randolph of West Virginia, a jovial and understanding man. I told him the story.

He said, "General, you know, I find this kind of hard
to believe, but I have to take your word for it. But why
don't we just double-check?"

He picked up the telephone, got his administrative assistant, and said, "Get me the Governor." He explained,
"Governor, I have a gentleman here who's telling me
quite a story, and I wish you would check into this, because it's not fair, and I don't think you would order anything like this."

He told the Governor the story, and the Governor
replied, "You know, Jennings, I can't believe it, either,
but I'll tell you, if it's going on, we'll stop it."

And it was stopped. Jerry's trucks were never pulled
over and weighed again. I assume then that he went back
to overloading his trucks, along with his competitor.

The reason I have given these examples (and there
were many more) is to indicate that I had worked my way
into the cogs of the corporation and was beginning to pull
my load.

On January 1, 1967, I was promoted to Vice-President of the Corporation in the Aerospace Group. My salary jumped, from my original salary of $25,000 a year to $47,500—quite a raise. At that point, besides being a vice-president, I was given the title of Washington Representative of Martin Marietta Corporation, and although I did most of my work for the Aerospace Group, there were other corporate entities I served, such as Rock Products, Cement and Lime Divisions, Southern Dye, etc.

It was a conglomeration of duties, but I liked my work very much. As a result I got to know a great number of people on Capitol Hill, in the services, and in industry, as well as in the business world in Washington. I kept this job until 1972, when I had to retire at the age of 65.

All in all, the experience with Martin Marietta was very satisfying, and I met some wonderful people. George Bunker, for one, was a unique individual. I never met any person like him. I had a deep and abiding affection for this modest, unassuming and generous but incredibly brilliant business man.

One of the things that impressed me very much about Martin Marietta was its unannounced, undescribed, undefined code of ethics. When I was Chief of Information of the Army, I met an awful lot of people from industry, people who had no particular qualms about courting favor and were unbelievably open about giving gifts, wining and dining, and offers of trips, sports events, and the like.

My initial apprehension in joining Martin Marietta Corporation was soon dispelled when I discovered that they tried to *sell* their products rather than *buy* their customers.

I've always been proud of my association with this great corporation.

62

ALMOST AN AMBASSADOR

Hi, Barry, who are you going to pimp for?"

Senator Goldwater didn't have a chance to answer President Nixon as he was being escorted to his car through a milling crowd around the balcony on the second floor of the Capitol Hilton Hotel.

This remark was made immediately after the 1969 Alfalfa Dinner, which followed President Nixon's inauguration.

I had been standing outside the V.I.P. or head table assembly room waiting for Barry Goldwater, when Vice President Agnew wandered out. After greeting each other, we began to discuss a mutual friend of ours, Colonel Jim O'Hara, in whose unit Agnew had served in Germany during World War II. Shortly thereafter, Barry came out and had just begun to enter our conversation when the President passed us and made that startling remark.

Seven months later, on August 12, 1969, there appeared in the *Chicago Tribune* an article entitled, "An

Achilles Heel, the Greek Post," by Phillip Warden, with a
date line of August 11, 1969. The article reads as follows:

> The choice of ambassador to Greece threatens to become
> an Achilles Heel for the Nixon Administration. Greek-
> Americans want to see one of their own chosen. They look
> to Vice President Agnew as a son of a Greek immigrant to
> influence the Administration in its choice. Agnew, however,
> has refused to become involved. The State Department
> poses to give the post to one of its career diplomats, Henry
> J. Tasca, now ambassador to Morocco. His former posts,
> i.e. Doctoral Studies of the London School of Economics,
> and his service as Economic Advisor to W. Averell Harri-
> man on North Atlantic Treaty Organization matters, makes
> his political views suspect to many Republicans. The Liber-
> als are trying to ram him through, however, as ambassador
> to Greece. A member of Congress who had worked closely
> with the Greek-American community in Chicago said last
> week that the reports received from Sweden say that the
> State Department has chosen Tasca. Kennedy and Johnson
> carry-overs in the State Department have been pushing
> him.

In this same article, later on, it said:

> Senator Barry Goldwater has pushed Lieutenant General
> William W. Quinn, Chief of the Army Section, United
> States Military Advisory Group of Greece from 1953 to
> 1955, as a nominee. Quinn has been extremely popular with
> the Greek-Americans. If they cannot have an ambassador
> from their own ethnic group, members of Congress say
> Quinn will probably be the first choice of the group.

Several Greek-Americans had been nominated, but
apparently, for one reason or another, were not acceptable. In any event, Tasca was now the front runner.

In connection with this situation, it should be understood that the traditional position and policy of the State
Department, strongly influenced by the Foreign Service

Officer's Association, holds that U.S. ambassadors should be professionally trained diplomats and not businessmen, campaign contributors, or political appointees, and in my case, a soldier.

I don't know how much the Greeks influenced my selection, but I am led to believe that the "Junta" informed the President, by some manner or means, that I was highly acceptable. In any event, the Greeks got the word that I was being seriously considered, which they took to mean that I was to be selected. This is probably the reason that this information was leaked to the Greek press and the articles on my appointment published.

These articles in the Greek and, subsequently, the U.S. press, were almost correct, and the President did in fact select me in late August 1969 to be ambassador to Greece and told either Bob Haldeman or John Erlichman, Pat Flanagan or somebody, to call the State Department and tell the Secretary that he had selected Quinn to go to Greece.

At that time, I believe that Secretary Rogers was out of the country and Under Secretary Elliott Richardson was in charge and received the information. I was told that his office immediately called the White House to ask that no announcement of my appointment be made until he had conferred with the President.

It is my understanding also that Under Secretary Richardson, together with Under Secretary U. Alexis Johnson (for Political Affairs), did contact the President and convinced him that I should not be selected; that their opposition to me was not personal; but that it would not be prudent to send a military man, who might "get in bed with the 'Colonels' and hence the Greeks might never break the yoke of the Junta," or words to that effect.

This logic, along with the case they made for Tasca,

persuaded the President to change his decision and agree to select Tasca.

Upon the announcement of Tasca's appointment, the *International Herald-Tribune* published an article which covered the Greek States' acceptance of the new U.S. envoy: "The Greek Government tonight announced that it approved of the appointment of Henry J. Tasca as U.S. ambassador to Athens."

That briefly explains why Bill Quinn did not return to Greece as ambassador.

• • •

This near nomination for ambassador to Greece by President Nixon in 1969 had its beginnings in Greece during a period between 1953 and 1955. I had been appointed Chief of the Army Section of the Joint United States Military Assistance Group (JUSMAG) with a mission to assist the Greek General Staff and the Greek Army units in training, supply, and in United States' procurement. During these two years, Bette and I became very much integrated in the social life in Athens. Being a brigadier general, I was placed on the diplomatic list, and hence we were invited to practically all receptions hosted by foreign diplomats and Greek friends, and to many official dinners hosted by the Greek government. In other words, we got around, and I must say immodestly that we became very well known and quite popular.

Now, this is important because it laid the foundation for what was to transpire 14 years later.

One of the first evidences of my good fortune in Greece came as a result of my meeting Fleur Cowles. She was formerly the wife of Gardner Cowles, editor and publisher of *Look* magazine, and she was, at one time, the editor of *Flair* magazine. We met through Professor Stratis Andreadis, a banker, hotel owner, ship owner, et cetera. He was what you might call a Greek tycoon, and through him, Fleur and I became very good friends. On August 16, 1954, she wrote a flattering letter to General Matthew B. Ridgeway, the Chief of Staff of the United States Army, regarding my service in Greece. The letter eventually found its way to the White House.

On our departure from Athens for Germany, my wife and I were deluged with farewell parties and dinners by our Greek friends, and I received quite a number of letters from Greek military leaders. Although there was a lot of redundancy in them, they were very meaningful to me. They may be read in the appendix. One of the letters was from Athanassiades Bodossaki, who might have been classed as the "DuPont of Greece."

Mr. Bodossaki received one of the first contracts to make American 155mm artillery shells for the howitzers that we had provided the Greek Army and to produce the shells in Greece. It so happened that on the day that the first run was to come off the line, he had a dedication in his plant, with a reception. He asked me if I would make the principal address, although their Majesties were to be there—King Paul and Queen Frederica. It was a red-letter day for Greece to be able to make their own artillery shells. It signaled a great stride on the part of Greece into the munitions field.

Well, I went to this dedication and made the speech, and Bodossaki and I became good friends. I mention this, because when you have someone of this stature ask you to do something like this before their Majesties, that was "tall cotton" in Greece. As a result, favorable newspaper editorials appeared, as well as letters, which came somewhat as a surprise, because I had not sought this kind of approbation. That was Greece, and off I went to Germany to join a Division.

• • •

The scene reopens on the Greek subject in Washington, D.C., after my retirement and during the Nixon election. Being a Republican, I was soon contacted by my Greek friends in Washington and in other places in the United States, and a few friends in Athens, who began to implore me to seek an appointment as ambassador to Greece. Well, I really had no more idea of being ambassador to any place than to be the man in the moon, but I went to talk it over with Senator Goldwater. I told him of the experience I had with the members of the AHEPA (American Hellenic Education and Progressive Association), made up of people of Greek heritage, and of the insistency on the part of a friend I had in Athens, Elias Demetracopoulos. When I was in Athens in the 1950's, Elias was an ace political and military writer on one of the leading newspapers, and we became friends. Much later, he was exiled because of the "Colonels," and eventually came to Washington. He became a leading opponent of the Athens regime.

Senator Goldwater thought the suggestion of ambassadorship was a good one. He began to ask some people around town what they thought of my being ambassador to Greece, and most said, "Why not?" Consequently, Barry put my name "in the hopper." And on December 30, after Nixon had been elected, but before the inauguration, I received the following letter:

OFFICE OF THE PRESIDENT-ELECT
Richard M. Nixon

450 Park Avenue
New York, N.Y. 10022
(212) 661-6400

December 30, 1968

Lt. Gen. William Quinn
Martin Marietta Corp.
815 Connecticut Avenue, N.W.
Washington, D.C. 20006

Dear General Quinn:

Your name has been suggested to the
incoming Administration for appointment to high
Federal office. It is our responsibility in
such cases to obtain full information concerning
your qualifications and possible availability
for such an appointment, although our doing so
does not imply that such an appointment is being
sought or will be offered.

If you might under any circumstances be
available to accept such an appointment and serve
in the new Administration, either now or in the
future, we would greatly appreciate your prompt
completion and return of the enclosed form to this
office.

All responses will be held in confidence
and used only for the purpose described above, i.e.
to obtain information concerning your qualifications
and possible availability for appointment to high
Federal office.

Thank you for your cooperation and
assistance.

Sincerely,

C. Calvert Knudsen

Encl.

On January 5, 1969, Goldwater sent a message to Tom Pappas, a well-known Greek-American in the oil business in Greece. He ran ESSO PAPPAS. The message read:

> I am informed that my dear and close friend, General William Quinn, is being considered for ambassador to Greece. Knowing of his long devoted service to Greece during his Army days and his devotion to that country, its people and its problems, I strongly urge that you lend your support to this outstanding man as our ambassador to Greece.

The very next day a telegram was received by Goldwater:

> Dear Senator Goldwater:
>
> You know that any friend of yours is a friend of mine, and I will see you in Washington this week, will call your office and assure you of my support. Looking forward to seeing you in Washington.
>
> Regards, Tom Pappas

Things began to move then, and I got a lot of encouragement, but I thought I should talk to somebody who had been an ambassador. So I went to see Joe Farland. Joseph Farland had been ambassador to Pakistan, and we had become good friends. He gave me some good advice as to what I might expect at confirmation hearings and if confirmed, what my problems would be living with the State Department.

In January, I wrote the following note to Goldwater:

> Regarding the Greek job, I saw Senator John Tower at Col.

J. Hunter "Trapper" Drum's dinner and told him about it, and he asked me if I wanted him to put in a plug, which he would gladly do. I told him that you had turned out to be my campaign manager, and that I asked you what was the best way. He said to let him know. I have another supporter in William J. Casey, a New York lawyer, who is writing to Secretary Rogers who will also call his very old friend, Tom Pappas, in my behalf. I learned yesterday that I could expect acceptance by the 'Junta.' This came from the Greek military attache here, Colonel Psiliopoulos, the personal representative of the Premier.

Thanks, Bill

The Senator thought he should get the aid of Vice President Spiro Agnew, and so he wrote the Vice President a letter to ask for support. Agnew wrote back saying in part:

Dear Barry:

Thank you for your letter regarding General William Quinn. As you know I had the pleasure of talking briefly with General Quinn at the ALFALPHA dinner. I was most impressed with him. Unfortunately, I had made a previous commitment to support Mr. George Christopher for this post. This makes it extremely difficult for me to take any other course.

Regards, sincerely, Ted

Goldwater sent me a copy of this and wrote "This isn't good," and adding, "George isn't either."

Now started a journey toward defeat and the disappointment of friends who had supported me. One of them was Fleur Cowles who sent me the following wire on December 31st from London:

Dear Bill:

Cable service was resumed last night after negotiations. I couldn't get through until this morning. I did send Mike Cowles the following for the record: My very dear friend, General William Quinn one of two being considered for ambassador to Greece ... stop ... Urge you immediately communicate with Nixon that other Greek foreign candidate would immediately offend Middle East—especially Turks—stop. Quinn wants Embassy, Athens and is outstandingly admired by all factions. Love and thanks, Fleur

And then she added, "Keep me posted, Bill. You've got to go to Greece. Love to Bette, too."

On the 4th of February, Senator Goldwater called me to talk about the UPI piece that was in the paper that day. He had talked to Pappas in Athens and had told him about George Christopher. Pappas said, "He can't go because you can't send a native born to the country of his birth to serve as a diplomat. You can be of the extraction, but apparently, Christopher was born in Greece." Barry also told me that he had talked to the Vice President on the floor of the Senate and told him that the State Department rules precluded George Christopher's going; whereupon, Agnew said, "Well, if that's the case, I'll back Quinn."

Now I received some good news—and I think it was from Demetracopoulos on the 5th of February—that Mrs. Marian Mitchell, on the Greek desk, had called him. Instead of clobbering me as anti-Junta man, she identified me as being acceptable to all factions.

Now, from Greece came the word that I was coming as ambassador, and one of the Athens newspapers on February 5 had a story about it. As reported, it said:

> Retired Lieutenant General William Quinn, former Commander of the Seventh Army, has been appointed new ambassador to Greece. The Athens English newspaper, *Daily Post*, reported yesterday he will succeed Ambassador Phillips Talbot who resigned in November of 1968.

This, of course, turned out not to be true, but in any event it came out in several newspapers.

On February 7th I received a cable:

> Have just heard you have been nominated for a new ambassadorship in Athens, and would like to tell you how very happy and thrilled we are at the prospect of having Bette and yourself here with us. Stop. Looking greatly forward to hearing from you on confirmation of good news. We are sending you both our very best regards. With love, Dorette and Stratis Andreadis.

Stratis is the person I mentioned earlier who introduced me to Fleur Cowles. He owns the Hilton Hotel, a ship line, the railroads, and is the president of the largest commercial bank in Athens and obviously a very substantial person in the country.

The situation at this time was that the Greek regime was raising a storm with the Council of Europe over Greece's alleged violations of human rights, about which there were investigations and editorials and all kinds of charges. The articles still kept coming out that I was going and that I had been selected. On the 6th of February, I sent the following note to Barry Goldwater:

> I have it from the grapevine that the minions in the State

Department are not happy about me. In fact, members on Kissinger's staff are broadcasting the following: 'Quinn is another Komer in Ankara,' i.e., ex-CIA. Greeks will react as Leftist Turk papers did.

Bill Casey wrote to Secretary of State Rogers saying that he would like to recommend me as ambassador to Greece. Following that, Secretary Rogers wrote to Bill on February 11th:

Dear Bill:

Thank you for your letter of February 4th, recommending Lieutenant General William W. Quinn for an ambassadorial assignment. I appreciate knowing of the high regard in which you hold General Quinn. We will keep your comments on his qualifications very much in mind.

Sincerely, Bill

On the 11th of February, I received a note from Fleur Cowles in London. She wrote:

Dear Bill:

This is just a quick flash to tell you that I have had a word back from Mike Cowles who says that he will certainly do what he can to be helpful to you. Will you, in return, keep him posted? Affectionate regards to you and Bette."

Fleur

On Thursday, February 13th, in the *Atlantis*, America's largest Greek-American newspaper, there appeared a headline which read, "Quinn named U. S. Envoy to Greece." The article stated:

Washington—President Nixon has nominated William Wilson Quinn, retired Army General and local businessman as the next ambassador to Greece, succeeding Phillips Talbot.

According to reports here, the nomination has gone to the Senate. Quinn is Vice President of Martin Company, Washington, and a 1933 graduate of West Point. A native of Crisfield, Maryland, the 61-year-old ambassador designate has a distinguished military career, earning the Legion of Honor, the Croix de Guerre, the Presidential Unit Citation for Korea action, and the Legion of Merit with cluster. He was at the War College here in 1948—49, was Director of Strategic Services 1946—47, Korea in 1950 and Army Chief of Staff's Office in 1952, Chief of Army Section Joint United States Advisory Group to Greece in 1953—55, Deputy Director of Defense Intelligence Agency 1961—64, Commanding General of Seventh Army in Germany 1964—66.

On the 20th of February, I received a letter from Bill Casey, from New York, saying:

Dear Bill:

I hear via the grapevine from Greece by way of Tom Pappas that you are the next ambassador to Greece. The enclosed came in from Bill Rogers, which is the letter I have just read. You can't leave before the next Veterans of Strategic Services dinner on April 22nd, at which we are admitting Russ Forgan to the distinguished company of Donovan Medal Holders.

Sincerely, Bill Casey

On the 24th I received another letter from Casey. He wrote:

Dear Bill:

I saw Barry Goldwater Saturday at the University Club. He tells me that he hears from Greece that you are indeed the next ambassador, but that he's heard nothing from Washington. That's probably par for the course.

Bill Casey

I should at this point identify those in Congress and others who were supportive of my appointment. They were: Senator Strom Thurmond, Congressman Bob Wilson, Senator John Tower, Senator Peter Dominick, Senator Mac Mathias, Allen Dulles, Nate Twining, former Chairman of Joint Chiefs Gen. Hoyt Vandenberg, Dick Helms, Former Director of CIA, Ambassador George Ball, with whom I went to Pakistan in 1963, Ambassador George McGee, Fleur Cowles, Bill Casey, Secretary of State Rogers, Tom Pappas, Jack Ashby, and many others.

In a *Philadephia Inquir*er article on Sunday, March 31st, there was an article by Evans and Novak, which was syndicated and went practically everywhere. Also, on the same day, an article in the San Francisco *Examiner* was headlined, "Christopher Rejects Job as Envoy," and went on to say that the former San Francisco Mayor, George Christopher, one of the nation's best-known Greek-Americans, had declined to serve as ambassador to Athens. "As a result, the problem of filling this sensitive diplomatic vacancy is beset with complications for the Nixon Administration, Washington. The immediate prospect for the assignment now is William Quinn, retired Army Lieutenant General who once did a military tour of duty in Greece. He holds a Washington executive post with Martin Marietta Corporation, a leading aerospace and chemical firm. However, some State Department officials and liberal senators argue that Quinn's military industrial background make him less than an ideal American choice to deal with the Greek military dictatorship."

The article goes on to say, "Meanwhile, the White House is continuing its search for another Greek-American. 'Don't count General Quinn out,' one source says. He is highly respected. He did a good job as head of our military mission in Greece about 16 years ago. But the liberals on Capitol Hill are concerned. They feel that Quinn is inclined to excuse the 1967 military take-over in Athens as an inevitable response to Communist dangers."

The *Washington Post* had also run the March 30th Evans — Novak article, but had left out the part that says, "Other foes of the Greek Junta, however, say Quinn favorably impressed all elements of the Greek political spectrum, while heading the Army mission there in the early 50's and would be vastly more even-handed as ambassador than pro-Junta foreign service officers."

Shortly thereafter, I received a note from Bob Novak, in which he said, "General Quinn, the underlined portion of our item about you in Sunday's column was not included in the *Washington Post* version of our column, though it did appear in the *New York Post* and other papers. I think the omitted sentence puts the item in considerably better perspective."

Now, what was eliminated followed the line, "Liberals on Capitol Hill feel Quinn is inclined to excuse the 1967 military take-over in Athens as an inevitable response to the Communist dangers." The favorable portion was deleted.

In addition to the supportive people that I have mentioned, I had another good friend, Jack Ashby, who was President of Kaiser Steel Corporation. On April 7th, Jack sent a telegram to the President recommending my appointment.

On April 9th, I received a note from Senator Goldwater:

Dear Bill:

This morning I contacted Kleindienst and then in turn called Mitchell in Key Biscayne; and this is the information I received "vis-à-vis the competition". The name of the man is Angelus, and he lives in Chicago. This was a promise made to Mr. Clement Stone, who was an extremely heavy contributor in the campaign in the early stages when money was scarce. I am going to meet with Mitchell next week and go into this farther, so unless something happens in the interim, you won't hear from me until I've had a chance to see him.

> With warm wishes, sincerely, Barry

In addition to what has happened, the President received several letters from personal friends of mine, who were not necessarily well known.

On May the 7th, I received a copy of a letter from the office of the Vice President. Addressed to Mr. Delos Ellsworth, who was an assistant to Barry Goldwater, the letter says:

Dear Mr. Ellsworth:

A friend of mine who used to work as a staffer in the Senate picked up a rather unusual quote from a speech by Senator Kennedy. At my request, he wrote the enclosed comment on it. If you think it's appropriate, you might want to work it in on one of the Senator's speeches. The Senator might be interested to know that the Vice President wrote another letter to Secretary Rogers last week supporting the candidacy of Bill Quinn for ambassador to Greece.

> Sincerely, Kent B. Crane
> Assistant to the Vice President

On the 12th of May, I wrote to Bill Casey, in order to keep him abreast of the situation. I said:

Dear Bill:

Apparently the field is narrowed to two for the Greek spot, Quinn and Rockwell, a foreign service officer. The State Department, i.e., the 'State boys,' are campaigning with

Pell and Fullbright in passing out ideas as per Don Edwards insert attached. The one thing they are hammering on is the fact that I am military and that the 'Junta' are military. Barry says I'm alive, but he's done all he could and agrees I can use help from any source on that score. I've attached a copy of a letter directed by my local Greek-American supporters, which they think if dispatched by someone, i.e., someone the President respects, might help do the trick. Can you think of anyone in that category in New York, Sheehan or Forgan or anyone else? For your information, the Vice President sent a note to Rogers last week and recommended me again for the job. In any event, thanks for your interest.

Sincerely, Bill Quinn

Although I was not involved in it, the situation in the month of May 1969 became very acute because of the accusations by the Amnesty International and other humanitarian organizations around the world, who began to put the heat on "the Colonels" because of the human rights issue. The question of who should be ambassador there became a part of that particular situation and specifically, the need of an American ambassador who could best handle the problems associated with the accusations.

On the 10th of June, Goldwater sent a letter to Attorney General John Mitchell in my behalf. Kent Crane called and said there was no news, that it was all kind of quiet, and he said, "In all probability, another foreign service officer, a career diplomat, will be nominated or will be looked at." And he said, "But, your letter from the Vice President is still on Rogers' desk."

On the 10th of June, I went to a dinner for Ambassador Ellsworth who was on his way to NATO. There was Senator Mathias, Rogers Morton, Senator Scott, and Bryce Harlow, who came up to me and said, "I've heard plenty about you in the last few months. Barry is really bird-dogging for you, and I'd like to talk to you again."

On the 11th of June, the Senator called me. He said, "We've got problems. The word's around that they don't want a general, or a colonel, or even a corporal, and I haven't heard from Mitchell." The *Washington Star* article on July the 18th read: "Nixon delay on Greek Envoy shows displeasure with the 'Junta.' " The article goes on to say why the writer thinks that the aspect of the torture and the attitude of the "Junta" vis-à-vis NATO and the United States were the reasons for the delay. But in fact, it wasn't so much that as the fact that they couldn't pick the ambassador.

As explained earlier, the President was influenced by State to select Tasca, a career Foreign Service Officer. The aftermath brought a squibb in the *U. S. News and World Report* on October 13th, in the column called "Washington Whispers." It said that Senator Barry Goldwater is described by friends as very unhappy that the President sided against the Senator's recommendation of a retired Army general as the U. S. ambassador to Greece; instead the White House picked Henry J. Taska, a career diplomat, spoken of as a liberal. In the *Congressional Record*, Washington, Friday, December 19th, 1969, under the subject of Executive Session The Assistant Legislative Clerk read the nomination of Henry J. Taska as the U. S. ambassador to Greece, and this was followed by discussion by Mr. Goodall and there were individual comments by Mr. Bayh and Mr. Moss, Mr. McGovern and Mr. Church. The nomination of Mr. Tasca was then confirmed.

NOTE: In the preparation of this chapter I requested the following persons to confirm my account: Mr. Halderman, Mr. Erlichman, Mr. Flanahan, Secretary

Richardson, Secretary Johnson, and President Nixon.
Most responded. None contested its accuracy. The President sent me the following letter:

RICHARD NIXON

December 20, 1983

26 FEDERAL PLAZA
NEW YORK CITY

Dear General,
    I read your letter of December 5th and the
attached manuscript with great interest.

    Unfortunately, I do not have my papers
covering that period in my office in New York.
Consequently, I can not verify your account about
the appointment as Ambassador to Greece. I do
know, however, that not only our mutual friend
Barry Goldwater but several others strongly
endorsed you for that post.

    I had known Henry Tasca since 1947 when I met
him in Italy as a member of the Herter Committee.
I considered him to be several cuts above the
average foreign service officer and felt that he
could serve with distinction in any post he was
assigned to.

    I want to assure you, however, that his being
named as Ambassador to Greece was in no way a
reflection on your outstanding qualifications. I
have no prejudice whatsoever against military men
in key diplomatic positions. Quite the contrary.
In that connection, I think you might find the
enclosed copy of the private edition of my new
book, Real Peace, of some interest.

    With warm personal regards,

                        Sincerely,

Lt. General William Quinn

63

PAN MUN JUONG— THE DMZ

In 1982 when Senator Goldwater was Chairman of the Senate Select Committee on Intelligence, he decided to make a trip to the Far East to visit certain commands and classified military intelligence installations in the area. This brought the two of us to South Korea. In Seoul we were greeted by the highest civilian and military dignitaries. We met the President and the Defense Minister. We were briefed by the Central Intelligence Agency and also by the Commanding General of the Eighth Army, a unified and united command. We were then taken up to the Pan Mun Juong, which is the armistice area at the demilitarized zone (DMZ) that crosses Korea north of the 38th parallel.

While we were in the Pan Mun Juong briefing room, before we went up to the line itself, we were being briefed by a young officer on the background of the armistice negotiations and some of the current circumstances and happenings that had transpired. In the middle of this briefing, however, the briefing officer stopped and said,

"General Quinn, we have a surprise for you."

"What is it?"

In the front of the briefing room came a lieutenant colonel, who introduced himself as the battalion commander of the First Battalion of the 17th Infantry Regiment (The Buffaloes). He asked me if I had my buffalo nickel. In Chapter 46 of this book I tell the story of the nickel. It is a tradition of the regiment that all members have a specially designed buffalo nickel. Once it is presented to another Buffalo, if the latter does not have the nickel on him, he has to buy the drinks. I had mine.

At this time, Senator Goldwater was presented with a nickel and also alerted to his responsibility in having such a token. Then to my great surprise, the battalion commander held up a photograph of me, which was about 18 inches wide and about two feet tall, a blow-up of an old photograph.

I asked, "Where did you get this?"

"It came from my predecessor and his predecessor, and I understand that when the regiment was deactivated and the First Battalion that I now command was left and attached to the Second Infantry Division, this picture was handed to us to hold. It has been hanging in the First Batallion's Headquarters orderly room for over thirty years."

Well, I was aghast; I never was so dumbstruck—that out of a hell of a lot of commanders they had selected me to be so honored and that my picture had been hanging there all of those years; I can't begin to express the tremendous emotional impact of that experience. It was one that was topped only by my having been chosen to be the Honorary Colonel of the Regiment by the Secretary of the Army.

64

COLONEL OF THE REGIMENT

In September 1984, I received a letter from the Commanding officer of the Third Brigade of the Seventh Division (Light) at Fort Ord, California. He indicated that several battalions of the 17th Infantry Regiment (Buffaloes) were to be re-activated, as the only active battalion was the 1st, which was attached to the Second Division in Korea.

He also stated that the Chief of Staff of the Army, General John Wickham, was coming to Fort Ord on an inspection trip and that he was planning to dedicate the building selected to house the new regimental headquarters, and it was to be named Quinn Hall.

Now this was exceedingly flattering, because the 17th Infantry Regiment had many illustrious commanders from the time it was activated in 1812 until the present. To be selected as the regimental commander more prominently remembered for one reason or another was highly significant to me and really a capstone to my military career, with one exception, an incident which took place the fol-

396

lowing May.

I was invited to go to Fort Benning by the Commanding General of Fort Benning and the Commanding General of Fort Ord, California, to attend the graduation ceremony of the 4th Battalion of the 17th Infantry Regiment, which was to be activated and formed. This event was the result of a new program in the Army called COHORT.

What happens here is that the Army takes its volunteers or enlistees from enlistment centers, maybe a thousand of them, and assigns them to a unit in a basic training camp, in this case, Fort Benning. After basic training, this same group of a thousand men, still together, are given advanced infantry training. Once they are through with that, they are ready for combat. They are well-trained soldiers and will stay together throughout their first enlistment.

While the latter part of the advanced infantry training for this group of soldiers is given, the Army selects a cadre of officers and non-commissioned officers, a lieutenant colonel to command the battalion, several majors to be executive officers and so forth, captains for company commanders, and a score of lieutenants. They are taken from different units of the Army, officers and enlisted men, non-commissioned officers. Once chosen, they are sent to Fort Benning for a refresher course in Infantry tactics and general military subjects in training, and upon graduation are then joined with their men and the battalion is thereby formed, and they fly off (as they did in this case, to Fort Ord) as a battalion of Infantry ready to fight. It is a wonderful system, and it seems to be working out very well. What it means is that these young men come in off the streets of America and are together for two years, the same people, side by side. So they get to know each other intimately, and that breeds high morale with great spirit.

In any event, I was invited to the graduation of this 4th Battalion. It so happens that Senator Goldwater and I had been talking about going to Fort Benning for some time. He, being the Chairman of the Senate Armed Forces Committee, was in the process of visiting various Army, Navy, Air Force, and Marine installations. We went to Fort Benning, and were at the presentation of this group, and Senator Goldwater made some remarks, as did I, because I was a former commander of the 17th Regiment in Korea. During the latter part of the ceremony, I was asked to assist in giving out awards for best marksmanship, best all-around soldier, and for one thing or another.

At the very end, the Commanding General said, "Now, General Quinn, would you please stand beside me?" He then read from a certificate signed by the Secretary of the Army naming me the Honorary Regimental Commander of the 17th Infantry Regiment.

The fact that I had been selected as the Honorary Colonel of the Regiment for life was a tremendous surprise to me, and a day I shall always cherish.

PART XII

VIGNETTES

The Quinn Family, 1965

Sally, Bill, Jr., Donna
William and Betty

65

JOE JONES— ENTREPRENEUR

Although they say there's nothing new in this world, several years ago I ran into something that was new to me, and that was Joe Jones and his hardware store in Enterprise, Alabama.

To say that Joe ran a hardware store is at best only a very rough classification of his establishment. The building was loaded from floor to ceiling with everything you can think of, and just to be different Joe ran a "Bargain Balcony" instead of a basement. But it's really not so much the store I want to tell you about . . . it's the way Joe operated it.

The first time I went into his place, Joe greeted me at the door with, "Come on in, friend, and let me trade you out of some money." I laughed and told him I was just window shopping. He invited me to "climb around" and said if I couldn't find what I wanted he'd go out back to the warehouse; it would be there. I finally bought a nineteen-cent can opener. When I paid him he remarked, "That'll be twenty cents my friend, nineteen for Joe and one for the Governor."

When Joe first opened for business he startled Coffee County with his initial newspaper announcement. The full page ad invited the populace to come down to his store and look at the pile of "trash and junk" he had accumulated and was going to attempt to sell. Joe told me people flocked in to see the "trash" and some were disappointed because it wasn't. In this connection, his weekly radio advertisements were classics of understatement and violated every rule of sales appeal, yet the people still come in to buy the very merchandise he ran down.

Once Joe advertised over the radio that he had a lawn mower he was tired of looking at. He said that its price was $19.95 but each day until he sold it, he would reduce the price by one dollar. He then went on to advise his listeners, "If you're smart you won't come in right away. Wait until the price gets down to $ .95." Needless to say, the grass cutter was sold the next day for $18.95.

You never knew what Joe was going to give out with. One of my neighbors, Jimmy Kelsoe, told me about a couple of his visits to Joe's store. It seems Joe was having a sale on fishing poles and Jimmy was inspecting one of them. It was priced at ninety-nine cents. Jimmy asked, "How much was this before the sale?"

Joe replied immediately, "Eighty-nine cents."

"How come it's ten cents more with a sale on? I never heard of such a deal," Jimmy retorted.

Joe's answer was, "How about that? I guess it's because I have to cover the cost of advertising the sale."

Another time Jimmy was looking at a garden tool which was priced higher than a similar one in another store down the street. Jimmy challenged him on the fact. Joe's answer was, "Yeh, I know. You see, we operate on an entirely different basis. I make more profit." What can you say to a guy like that?

Jimmy's wife went in one day looking for a can of inexpensive paint. Joe showed her some. He said, "Now here's a can of cheap paint. I guarantee it to be no good." She thought he was kidding. When she got home and used it on a porch chair she found that it was just what he had claimed it to be . . . terrible.

The latest advertising gag pulled by Joe had to do with the souvenir program published in connection with a Coffee County rodeo. Joe took a half-page ad on which he placed just four letters—*L P Q T*. The ad salesman said, "Joe, you got to put your name on the ad. No one will know whose it is."

Joe said, "You're wrong, my friend; people will find out that those initials mean Low Profit—Quick Turnover, if they have to ask everybody in Coffee County. They'll also find out it's the motto of Joe Jones' hardware store."

I'll say this for Joe, while Arthur Godfrey used to run down the product of his sponsor, Joe had the courage to ridicule his own wares, which combined with the humor by which it is done, tickles the imagination and sense of humor of the average American. It occurs to me that if we all could practice a little of Joe's philosophy, and get a few laughs out of our daily labors, the strain of our association with each other in this competitive world would certainly be materially lessened.

66

GEORGE DIXON

George Dixon was a very popular Washington columnist for many years. He was a satirist, somewhat along the Art Buchwald line, with a very delicate sense of humor.

George and Imelda Dixon came to visit us in Germany when I had command of the Seventh Army in Stuttgart. This particular weekend I had been invited by the new Ambassador to Luxembourg, Mr. Rivkin, to visit him on Saturday evening. He was honoring the visiting Pittsburgh Philharmonic Orchestra at a reception. The orchestra was to give several concerts in the city of Luxembourg.

I had my aide call the Ambassador's secretary to say that we had some house guests and who they were, and also that my daughter Sally was home at the time. The Ambassador's response was to extend an invitation to my guests and Sally.

At this time the Seventh Army Commander had his own train. This acted as a mobile command post with its own communications, salon, sleeping compartments, and a dining room with an excellent chef—strictly a first class operation.

I asked George and Imelda if they would like to go to Luxembourg with us, go to the reception, spend the night on the train, and return to Stuttgart the next day. They graciously accepted the invitation, as they had never been to Luxembourg.

Well, on the train the next morning we were having a few drinks and a lot of laughs before lunch, listening to George regale us with stories about Washington and some of its characters. Finally, during a lull in the conversation, Sally got in the act by saying, "George, I have something that I picked up in Germany recently, and I doubt if anybody except me can do it."

George said, "What the hell is it?"

"You take a standard wire coat hanger, round it into a circle without undoing the top wire and pass it over your head and shoulders and down over your hips until it drops to the floor."

"Okay, you've got a pretty broad butt, so let's see you do it," George said.

Sally took the coathanger, rounded it out, put it over her head, and with some swerving and pulling and tugging, she got it down over her shoulders and behind.

"No big deal," George teased, "give me the hanger."

So he took the coathanger and started struggling. He got down on the floor squirming and snorting, trying to get through the hoop, and he finally made it. He ended up with welts and ridges on his shoulders and neck, but he certainly was a riot.

Then George dropped his bomb. "I've been thinking about this party tonight. I don't mind going to receptions, but I have never liked oboe players, and anybody who plays an oboe or piccolo is for the birds."

I said, "George, they've got trombone players and

drummers as well. You got a problem with them?"

"No, it's just that I don't like the word oboe and any-body that plays one can't be any damn good."

"So," he continued, "I'm not going to the reception. You all can go, but I'll stay on the train or go to a local bar."

"You can't do that," I replied, "We've already accepted for you."

"All right. I'll tell you what will happen if you force me to go. I'll make a scene, and I promise you this, you'll be sorry that you ever dragged me into that Embassy."

We said, "Okay, George, we'll take our chances on that, but you've got to go. The Rivkins are expecting you."

We were met at the Luxembourg City Train Station at around 6:00 P.M. and driven to the residence in embassy cars. It so happened that that week, a magazine named *The Diplomat* had a feature article entitled "The Rivkins of Luxembourg." It was a flattering article, describing their background in Chicago, their many graces and accomplishments, and so forth. It had not yet arrived in Luxembourg, and Mrs. Rivkin had not seen it, but knew that an article had been written about them.

Assembled at one end of the room, in a huddle, was George, Imelda, Mrs. Rivkin, Bette, and myself. Mrs. Rivkin said, "You know, Mr. Dixon, I understand that there's an article about us in the new *Diplomat* magazine."

George said, "Yes, I know, but I wouldn't worry about it, if I were you."

Mrs. Rivkin, with a dramatic double-take, said, "What do you mean, I shouldn't worry about it?"

"Oh," George replied, "I wouldn't worry just because they call you a lush, or because some editor thinks you drink too much."

I thought Mrs. Rivkin was going to have a stroke. I said quickly, "Mrs. Rivkin, don't pay any attention, because I hear the article is very complimentary."

But she wasn't listening and rushed to tell the Ambassador. Bette, Imelda, and I looked at George like we wanted to wring his neck. With a smug smile he said, "I warned you. I told you I was going to make a scene. Wasn't that a beaut? Maybe one for the *Guinness Book of World Records.*"

67

BILL QUINN
OF HAWAII

While I was in command of the 7th Army in Germany in 1965, I was invited by the veterans of the Office of Strategic Services to return to Washington to receive the William J. Donovan Medal. This award had previously been given to Allen Dulles, former Director of CIA, and to the Honorable John McCoy. Later it was presented to President Eisenhower, Admiral Mountbatten, Margaret Thatcher, David Bruce, Bill Casey, and others.

The dinner was held at the Mayflower Hotel, and the former Secretary of the Army, Dr. Elvis J. Starr, presided. There were reporters and photographers there from the *Times-Herald/Washington Post*. The next morning there was a story of the event featuring pictures of my mother, Bette and Barry Goldwater, and a photograph with a caption that read, "Lieutenant General William W. Quinn received the honor of the Donovan Award last night at the Mayflower Hotel." The photograph over the caption was of William F. Quinn, former Governor of Hawaii. I had never met the Governor, but I had heard of him. Just for the hell of it, I cut out the article with the photo and caption and mailed it to him, after writing across it in black crayon, "Quinn of Hawaii, get off my back. Quinn of Washington."

Well, I got a very funny note from him saying, "I'm really not climbing up your back. It's the morgue that the *Washington Post* has that's so bad, and you must know that you have to get known real well before you get your picture in the paper."

Through the years we became penpals and finally met at the Bohemian Grove in California. The next incident involving the two of us was on my retirement from the 7th Army a year or so later. I had been awarded the Legion of Honor by President de Gaulle for my intelligence work in the 7th Army during World War II in the grade of Chevalier. On my retirement from command of the 7th Army in 1966, de Gaulle raised the order of my Legion of Honor from Chevalier to Officer. I did not receive this medal in Germany, so the French Government sent the medal to the French Embassy in Washington for presentation to me there.

But here's what happened to it. Some clerk in the French Embassy sent it to the Consul General in San Francisco, instructing him to make the necessary arrangements to present this medal to William Quinn of Hawaii, the former Governor. Bill, who was then president of the Dole Company, later told me what happened. He was in his office one day when the phone rang. It was the French Consul General in San Francisco, who told him he had this award for him, and would like to make a presentation of it, hopefully in San Francisco, and that Bill was at liberty to invite any of his friends from San Francisco or Hawaii who would like to attend.

Bill said, "Well, I don't know what I've done, but I

appreciate it." He told me later it wasn't too clear and he didn't know what the hell was going on. So within the week Bill had business in San Francisco, called the Consul General, said he'd be in town, and arrangements were made for this presentation.

Suddenly, Bill remembered that newspaper clipping—so he called the Consul General and told him, "Listen, I think you've got the wrong man."

"Oh, no, Governor, we know precisely."

"What does the citation say?"

"It says for meritorious service and so forth while in command of the 7th U.S. Army in Germany."

"Well, that's not me. I've never been to Europe. I was in the Navy. I think you want General Quinn in Washington, D.C."

The Consul General then asked, "Where did you serve in the Navy?"

"I was in the Pacific during the war."

Well, the French Ambassador and Consul General were really embarrassed about this.

Later on the French Military Attache presented me with the medal at a party in my honor in Washington and was very apologetic. To compensate for their goof, they presented Bill Quinn of Hawaii with the *Croix de Guerre with Palm* because they learned that the ship he was on during World War II had sailed past a French-owned island!

I might say that we've had lots of laughs over this, and when Bill Quinn and Nancy and some of their seven children came to Washington, we had a great visit with them. On our trip around the world with Barry Goldwater in January 1986, we stopped in Hawaii and had a drink with them. They are delightful, gracious people.

68

CARDINAL SPELLMAN

During Thanksgiving week of 1965, Cardinal Spellman came to visit my troops in the Seventh Army. As Commander, I was his escort on several occasions and was smitten with him because he was a great man, a great spirit. At our quarters in Stuttgart one evening, we had a small dinner party for him with some of the Seventh Army and Seventh Corps Catholic chaplains and some of the officers of my headquarters. During dinner, the Cardinal was asked if he was going to Vietnam for Christmas, and he said, "Of course, I am. Do you think for a minute I'm going to let that Bob Hope get ahead of me?"

He was a lot of fun. At dinner that night my wife Bette was on his left. They were talking about driving in Germany, and for some reason, the subject of St. Christopher came up. It seems that St. Christopher had just been removed from his status as a saint, I assume by the Vatican. Bette was explaining that although she was not a Catholic, she had a great deal of faith in St. Christopher and always kept a St. Christopher medal in her automobile when she traveled. Bette was also lamenting the fact that she recently discovered she couldn't find hers, and she was sick about losing it. No more was said on the subject.

After visiting the troops and giving blessings in several mess halls Thanksgiving Day, Cardinal Spellman returned to New York. About three weeks later, a little package arrived from New York, addressed to Bette. When she opened it, she found a St. Christopher's medal and a note from Cardinal Spellman saying, "I, too, am somewhat depressed over the busting of St. Christopher from a saint, and I, too, still have a great deal of faith in him, as you do. And as you have that faith, I have enclosed a small token of my esteem and thanks for a generous evening, a beautiful dinner, and the hospitality of your home. The medal may give you additional pleasure, as it was blessed by the Pope."

Well, Bette looked at the medal, which was rather dull looking. At that time she was working on a charm bracelet, which consisted of gold ornaments. She said to me, "You know, I'd like to put this on my charm bracelet, but it doesn't match the other gold; so I'm going to have it gold-plated."

So she went downtown in Stuttgart to a jeweler's and asked to have the metal gold-plated. The German jeweler looked at it, looked at her, and said, "Lady, this does not need to be gold-plated. It is already 18 carat."

69

GENERALISSIMO CHIANG KAI-SHEK

In the winter of 1960 the Secretary of the Army, Dr. Elvis J. Starr, decided to make a tour of the Army installations in the Far East. As his Chief of Information, I was invited to be in his party, which included Bette. It so happened that Mrs. Starr was ill and unable to make the trip; so it then fell as Bette's responsibility to act as hostess for the Secretary and the group. Our itinerary was to confer with Army commands and advisory groups in Hawaii, Korea, and the Republic of China in Taiwan.

On our arrival in Taipei, besides flowers and gifts in our rooms, we found an invitation for dinner at the palace—an invitation extended by the Generalissimo and Madame Chiang Kai-Shek.

When we arrived in the palace, we found the Generalissimo seated by a fireplace with a fire going. The Madame was across the room at a small table. Several aides were moving around. It turned out that Bette was the only lady invited, for the simple reason that Madame Chiang Kai-Shek did not have the time for women. She liked to talk to men and pick their brains. She felt that any time spent with women really was wasted, as it had nothing to do with politics, economics, etc., but only with children, clothes, or shopping.

The Generalissimo and the aides had an interesting routine. Aides would come up and say, "The Generalissimo would like to have a short conversation with you." And so, you were guided up to a chair next to the Generalissimo. He would ask you what your position and background were and inquire into matters bearing on Taiwan, U.S. opinion, etc., and ask a couple of questions about what you thought about his army. It was an interesting exercise, but it was only on a question and answer basis. You didn't ask him any questions. He did all the asking, and you supplied all the answers.

Once the Generalissimo had milked you, he would signal an aide, who would approach the Generalissimo and be spoken to in Chinese. In my case, the aide said that the Generalissimo would like to have a few words with Colonel X, which signaled my departure. Great system. Smooth.

After dinner Bette and I were guided to the small round table by the Madame. In our discussion, we covered several subjects, one of them being diet and weight. The Madame acknowledged that was her big problem, in view of so many official dinners, etc.

The "bible" for weight watchers in the U.S. at that time was a newly published book entitled, *Calories Don't Count*. As the Madame seemed fascinated by the concept and indicated a desire to read the book, I told her I would mail her a copy on my return home.

Just before we were to leave for our hotel, the Madame asked Bette and me to follow her. She led us through some of the large hallways and foyers to show us her paintings and water colors. We were very impressed with her work. We returned to the living room and shortly afterwards departed for the city.

On our arrival at our hotel, we found a large folder about two inches or more in thickness. Attached was a note which thanked us for our generosity in offering to send her the book. It was signed by Madame Chiang Kai-Shek. The folder contained lithography copies of all her art. It is a souvenir which we continue to treasure.

70

LIEUTENANT GENERAL ALEXANDER M. PATCH

General "Sandy" Patch was one of God's noblemen—a true gentleman, a man of personal dignity with a simple and easy manner in dealing with others. If you were lucky enough to call Sandy Patch a friend, you really had one—to which George Patton could have readily attested.

In attempting to paint a verbal picture of General Patch, I sense that I am a biased artist, in that my admiration for him was limitless. If he had one fault (and it may not be one), it was that he "hid his light under a bushel."

In other chapters of this book can be found references to him and our relationship. Of great pride to me was his selection of me, from among scores of officers in the 7th Army Headquarters in Germany, to accompany him on his reassignment by General George Marshall to the Far East. He had been selected to command an army for the invasion of Japan. Of course, the atomic bomb precluded the necessity of that operation. It is not my purpose to enumerate his many accomplishments or construct a biographical sketch or relate his great successes of command both in the Pacific and in Europe. For that purpose I heartily recommend a brilliant biography of Patch written by William R. Wyant, who was the secretary to the General Staff of the Seventh Army during Patch's period of command.

To shed one light on the personal characteristics of General Patch, here follows an excerpt from Barry Goldwater's book, *Goldwater*:

> I was about to meet the man who would straighten my direction, stiffen my purpose, strengthen my mind, and show me a discipline I had never known before—Sandy Patch.
>
> Major Alexander M. "Sandy" Patch was in charge of the Reserve Officers Training Corps and my military instruction at Staunton Military Academy. He was Army from birth to death—and a native Arizonian. Patch had been born at Fort Huachuca in the southern part of the state and died of pneumonia at Fort Sam Houston in Texas. Like his father, who had lost a leg fighting Indians in the Southwest, he was career Army and eventually became a general. Both of them were West Point graduates.
>
> Patch was about six feet tall, with blue eyes and reddish hair, weighing some 170 pounds, and light on his feet. The thing that marked him as a man and officer was his personal discipline. He wasn't tough or mean. He was calm. He never lost his temper, no matter what.
>
> Behind those steel blue eyes was a taskmaster. If he said to be some place at 10 A.M., you had better be there on the dot. If he asked you a question in class, you had better be prepared with an answer. If you broke the rules, you paid the price.
>
> Patch stressed basics. He was a painstakingly practical man. He always said we would use what we learned—in some way—for the rest of our lives.
>
> I remember one evening when the class was fighting a mock Battle of Gettysburg. We were using a large sand-table model of the terrain.
>
> Each cadet would start as a platoon leader. We'd work up to the problems facing captains and other officers. If anyone went off on a wrong track, the major would patiently allow

him to go. He would let him dig his own trap. Then, he would stop and ask questions. He would slowly lead the cadet out of the trap but would make him find part of the way himself. The gentle but firm manner in which he did this was a work of art—like a master chess player. He was a gentle fox.

Sandy would always tell us to remember our basic orders, to keep in mind our original estimate of the situation. Not to just jump into a fight. Not to make big changes unless the battle shows the estimate was wrong. If you remember that, you may be able to avoid getting yourself and your men hurt.

After completing an assignment, I once asked Patch, "Major, is there any other way we can know our orders are right or wrong?"

He replied, "Son, you'll never know that until the enemy starts shooting at you."

As indicated in Chapter 5, and in Chapter 75 on Barry Goldwater, Professor Gardner, the principal of my high school on the Eastern Shore of Maryland, would recite to his pupils a list of what he termed the very basic elements of character. He challenged us to use them to measure ourselves and to measure others. So saying, let me enumerate some of the important ones now, so that you might measure this man Patch:

Integrity, Industrious, Persistent, Courageous, Kind, Thoughtful, Humorous, Considerate, Friendly, Dependable, Polite, Patient, Generous. He had them all.

That tells you just about all you need to know about Sandy Patch.

Except probably, what Generals Eisenhower and Marshall thought of him. Upon learning of his death, General Eisenhower, then acting Army Chief of Staff, stated: "I wish to express my sorrow at losing a valued friend and colleague. General Patch was one of the nation's outstanding troop leaders, and the Army mourns his passing. As a close personal friend, I am deeply grieved. He was a soldier's soldier. His leadership in bat-

*Lt. Gen Alexander M. Patch pins the Legion of Merit
on Col. William W. Quinn.*

tle, both in the Pacific and in Europe, and his skill in the training of our men, contributed immeasurably to the defeat of our enemies. In Europe, his outstanding achievement was his brilliant leadership of the Seventh Army."

Mrs. Patch received the following message from General George Marshall, who was about to become Secretary of State: "We all send you our deep sympathy, with our profound regrets at the great loss to the Army, in the death of your husband, and our sympathy for you. He rendered a magnificent service to the country and died commanding the respect, not only of the Army, but of the people."

71

GENERAL OMAR N. BRADLEY

A great many historians have followed the career of General Omar Bradley and have eulogized him in many ways as a fine man, a good soldier, and a superior tactician, or strategist. I guess my first encounter with General Bradley was in the Louisiana Maneuvers when he commanded the "Blue" forces and was opposing the so-called "Reds," i.e., the American troops acting as the enemy. At that time I was working for General Oswald Griswold as the corps' G-2. I started out as a major and one day was called to General Bradley's headquarters and in the presence of General Griswold I received from General Bradley my silver oak leaves as a lieutenant colonel.

I saw General Bradley quite a bit during that period and observed him in my position as a corps G-2, when he was in command of a division and also of Camp Livingston, Louisiana. I visited with him again, as I relate in Chapter 73 on General Patton, at his headquarters in France during World War II.

My purpose here is not to discuss or otherwise attempt to tell you all about General Omar Bradley, as
again many historians have done just that. I do want to
tell a story about him, which to me kind of salts him down
in a way that is very pleasant and very human. This man
was Lincolnian in his humor, his intellect, and his philosophy. In every way he was a great leader, with a very
quiet manner, but anyone who dealt with him had a great
appreciation for his sincerity, his knowledge, his understanding, and his dedication.

Here then is my favorite story about General Omar N.
Bradley. When he was in command of Camp Livingston,
Louisiana, and an infantry division, his responsibility was
in the hurry-up-and-train-and-get-overseas (1942–1943)
period. On this particular occasion, it was winter, and
we'd had a tremendous amount of rain in that part of
Louisiana. The roads at Camp Livingston, which were not
improved, were almost impassable. As the camp was
newly constructed, the roads turned out to be a
mire—not roads at all—just mud. This had a detrimental
impact on movement and training, and troops were
muddy all the time. The camp was not really in good
shape, even though General Bradley was trying his utmost
to get it straightened out.

General Bradley had a small office building which was
the Division Commander's Building, in which there were
two entrances, the front and the back. There were two
rooms and a bathroom in the cottage. As you entered the
first room it had desks for an officer aide and a duty officer, a few chairs, and bookcases. The other room was entered through a back door or through the door of the
aide's room. This was General Bradley's office.

This Saturday night the aide for General Bradley was
on duty. The headquarters had to be manned 24 hours a

Gen. Omar N. Bradley, Commander of the 1st and 3rd U.S. Armies in France, in a car at his roadside Command Post.

day, i.e., someone had to be there to answer the phone for General Bradley in case the Department of the Army called him or he was called by the Chief of Staff of the Army.

This aide had a friend who was a friend of mine, Eldon "Bud" Larecy, who told me the story. Bud was the logistics officer for the 4th Corps which was stationed at Fort Beauregard and in which General Griswold was in command. This included the area which involved Camp Livingston, General Bradley's division, and other troops. So Bud went over to see his friend on this Saturday night, bringing a small bottle of cheer and mixings. While they were sitting there in the aide's room having a drink and talking, unbeknown to them, General Bradley entered his side of the building and started to work at his desk, without making his presence known to the two people in the aide's area. The door between the rooms was open, and General Bradley could hear the conversation.

Bud Larecy said, "You know, General Griswold is really upset about this camp, its conditions, the lack of training facilities and the fact that the troops are not, or don't seem to be, getting as well trained as they should. What would you do if you were General Griswold, the corps commander?"

"Well," said the aide, slamming his fist down on the table, "the first thing I'd do, I'd say, 'Omar, come in here!' "

General Bradley heard this, got up, walked through the door, came to attention, saluted the aide, and said, "Did you call, sir?"

72

FIELD MARSHAL
VON RUNDSTEDT

F ield Marshal Von Rundstedt was probably the finest
ground soldier we interrogated in the 7th Army—a very
profound professional, straight as an arrow and immaculate, Prussian. When he was captured, he was brought directly to 7th Army Headquarters. General Patch held him
in great esteem. They spent many hours in conversation.
Patch liked Von Rundstedt much more than Goering.
Von Rundstedt was more his type. He was an infantry
"ground pounder," if you will, and so was Patch. They saw
eye-to-eye immediately.

Von Rundstedt explained the fallacy of his strategies
to Hitler, but he said there was nothing anybody could do
about it. With the S.S., Hitler had complete control of the
situation, from both police and political standpoints. Von
Rundstedt said that Hitler was obsessed with the idea
that not one Western soldier, British or American, would
gain a foothold on the French coast. Consequently, Hitler
ordered the dispersion of forces, which formed, actually, a
crust from Normandy all the way down the coast to Cher-

bourg Peninsula.

Von Rundstedt told Hitler on several occasions, "You must not do this, because we have no idea where they are coming, and if they come at any one particular point with a tremendous amount of force, they will break through this shell we have. We have no armor in reserve with which we can counterattack; it's all up front." Von Rundstedt's idea was to lightly defend the beaches and to place the major reserves and tank armies in concentrated areas so that wherever the landing came, he would be able to inflict a counterattack which would probably overpower the invading forces in disarray. In any event, he told Hitler that the logistics of recreating and assembling a counterattack force would be too difficult to insure a timely reaction.

An interesting episode occurred while the Field Marshal was incarcerated. We in the 7th Army had taken over a complete worker's village associated with a large industry in Augsberg. The field marshals, generals, admirals, and other high-ranking government officials were billeted in the village. Quarters were small, but adequate, comprising a living-dining area, a bedroom, and a bath. The staff of the prisoners, if any, slept on cots in the living room. Marshal Von Rundstedt was assigned one of these quarters, as were Goering, Kesselring, Von Wachts and Schoerner—all marshals.

It so happened that just before our troops took Augsberg our bombers had hit the village and knocked out the water supply; hence, the houses had no running water. There was a well with a manual pump, however, at the foot of the main street.

Almost immediately on the occupancy of these quarters, I went to see Von Rundstedt with Major Kubala and explained the circumstances. We discussed the options of

Colonel Quinn, interpreter,
Field Marshal Von Rundstedt, General Patch

procuring water at the pump until our Army engineers could repair the damage. Von Rundstedt said, in essence, "For good order, I suggest that I have a formation at frequent intervals during the day involving all the officers in this area. If you will provide me with a loud whistle and inform all concerned of this plan, I will assemble them and form them into a column of two with their buckets, or pots and pans, and march them to the pump."

We sent German-speaking messengers to each billet to pass the word and provided the Marshal with a small MP whistle. It was an incredible sight to watch this first formation. There were 45 or 50 field marshals, generals, and admirals with pots and pans being marched to the pump. In bugler's terms, we called the whistle-blowing "Von Rundstedt's Water Call."

73

GENERAL GEORGE S. PATTON, JR.

Although I admired him from a distance, there were only two occasions when our paths crossed. As the circumstances were both amusing and atypical of General Patton, I have related them here in two episodes.

Episode One

At Fort Benning, Georgia, the Harmony Church area is the jumping-off place for the training areas on the reservation. The buildings at Harmony Church proper served as the headquarters for the Fourth Infantry Division. At that time in 1941, I was Headquarters Commandant, Provost Marshall, Division Police Officer, and Headquarters Company Commander. I had these four jobs as a captain. In later tables of organization, there are two lieutenant colonels, a major, and a captain to handle these functions. So much for that.

Up the road from Harmony Church to the north was the Second Armored Division and its headquarters. It was commanded by Major General George Patton, Jr. Most of the senior officers had quarters on the post at Fort Benning and departed them in the morning to join the troops in the division areas. This one morning, General Patton was apparently late leaving Fort Benning on his way to his division area. He was close to the Harmony Church area in his Packard coupe, as I recall, exceeding the speed limit by quite a wide margin. Now, the Fourth Division was responsible for the traffic control of that particular road, and my Military Police company patrolled it with motorcycles to insure that there were no violations of the speed and traffic regulations. Patton sped by Corporal Dutton, one of my MP's, who was at an intersection when General Patton went past him like a bullet. Dutton took out after him, not knowing whom he was chasing. General Patton turned left at the Harmony Church intersection, ignoring the MP's sirens on the motorcycle. He just kept going and stepped on the gas. Dutton followed him in hot pursuit, and when the first road that was under the control of the Second Armored Division—Patton's own turf—came into view, the General pulled off on it. He was now in his territory, and he got out of the car. The MP came skidding in on the motorcycle, went up to General Patton, saw who it was, and saluted.

General Patton said, "Get your ass out of the Second Division area. This is my division and my area, and you, as far as I'm concerned, are trespassing; so get the hell out."

Well, the MP knew damn well he would probably be court-martialed, and probably drawn and quartered. He came immediately back to the Harmony Church Headquarters where the Fourth Division was, came in the orderly room, and asked to see me. He walked in shaking and reported, "Cap'n, I just made a helluva mistake."

I said, "What did you do?"

"I tried to arrest General Patton."

"You did? Well, tell me about it."

When he did, I reasoned that this was not right. General Patton should not have chewed that soldier out for what he'd done; he should have commended him for doing his duty instead of giving him hell.

Now it so happened that the senior officer at Fort Benning was Major General Lloyd Friedendal, and Friedendal was senior to Patton. He commanded the Fourth Division, which was where the offense had been committed. I found General Friedendal and said, "Good morning, General, I have a report to make to you."

"What is it, Quinn?"

"Well, one of my MP's just tried to arrest General Patton."

Now there was no love lost between these two people. As a matter of fact, they kind of disliked each other. I don't know whether they hated each other's guts or not, but at any rate, Friedendal turned to me, very enthusiastic, and said, "Have you got him in the pokey?"

"No, sir, he's not apprehended."

"What happened?" he asked.

So I told him.

"That son of a bitch. He's not going to get away with this. You come with me."

So we went up to the headquarters building, went into his office, and he said, "I want you to hear this."

He picked up the telephone and called General Patton. He said, "George, what's this I hear about this MP trying to arrest you for speeding and you chasing him out of your area?"

I don't know what General Patton said, because I couldn't hear the other side. But General Friedendal said, "Well, George, I don't think that was right. That young man was trying to do his duty, and he didn't know who you were."

There was a silence. Then General Friedendal said, "George, I think the best thing for you to do is to come on up here to this headquarters and apologize to this soldier."

Another silence. "That's right, George. I said apologize to this soldier for your conduct and your remarks to him."

I stood there flabbergasted. Damn, this was going to be a whingding. When Friedendal said, "I want you to come up here and apologize to this soldier." He added, "And now. Right now."

Another silence. He said, "*NOW*, George. Now's the time." Then Freidendal said to me, "General Patton will be here, and I want you to go get that soldier and bring him in."

I didn't know what the hell to do about this. I got Corporal Dutton, and made sure he was "spooney"—in other words, looking real sharp.

So the two of us went up to Division Headquarters and sat and waited till General Patton came. He arrived, of course, immaculate. His boots were like mirrors. He was a handsome, soldierly man. He said to the aide, "Tell General Friedendal General Patton's here."

The aide went in, came out, and said, "Come on in, General."

General Patton went into the room with General Freidendal. I have no idea what was said in there, other than I'm sure that there was some remonstration toward Friedendal. But the door opened, and Friedendal was standing in the door saying to me, "Quinn, where's that soldier?"

"He's right here, sir."

Dutton went in alone. I was not invited. When he came out, I asked, "Are you relieved?"

He said General Friedendal told him to go back to the barracks. Walking back to the barracks, I said, "Tell me about it."

"I walked in, and General Friedendal said, 'Corporal, General Patton has something to say to you.' And General Patton said, 'Soldier, I'd like to tell you that you did a good job this morning in trying to apprehend somebody who was violating the rules. And as for the remarks I made to you, I sincerely owe you my apologies and sincerely hope that you will accept them.' And so I said, 'Yes, sir. Yes, sir, yes, sir, General. No problem.' "

Episode Two

In World War II I was the G2 (intelligence officer) of the Seventh U.S. Army during the invasion of Southern France and for the remainder of the war. At the point we were making a great rush up the Rhine Valley and the Normandy invasion forces were moving to the East, it became obvious the two forces would eventually join up, entrapping thousands of German troops of the 19th German Army that had been in southwest France and were desperately trying to escape to the northeast. It was necessary to coordinate and plan identifying communications so that when our forces joined, we didn't shoot each other, and so there would be no confusion. We also had to make plans to withhold any pressures on the part of the escaping German army. In addition, we had to face backwards or to our flanks in a sense. Another problem was that we had to prepare to accept the surrender of hundreds of thousands of prisoners. The overall tactical and logistical requirements were enormous.

Gen. George S. Patton, Jr., Commander of the U.S. Third Army, smiles as he slips a new pistol into a holster.

For this coordination, General Patch sent John Guthrie, who was the G3 of the Seventh Army, myself, and Major General Arthur A. White, the Chief of Staff of the Seventh Army. The three of us, with our assistants, then went to General Bradley's Army Group Headquarters in the vicinity of Saint Lo. We worked with his staff and also the staff of the Third Army under General Patton to insure a smooth coordination and link up.

While there I had a few minutes break, and I went over to General Bradley's trailer. The Army Group headquarters was housed in buildings and tents, but General Bradley had his own personal van. This van contained his bunk, some communications, and a big wall map. This situation map was updated by briefing officers who came periodically to make up the changing situation, both of the friendly forces and the enemy dispositions.

So I rapped on the van door when I learned he was there, and a voice said, "Come in." I walked in, and General Bradley was alone. He and I had participated in maneuvers in Louisiana a year before, with him as the head of the "Blue Forces," and our socalled enemy being the "Reds."

After he greeted me, he said, "You know, Bill, there's been a lot of water over the dam since you and I were fighting those Reds down there in the Louisiana maneuvers."

I said, "Yes, sir, it sure has, and it's been a great transition from Louisiana woods and swamps to the battlefield here that we're on now."

At that precise moment, the door opened without a knock, and in stalked General Patton. General Patton, without any greetings, walked up to the situation map, took a pointer that was on the tray, pointed to the map and turned to General Bradley. In his famous highpitched voice he said, "Omar, I'll tell you what I'm going to do."

He pointed to the map and continued, "I'm going to send a column up that road over here on the left, and I'll send a column right up the center here, and I'm going to send another column here along this road to the right, and I'm gonna kill those bastards."

General Bradley watched. Parenthetically, I have always thought that in some ways General Bradley must have been a relative of Abraham Lincoln. He was so quiet, so gentle, so understanding and so wise that I consider him one of the great men of our time. Well, in a Lincolnian kind of remark, General Bradley said, "George, you know that's kinda like sticking a pitchfork in a loose pile of hay."

Actually, the remark was so apropos from a military standpoint that the truth of that particular comparison was almost startling. "Now," he said, "George, you ought to think about this; you might want to send a force up this left road, a small force, as a kind of decoy. I would also suggest that you don't impose radio silence, and let your people talk to each other about what they're going to do almost to a point that they're breaching security, and you ought to take the noisiest vehicles that you've got—and at night when sounds can be heard at great distances. And if, with that small group, you make enough noise, it may attract the German forces to the point that they assume that a major attack is coming in that direction. I would then take the rest of the Third Army, and move it on the road on the right flank, two or three hours after this decoy force had been dispatched. If you do send the rest of the Army up the right avenue, it's very possible that you may hit them in a flank, and destroy those German divisions in front of us."

George looked at General Bradley, then looked at the map, thought for a minute, then said (again in his high voice), "Omar, I tell you what I'm gonna do. I'm gonna send every damn band I've got in the Third Army, all the noisiest, clanking tanks I've got up that left flank, and I'm gonna make so goddamn much noise that they're gonna think the world's coming to an end. I'm gonna take the rest of my Army, and I'm going up that right flank, and I'm gonna kill those bastards!"

Omar Bradley said, "George, that's a good idea. Why don't you do just that."

And Patton did. Just that. And he killed one hell of a lot of those bastards—as they were called then.

Note

General Patch and General Patton were great friends and great admirers of each other throughout their military careers. There were never two more different men. Patch was quiet and conservative with deep mental power, easily sensed by those around him. He was thoughtful, intelligent, and unobtrusive, and he shunned publicity. Patton, on the other hand, was flamboyant; he was in front of the cameras at all times, as well as in front of the troops. Both men had the qualities of great leadership, but they exercised them in ways that were 180 degrees apart.

They both went to West Point. Patton was ahead of Patch, but I believe they were in the same company. When Patton went to Infantry School at Fort Benning, Georgia, even though he was in the cavalry, he attended the same year as Patch. By virtue of the accident of their names, they sat side by side, Patch and Patton, for a year. They then went their separate ways until several years later when they attended Staff College at Fort Leavenworth at the same time. Again, their names put them side by side in the classroom. Again, they spent a year in an intimate relationship. Later, when they went to the Army War College, they sat beside each other once more.

During the European war when Patch had the Seventh Army and Patton had the Third, it so happened that in the early part of joining up General Bradley's forces with Patch's Seventh Army, the Third Army was located next to the Seventh. And here they were again, Patch and Patton beside each other—not in chairs this time, but as heads of armies.

It happened from time to time when there was a lull in fighting and things were relatively quiet, General Patton would come over to Seventh Army Headquarters, usually in the evening, and sit beside his old buddy again as they had so many times before.

In these meetings, which included the Operations (G3) and Intelligence (G2) officers, it was interesting to note how Patton sought Patch's opinion on a myriad of subjects relating to current operations. In my mind General Patch was the greater scholar and tactician. Patton, I think, was superior in physical leadership qualities and willingness to assume risks in a flamboyant way—not that Patch didn't have courage and didn't place himself at risk; he did, but in a much quieter way.

In any event, their relationship was admirable, enviable, and brotherly.

74

PAKISTAN AND AYUB KHAN

In 1963, Pakistan was playing political footsy with the Chinese Communists. They were doing this on purpose because of their feeling of animosity towards the United States. This was due to the fact that we were heavily arming or otherwise giving the Indians too much military hardware. The Pakistanis were in the process of making arrangements for mutual landing rights in the various airports in Pakistan for the Chinese Communist airlines. They were also meeting and attempting to resolve some old border disputes.

The President, John F. Kennedy, and the Secretary of State, Dean Rusk, decided that conversations with Pakistan were necessary to patch up whatever differences we had with them and to get them to slow their momentum toward any alliance with the Chinese Communists. Consequently, George Ball, who was Assistant Secretary of State at that time, was to select a team to go over and talk to the Pakistanis and to discuss with Ayub Khan, then President of Pakistan, all problems impacting on Pakistan-

U.S. relations.

I was then Deputy Director of the Defense Intelligence Agency and was selected to be the military member of Mr. Ball's team. In September 1963 we took off for Pakistan. At Rawalpindi we were met with a great deal of courtesy from Ayub Khan. We talked several days in regard to various subjects of mutual concern. During many of these meetings, I met Mr. Bhutto, who was then the Prime Minister and a very powerful man. He was quite charming and highly intelligent, and I can appreciate why Zia's regime executed him, because he was a threat: a dynamic, political threat to any successor to Ayub Khan.

In any event, one day (and the purpose of this story is to recount a pretty interesting sidelight on diplomacy), we were having luncheon at the palace, and at the table were Secretary Ball, the Minister of Defense, the Chairman of Joint Chiefs of Staff, President Ayub Khan, and myself. We were going to play golf that afternoon, as we had finished our talks for the morning.

At luncheon, Secretary Ball said in a very jocular way to Ayub Khan, "Mr. President, you should know that General Quinn has been thoroughly briefed on the protocol of playing golf with the head of another state. And I have no doubt that I can depend on General Quinn to observe the amenities of diplomacy in that you will, of course, emerge victorious in this match with him and that you might well, knowing that, bet rather heavily."

Turning to Secretary Ball, knowing that I was being ribbed, I said, "Mr. Secretary, I don't know what the diplomatic term for a rebuttal is for such a condition as you have placed me in, but in the Army, we would call that an illegal order, not necessarily to be obeyed, per se."

Ayub Khan said, "You're absolutely right, General, that is an illegal order. He has absolutely no right to order you to lose."

"Well," Secretary Ball said, "we'll just have to see what happens. But I wouldn't worry if I were you, Mr. President."

I had the Minister of Defense as my partner, and Ayub Khan had the Chairman of the Joint Chiefs of Staff as his. After lunch, off we went to the golf course. The course was at the Officers' Club in Rawalpindi, and was really one of the most unusual golf courses I have ever played. It had been virtually carved out of a jungle. It was rough in the sense that it was impenetrable. The fairways were fairways right up to and bordering on the jungle.

When we teed off, each of us had a caddy to carry our bags. Each of us also had a fore caddy, that is, a caddy who watched you hit the ball, watched where it landed, and went to locate it. There was a master fore caddy, who commanded all eight caddies, and then there was a master caddy, a big guy with a Sikh's garment and turban. So we had ten caddies all together.

When you hit a ball, if you sliced it into the jungle, you would say, "Well, I'd better hit another one."

The master caddy would say, "No, no, we'll find it, don't worry about it."

I would go up to where the ball went in, about ten or twenty feet on the fly, and there it would be, teed up beautifully, on a clump of grass, and I could see the green from where the ball was placed. It was hysterical. Also, at every third hole, out of the jungle would come men in turbans, in snow white uniforms, or long, flowing gowns, and bearing trays of drinks, orange juice, lime juice, gin and tonic, and iced tea. You had a choice of whatever you wanted to take along. A drink caddy would walk along with you to hold your glass on a tray while you were hitting the ball and would carry it until you finished the drink; then he would disappear into the jungle.

Well, we had a lot of fun playing the course. On the 17th green, my partner and I won the hole, which put us one-up on the match. As we were walking from the 17th green to the 18th tee, I was with the President, and I said, "Mr. President, remember that conversation at luncheon? This is going to be disastrous to me, because here we are one-up, and even if we should tie, we will have won, and as Secretary Ball indicated, I could never be a diplomat, and will have to go back to the Army."

He patted me on the shoulder, and he said, "General, what the hell is wrong with that?"

An interesting sideline on that trip was my association with Ambassador Ball—Secretary George Ball. I don't believe I ever ran into a more thorough person in the sense of being correct in everything he did or said. After each meeting we had in Pakistan, we would assemble at the end of the day in his suite in the government guest house, and we would draft a cable to the President and to Secretary of State Rusk. Secretary Ball would describe what had transpired that day. He would also write in the cable, almost verbatim, precisely what was said in the meeting, and his interpretation of what was said and meant. Had it been me, I would have written a message very rapidly and listed the points at issue and what was said about them, giving the essence of what was said. Not Secretary Ball.

Sometimes it was one or two o'clock in the morning before he would be satisfied with what he or the staff had written, or what we'd come up with. I couldn't leave and go to bed for the simple reason that he would not let me. He said, "This is going out as soon as we finish, to get into the hands of the President or the Secretary of State early in the morning, and the last two words in each message have to read, 'Quinn concurs.' "

Half the time I was so sleepy, I just said, "To hell with it. Of course I concur, I just want to hit the sack."

I might add that one of the reasons I was getting so tired and wanting to go to bed was that we had some drinks along with writing these messages, or, at least, I did. I asked one of the men, one of Ball's party, about Mr. Ball. This man was named Jeff Kitchens, a delightful guy and very effective, who should have stayed in the diplomatic service.

He told me that George Ball was a very meticulous person and probably the most dedicated member of the State Department. I could understand that from watching him work.

When we returned home, I got a call from Mr. Ball who said, "Bill, the President wants to see us about Pakistan. Can you meet me at the White House?"

I said, "Yes, sir, what time?"

I hotfooted over to the White House where I was ushered into a big conference room. The President said, "Mr. Secretary, this is your meeting." He was talking to Dean Rusk.

Mr. Rusk said, "Mr. President, Mr. Ball and his team have just returned from Pakistan where they went to see President Ayub Khan, and they also stopped at Lisbon on the way home and met with Salazar. Mr. Ball, would you take over?"

Mr. Ball said, "Mr. President, I think first I ought to tell you that we have a very delicate situation in Pakistan created accidently and unnecessarily by General Quinn here." He proceeded to tell the President about the conversations at the luncheon about the upcoming golf match and his instructions to me as to the protocol entailed. Then he said, "Mr. President, I'll allow General Quinn to finish this story, as it is only right that he have an opportunity to defend himself."

Well, I told the story of the golf game and when I came up about Ayub Khan saying, "What the hell is wrong with that?" I thought President Kennedy would fall out of his chair. He thought it was hilarious, and kept laughing. Mr. Ball then briefed the President on what had transpired in Pakistan and what his recommendations were and so forth. Finally he turned to me and said, "I believe General Quinn will concur in most everything I have said."

Which I did.

Mr. Rusk said, "General Quinn, thank you very much. We plan to talk about Salazar and Portugal, and as you were not part of those conversations, you may return to the Pentagon."

When I left I went around in back of the President, who was in a swivel chair. He wheeled around laughing and grabbed my hand, saying, "That's a great story."

I said, "Thank you Mr. President," and started toward the door.

He yelled, "How about a game of golf one of these days, General?"

Over my shoulder, I replied, "Well, okay, sir, but please don't give me that bad back routine on the first tee."

That was the last time I saw President Kennedy, and I'm very happy I left him laughing.

75

BARRY
GOLDWATER

My relationship with Barry Goldwater is detailed in the Prologue of this book, particularly events generated by his run for the Presidency. That chapter addresses the political environment at the time but does not shed much light on the character of the man.

In November 1988, at a dinner in Washington, D.C., Goldwater received the Annual Distinguished Service Award of the National Arthritis Foundation.

Barry Goldwater, Jr. and I were asked to make a few remarks, i.e., observations of a son and of a friend, regarding the Senator.

It occured to me, that having been a close friend of Goldwater and having observed him as a person, my remarks that evening might be worth repeating. Here then follows the transcript of my contribution to the Arthritis Foundation Dinner honoring Barry Goldwater on November 29, 1988, in Washington, D.C.

• • •

Gen. William Quinn and Barry Goldwater

Ladies and gentlemen, you have heard or you will hear, what Barry Goldwater has done in a lifetime. In my few remarks I'm going to try to tell you not what he has done, but what he is.

In my high school on the Eastern Shore of Maryland we were blessed by having Professor Gardner as our principal, a very wise old man. He used to drill us with the fact that there were twenty basic elements of character and that these basic elements are ones that we should judge ourselves by, as well as judging others.

Now, I'm going to use some of these which Professor Gardner gave us to describe Barry Goldwater. I'm also going to skip some of them: thrift, cleanliness, religious, and so forth. I'm just going to get to the nitty-gritty ones.

Let's try patience. Now, I'm suggesting, and this is supported by everyone who knows him, that every year when Barry gets his flu shot he also gets a shot *for* patience.

Honesty. As far as honesty is concerned, he could dish out enough for all of us in this room and have plenty left over for himself. He is honest almost to a fault. Oddly enough, some have criticized him for being *too* honest in politics.

Integrity. More of the same. There is no way you can bend this man in the direction of immorality or deceit.

Loyalty. I wish that he had stayed in the Army instead of going in the Air force. Now, of course, that kind of wish has to do with partisanship. He loves our flag. That flag of ours flies night and day high over his hilltop home in Arizona. He's loyal to his friends. And I mean loyal, as Bette Quinn and I can testify. And to his country, he is a loyalty freak who bleeds red, white, and blue.

Courage. I expect that if he'd been a little older he would have been the one, instead of Lindbergh, who touched down in Paris. He has crisscrossed the Atlantic X number of times, and in some instances, alone. In World War II he flew the Hump, the famous flight from India to China. He carried in his plane gasoline, ammunition, explosives, and once a Buick for Madame Chiang Kai-Shek. To show his courage, he's even flown an Army helicopter, and you know what that takes!

Sense of humor. Very droll. I think one of the amusing aspects of his humor is that he used to play a lousy trombone. It was so bad that in arguments, particularly with City Council in Phoenix years ago, if they didn't agree with him, he'd say, "I'm going home to bring my trombone here and play for you." That whipped them.

One Christmas, for instance, he bought a very tall radio antenna to be installed outside of his radio shack as a Christmas present—a ten-thousand-dollar Christmas present—for his wife Peggy. The next year, however, she bought him a twenty-thousand dollar white sable coat! Now, it was too small for him, so she consequently was forced to wear it.

During his presidential campaign he was flying into San Francisco for the convention and went up forward and asked the pilot to move over, and he took over the controls. While he was flying, he turned on a speaker (the reporters were in the back of the plane) and announced in a slurring tone, "This is your captain speaking. Would one of you reporters ask the stewardess to bring me up another double martini?"

His sister Caroline tells a story about him. In their home in Phoenix they had a downstairs john, and he wired it up so that when one sat down on it, a voice said, "Good Morning!"

Generous. Incredibly so. With family, friends, and the needy. He's a real soft touch. For instance, during the Vietnam War, he ran an operation in his radio shack with volunteers around-the-clock, twenty-four hours a day, taking radio messages at his expense from Vietnam, which were then patched through the telephone to loved ones at home.

I'll have to tell you a story about his generosity. Barry was down at our farm on the Eastern Shore one weekend.

We were having a cocktail party this Saturday night. We had a young colored woman, Marietta, who was our cook and helper. She and I were in the kitchen, where she was preparing some food. She turned to me and said, "General, we're having a rally at the church, and I hope that you can help."

"Yes, I'll be glad to, Marietta."

Unbeknown to us, Goldwater had walked into the kitchen and heard our conversation. He asked, "Marietta, what's a rally?"

She said, "Well, a rally is a fund-raising thing in which you try to raise money. Down here we call it a rally."

"What do you need the money for?"

"We need a new roof on the church."

"What's wrong with the roof?"

"Well, it leaks, and Sundays when it's raining, a lot of pews can't be occupied; so we need a new one."

"What's a new roof cost?"

"Oh, it costs upwards of a thousand dollars."

So I said, "Marietta, I'll send you a check," and that was that. Monday I sat down and wrote Marietta a check for twenty-five dollars. Wednesday, she received a check in the mail for one thousand dollars for a new roof from Barry Goldwater.

What I've outlined, I guess is probably about all you need to know about Barry Goldwater. Now, many of us will recall Neville Chamberlain, stepping off an airplane in London after the Munich Pact in 1938. He had just agreed with Hitler to the annexation of the Sudetenland by Germany. He raised his folded umbrella in the air and said, "Peace in our time."

Ladies and gentlemen, in a paraphrase of that statement, we'd like to thank our Lord that we in America have had a "Goldwater in our time."

An afterthought:

Barry Goldwater is unique in American history. A man severely defeated in a bid for the Presidency, yet who emerged as the nation's champion for the truth in life and in politics. He elicits the admiration and affection of all Americans.

The End

APPENDIX A

The following is a thumbnail sketch of my life story before I went to West Point, beginning, naturally, with my childhood. I guess this has to be done in most books to provide a background for what follows in one's life. So here goes.

I was born in Crisfield, Maryland, on November 1, 1907. My father was William Samuel Quinn, a member of the Quinn family of Crisfield, the most famous of which was his brother, Lorie C. Quinn, Sr., who founded the *Crisfield Times*, which has been in constant publication for over 100 years. Uncle Lorie was the second mayor after the town's incorporation.

His son, Lorie C. Quinn, Jr., was an entrepreneur in the news business and at one time controlled practically all the newspapers—weekly newspapers, that is—on the Eastern Shore of Maryland.

Uncle Lorie, who was 21 years Dad's senior, had five sons, Lorie, Jr., Wallace, Burt, Frank, and David.

My father married Alice Wilson, whose father was a sea captain, and it was from her line of Sterlings (my maternal grandmother was a Sterling) that I became a member of the Sons of the American Revolution, in that her forefather, Travis Sterling, fought in the Revolution with Captain Miles in the Potter's Company at Princess Ann, Maryland.

I enjoyed a normal childhood in a small town, doing what all kids do. I went to the local schools—secondary and high school; and during the summers I delivered telegrams or jerked sodas at the Sterling ice cream parlor and bakery in downtown Crisfield. I also worked one summer for Dr. Lewis in his pharmacy. I did other odd jobs. My father was not wealthy; he was an insurance agent, helped out at the newspaper, and was also in several businesses with his nephew, Wallace Quinn, who later became a multimillionaire. He had menhaden fishing fleets from Hatteras to Florida, shipbuilding in Pascagoula, Mississippi, and fertilizer plants on the Gulf between Galveston and New Orleans.

APPENDIX B

HEADQUARTERS FOURTH INFANTRY DIVISION
OFFICE OF THE COMMANDING GENERAL
APO #4, U. S. Army

April 20, 1944

Colonel William W. Quinn, GSC
Headquarters Seventh Army
APO #758, U. S. Army

Dear Bill:

Many thanks for your's of recent date.
Certainly am happy to see where you have arrived.
Only regret that you are not in my own zone of action. Do old Sandy Patch a dandy job for he is a
great soldier. Likely you yourself can't tell him,
I will, he has a topside soldier alongside him, in
you.

Go places, Bill, You've got the stuff, the
youth and everything that it takes. I shall be for
you always.

Warmly yours,

R.O. Barton
Major General U.S.Army

APPENDIX C

ARMY SERVICE FORCES
HEADQUARTERS FIRST SERVICE COMMAND
BOSTON 10, MASSACHUSETTS

4 April 1946

Colonel William W. Quinn, Inf.
Office of the Assistant Secretary of War
Strategic Services Unit
25th and E Streets, N.W.
Washington 25, D.C.

Dear Bill:

So glad to hear from you and to know that my
letter reached you safely. I tried to find you once in Washington in the Pentagon, where some kind soul told me you had
your office. After taking another 25-mile hike and becoming
hopelessly lost, I found out, too late to see you, that you
were in another part of the city altogether!

I tried hard to get you with me many times in the
Pacific, but luck was against me. Of my old IV Corps gang
I asked for, only Hugh Milton finally put in an appearance.
Duke got his division in course of time, and I had you figured for my next Chief of Staff, as his replacement. However I could never get you released, so finally Hugh got the
job and his B.G. He went with me through the Luzon show and
on to Japan, did a fine job and is a fine loyal officer - but
I wanted you!

I trust that your little family is well and comfortably situated. Please give Mrs. Quinn a good hug from both
Mrs. Griswold and myself - we were fond of her. I hear I may
come to Washington around the 10th for a conference, and will
try to look you up if I can.

Best of luck to you and yours.

Sincerely,

O. W. GRISWOLD
Lieutenant General, United States Army

APPENDIX D

WAR DEPARTMENT.
WASHINGTON, D. C.

20 March 1946

SUBJECT: Commendation

TO   : Colonel William W. Quinn, O-19283, Infantry
          Office of Strategic Services, War Department
          Washington, D. C.

     1.   As former commander of the IV Corps, I desire to commend you for outstanding services during the period 5 January 1942 to 12 April 1943.

     2.   As Assistant Chief of Staff, G-2, and Assistant G-2, IV Corps, during this period when the Army was expanding rapidly and training for combat was the paramount mission, your aggressive efforts were exceptional. In the establishment of intelligence schools, the supervision of intelligence training conducted by divisions and brigades of the Corps, as well as the continuous study of the world strategic situation, your services were outstanding. The successful endeavors of the Corps, both in maneuvers and in actual combat are due in large measure to your effective activities.

     3.   You are hereby authorized to wear the Army Commendation Ribbon by direction of the Secretary of War.

O. W. Griswold.
O.' W. GRISWOLD
Lieutenant General, USA

Copy: The Adjutant General for
       Officer's 201 file.

APPENDIX E

OFFICE OF THE DIRECTOR

UNITED STATES DEPARTMENT OF JUSTICE

FEDERAL BUREAU OF INVESTIGATION

WASHINGTON, D.C. 20535

December 11, 1964

Lieutenant General William W. Quinn
Commanding General
U. S. 7th Army
German Federal Republic

Dear General:

      I have been advised of the generous remarks

you made about me and the FBI during the Annual Dinner of

the Veterans of the OSS in Washington on December 4th.   You

may be assured the support and confidence you displayed in

my administration of the FBI are indeed appreciated by all of

us, and I want to take this opportunity to thank you.

      Sincerely yours,

      J. Edgar Hoover

APPENDIX F

NOTE FROM ALLEN DULLES AND READ BY

NED PUTZELL

AT THE

DONOVAN AWARD DINNER

WASHINGTON D.C.

DECEMBER 4, 1964

I am delighted that Bill Quinn is receiving the Donovan Award and only regret that my doctor won't let me join you in the presentation.

I worked with Bill in the war days. He understood, as few have, the importance of intelligence and he helped greatly to carry on the best traditions of intelligence as O.S.S. went through the transition from war to peace. Without him our profession would then have lost many of the "pros" who have carried on the Donovan spirit and traditions in our intelligence works of today.

I salute Bill Quinn as a man with the Donovan spirit. I thank him for his great contribution to intelligence and for what he has done to bring close cooperation between the military and the civilian side of intelligence. This cooperation is essential to the future accomplishment of our national intelligence effort.

A. W. D.

APPENDIX G

HEADQUARTERS
EIGHTH UNITED STATES ARMY (EUSAK)
APO 301, C/O PM
SAN FRANCISCO, CALIFORNIA

1 August 1951

THE COMMANDING GENERAL

Dear Bill,

It was a great pleasure to have your good letter of 15 July. Words fail me to express my deep feeling of gratitude and the great honor in becoming a Guardsman in the Order of the Buffalo. Please know that I am most happy to accept this membership and the great distinction it confers upon me.

All my life I have wanted to become a member of the US 17th Infantry Regiment. In 1916, as a 2d Lieutenant, I was a member of the 3d US Infantry which moved to Eagle Pass, Texas to take over that post which had just recently been occupied by the 17th Infantry. The 17th had gone into Mexico as a part of General Pershing's punitive expedition, and I can truly tell you that I was terribly disappointed not to be a member of your regiment at that time. Now, at long last I am given the welcome and membership which I have craved all these years. It is indeed a thrilling moment.

Since arriving in Korea I have followed the brilliant operations of the 17th Regiment with great interest and satisfaction. I have particularly noted the high morale of the regiment and of its skill and achievements in battle. While I am always ready to give credit to the great rank and file of any organization for its successes, I want you to know that I appreciate that the skill and desire to fight comes from Colonel "Buffalo Bill" Quinn. You have already had a brilliant career -- you are now, as a Regimental Commander, writing new pages of epic infantry battles in Korea -- I know the future for you and the Army you serve shines brightly.

Thank you, Brother Bill, and all your comrades. I shall do my best to be a worthy member of the Order of the Buffalo.

Faithfully,

JAMES A. VAN FLEET
General, U.S. Army
Commanding

Colonel William W. Quinn
Headquarters, 17th Infantry
APO 7

APPENDIX H

HEADQUARTERS 7TH INFANTRY DIVISION

OFFICE OF THE COMMANDING GENERAL
APO 7

26 July 1951

Colonel William W. Quinn
Headquarters 17th Infantry Regiment
APO 7

Dear Bill:

For the first time, I have begun to realize that you are actually leaving us and right along with that realization it occurred to me just what the loss of "Buffalo Bill" would mean to this division. While indulging in retrospect, I thought of Taemi San and the conduct of yourself and your regiment at a time when the odds were definitely against you. In that battle, you had the courage to prove what many of us believed and others hoped for—that the American soldier was not roadbound; that he could meet and overcome a numerically superior force on the enemy's own ground.

None of us who were engaged in the fighting in this sector of the Korean front will forget the brilliant penetration you effected at Yangu. Until I have the opportunity to do so personally, I wish to congratulate you, in this brief message, on the splendid pattern you have set for the men and officers of this division. We're going to miss Bill Quinn alright. Each of your operations from conception to conclusion showed tremendous thought and careful planning. I wish to express my appreciation to you and your unit for a magnificent accomplishment.

I sincerely hope that your next assignment is entirely to your satisfaction. We who knew you in Korea shall have a lasting interest in your career—both as fellow campaigners and as friends.

Sincerely yours,

C. B. FERENBAUGH
Maj Gen, USA
Commanding

APPENDIX I

GENERAL HEADQUARTERS
FAR EAST COMMAND
APO 500

COMMANDER-IN-CHIEF

24 July 1951

Dear Colonel Quinn:

    The thoughtful certificate of member-
ship in the "Order of the Buffalo" enclosed
with your letter of 15 July is acknowledged
with gratitude. The fine fighting reputation
of your Regiment reflects credit on its members, and makes the certificate a valued
keepsake.

    I feel certain that the future deeds
of the Seventeenth Infantry will match those
already inscribed in its distinquished record.

    With every good wish,

        Sincerely,

        M. B. RIDGWAY,
      General, United States Army.

Colonel William W. Quinn,
Commanding, Headquarters,
Seventeenth Infantry,
APO 7.

APPENDIX J

HEADQUARTERS IX CORPS
OFFICE OF THE COMMANDING GENERAL
APO 264

19 July 1951

Colonel W. W. Quinn
Commanding, 17th Infantry Regiment
APO 7

Dear Colonel Quinn:

I was highly honored to receive your letter of 15 July together with my appointment to the Order of the Buffalo. I shall always treasure this indication of comradeship and esteem from one of the finest of our regiments.

It has been a great pleasure to have the 17th Infantry in the IX Corps. I have always felt that missions assigned your regiment would be executed with dispatch and thoroughness. It has been an inspiration and example to the members of this command.

I have learned only recently that you are due for rotation in the near future, but I am sure that the high standards and traditions which you have inculcated into this regiment will continue after you have gone. I hope I shall see you before you leave.

With kindest regards, and best wishes for the continued success of yourself and the 17th Infantry, I am

Sincerely yours,

W. M. HOGE
Lieutenant General, U. S. Army
Commanding

P.S. Is it necessary that I raise a Buffalo mustache?
WMH

APPENDIX K

ROYAL HELLENIC ARMY GENERAL STAFF
CHIEF OF STAFF

      In Greece you leave admirers and friends, all those who have followed your work. Our Army feels very deeply the benefici: influence of your stay in Greece, appreciating the gesture of th military leadership of your country to elect you as Chief of the Military Mission in Greece.

      I beg you to transmit my greetings to Mrs Quinn as well as my sincere thanks for the friendly atmosphere she created between the families of American and Greek Officers, which has helped so much for the development of our friendship, understanding and collaboration.

      Wishing you the best of luck and the same success in your new duties, I remain your sincere friend.

Solon GHIKAS
Lt General
Chief of the G.A.G.S.

Copy to Major General G. BARTH

APPENDIX L

BODOSSAKI ATHANASSIADÈS
      ATHÈNES

    TÉLÉGRAMMES: BODOSSAKI   Athens, 15th June, 1955.

Dear General,

        If I may misquote an ancient philo-
sopher "All good things must come to an end" but
in your case I emphatically disagree with his
statement.

        You may be leaving my country but
after working so diligently helping us with our
problems, I do not believe that your interest in
Greece and your friendship for us will end with
your departure. In fact, I am confident that my
country and the Greek people will always have a
place in your heart in the same way as you do in
ours.

        Please be assured of my warm,
personal thanks, for your valuable contribution
to our Armed Forces and of my best wishes to you
and your charming family for a pleasant journey
home. When you return to visit my country --and
I am sure you will-- I hope you will to spend
some time free from your heavy duties and give me
thus the pleasure of taking you out un the Greek
islands with my yatch.

        With my very best regards to you
and your family and wishing you every success in
your new assignment,

                 I remain,

                 Yours very sincerely,

General William W. Quinn,
   Diamantidou Str.77
     P s y h i c o

        × T

OWNER + DIRECTOR,
HELLENIC POWDER + CARTRIDGE Co.,
ATHENS, GREECE.
(THE DuPONT OF GREECE)

INDEX